Who Do You Say I Am?

Who Do You Say I Am?
Introduction to Christology

JACQUES DUPUIS, S.J.

ORBIS BOOKS

Maryknoll, New York 10545

Fifth Printing, September 2002

Originally published in Italy as *Introduzione Alla Cristologia* by EDIZIONI PIEMME
S. p. A., Via del Carmine 5, 15033 CASALE MONFERRATO (AL), ITALIA

The Catholic Foreign Mission Society of America (Maryknoll) recruits and trains people for overseas missionary service. Through Orbis Books, Maryknoll aims to foster the international dialogue that is essential to mission. The books published, however, reflect the opinions of their authors and are not meant to represent the official position of the society.

Published by Orbis Books, P.O. Box 308, Maryknoll, New York 10545-0308 U.S.A., by arrangement with Edizioni Piemme S.p.A, Via del Carmine 5, 15033 Casale Monferrato (AL), Italia. Published in Italian under the title *Introduzione Alla Cristologia*.

Manufactured in the United States of America.

Library of Congress Cataloging-in-Publication Data

Dupuis, Jacques, 1923-
    Who do you say I am? : introduction to Christology / Jacques
Dupuis.
        p.   cm.
    Includes bibliographical references and indexes.
    ISBN 0-88344-940-4 (pbk.)
    1. Jesus Christ — History of doctrines — 20th century.   I. Title.
BT198.D83   1994
232—dc20   93-45599
                                                              CIP

Contents

Introduction

"WHO DO YOU SAY I AM?"

Characteristically, it is just before he announced his future passion to them for the first time that Jesus, in both Mark's and Matthew's narrative (Mk 8:29; Mt 16:15), put to his disciples this decisive question: "Who do *you* say I am?" Both evangelists report first who Jesus was in other people's view—John the Baptist or one of the prophets. Peter, however, spoke up and said to him, "You are the Christ" (Mk 8:29), or "You are the Christ, the Son of the living God" (Mt 16:16). Whatever the wording, the difference is probably less than it appears at first sight. Peter's answer might be seen as the first-ever christological statement, yet it was but an anticipation, a prefiguration of the christological faith that would be born with Easter. In fact, Peter's answer at Caesarea Philippi coincides with the content of the first kerygmatic preaching of the apostolic Church. When Peter stood up with the eleven to address the Jews in what is decribed as the first-ever Christian preaching, the decisive point in his message ran: "Let all the house of Israel ... know assuredly that God has made him both Lord and Christ, this Jesus whom you crucified" (Acts 2:36). The Christ, the Lord, the Son of God: these three titles form the core of the early christological faith. They show unmistakably the central place this confession occupied in the faith of the Christian Church from the outset.

It all consisted in predicating a particular title (Masiah, the anointed one, the Christ), borrowed from Old Testament theological terminology, of the man Jesus, whose proper name was Yeshua. The confession of faith "Jesus is the Christ" thus came to be born, later to evolve semantically into the apposition "Jesus-the-Christ" and further into the compound name "Jesus Christ." Parallel cases are not wanting in the history of religions; that of Gautama the Buddha is particularly striking. As the Christian faith gave Jesus the title "the anointed one," so the Buddhist tradition has honoured Gautama with that of "the Buddha" (the enlightened one). One tradition evolved from the Yeshua of history to the Christ of faith, the other from the Gautama of history (Shakyamuni) to the Buddha of faith (Amida Buddha). In both cases the religious traditions that ensued took their name from the titles bestowed on their founders: Christianity and Buddhism.[1]

But there is a difference. However exalted the rank of Gautama-the-

1

Buddha in the Buddhist tradition, it is not equivalent to that which the Christian faith attributes to Jesus-the-Christ. Admittedly, Gautama preached a message of liberation (*dharma*), as Jesus preached the Good News of God's Kingdom; he did so with the authority that an outstanding religious experience (*nirvāna*) bestowed upon him, as Jesus' own authority flowed from his experience of God as *Abba*. However, if Gautama is saviour, it is as the "enlightened one" whose example shows others the way to liberation. Jesus, on the other hand, *is* the way. From the apostolic age onward, Christian faith has professed him to be the universal Saviour. By doing so, the apostolic Church did not claim to innovate but only to recognize the significance and announce what God had done for humankind in the person and the event of Jesus Christ.

JESUS CHRIST THE CENTRE

The place and significance attributed to Jesus Christ by the Christian tradition appears distinct and original, from the viewpoint of comparative religion. From the vantage point of Christian faith, its distinctiveness stands out even more clearly. The person, life, death and resurrection of Jesus Christ are so central to the Christian mystery that sometimes it has been said — not without legitimacy — that "Christianity is Christ." This is said not in the mistaken sense that would identify the religion with the founder or the Christian Church with the one who established it, for the Church finds her *raison d'être* and her meaning in Jesus Christ, to whom she is entirely related and subservient. It is said in the sense that the person and work of Jesus Christ is the source, the centre, and the end — the alpha and omega — of what Christianity stands for and announces to the world.

Christian theology will be essentially christocentric. This does not mean that Christology exhausts the whole of theology, but it provides it with the necessary key of understanding; it is the principle of interpretation of the entire edifice. Protology and eschatology, anthropology and theology, ecclesiology and sacramentology all are distinct parts of a theological edifice that finds its unity and coherence, its meaning and hermeneutical key, in the person and event of Jesus Christ, on which it is centred. In him Christians learn to discover who God really is, who human beings are, what is their true origin and destiny, the meaning and worth of their world and history, and the role of the Church as she accompanies humankind on its pilgrimage through the ages.

The Second Vatican Council laid special stress on the relatedness of the Church to the mystery of Jesus Christ when it defined the Church as "sacrament," a "sign and instrument of communion with God and of the unity among all men" (LG, 1), adding that the Church is "the universal sacrament of salvation" (LG, 48). The Council consciously adopted the theological insight according to which Jesus Christ — who in his person is the mystery of salvation — is the "primordial sacrament" (*Ursakrament*) of humankind's encounter with God, while the Church is derivatively the sacrament of the encounter with the Risen Lord. A recent document of the International Theological Commission entitled "Select Themes of Ecclesiology on the Occasion of the Twentieth Anniversary of the Closing of the Second Vatican Council" (1984), declared:

> Since Christ himself may be called "the sacrament of God," the Church, in an analogous way, may be called "the sacrament of Christ." ... And yet it is self-evident that the Church can only be a sacrament by way of total dependence on Christ, who is intrinsically the "primordial sacrament" (8.3).[2]

The Christian mystery — and the theology whose function it is to articulate it — is by definition christocentric, not ecclesiocentric. Jesus Christ is the primordial mystery; the Church is derivative and related.

Christ-the-sacrament does not, however, exhaust the mystery of God; it rather points toward it. Christocentrism is not opposed to theocentrism; it implies it and calls for it. One reason for this has already been formulated: Jesus the man is the "sacrament of the encounter with God." This means that in Jesus' humanity and human countenance we come in contact with God, the Godhead and humankind being indissolubly united in Jesus as the Son of God made human. Jesus does not stand somewhere between God and human beings; he is not a go-between attempting — in vain — to bridge the gap that separates the Infinite from the finite. He is not an intermediary who is neither of the two ends to be united but the mediator in whom both are irrevocably bound together because he is personally one and the other.

CHRISTOLOGY AND THEOLOGY

As the God-man, Jesus Christ the Son Incarnate is the "way" to the Father who stands beyond the mediator. The Gospel of John expresses it clearly when Jesus says, "I am the way, the truth and the life; no one comes to the Father, but by me" (Jn 14:6). Christology entails a paradox, for while on the one hand we meet God in the person of Jesus, on the other the Father abides beyond Jesus. The Gospels, that of John in particular, testify to this paradox. To Philip, who wished to have the Father shown to him, Jesus answered, "He who has seen me has seen the Father" (Jn 14:9). Yet, reflecting on the mystery of God's manifestation in Jesus Christ, John remarks: "No one has ever seen God; the only Son, who is in the bosom of the Father, he has made him known (*exègèsato*)" (Jn 1:18). The Son incarnate is the exegete, the interpreter of the Father. In him God stands revealed and manifested, while yet remaining invisible and unseen. The

Father endures beyond; he is "greater" (Jn 14:28), who alone "is good" (Mk 10:18).

Thus the mystery of God remains secret and hidden, even while in Jesus Christ it is manifested to us in a unique, qualitatively unsurpassable, manner. Jesus revealed the mystery of God as experienced personally by him in his human awareness. Once transposed to the human consciousness of the man Jesus, the ineffable mystery of God's inner life could be enunciated in human terms; it thus became the object of divine revelation. Yet, for all its unique character, God's revelation in Jesus did not and could not exhaust the divine mystery; nor did Jesus' own human awareness of it. The God revealed in Jesus Christ remains a hidden God.

Nor does Jesus, the mediator who is the way to the Father, ever take the place of or substitute for the Father. On the contrary, he refers everything, including himself, to the God whom he calls Father. Never, in fact, did Jesus call himself God. The title *God,* in his language, refers exclusively to the Father. More precisely, Jesus' God is Yahweh, who in the Old Testament was revealed to Israel and to whom Jesus relates with the singularly intimate familiarity implied in the term *Abba.*[3] Jesus' human consciousness is essentially filial.

Through the Son we are thus directed to the God who is Father. Christocentrism calls for theocentrism. Jesus revealed God by revealing himself as Son; that is, by living his sonship of the Father under the astonished eyes of the disciples. In him and through him the mystery of the unknowable Father was unveiled to them. The same law applies to disciples today: Christology leads us to theology, that is, to God revealed in the most decisive manner in Jesus Christ while at the same time remaining shrouded in mystery. The development of christological and theological studies in recent years witnesses to this process: theological reflection ascends from the Christ of God to the God of Jesus; from Christology to theology.

CHRISTOCENTRISM AND ANTHROPOCENTRISM

Jesus Christ's posture at the centre of the Christian mystery does not make him usurp the place of God. God remains the end of all things as well as their origin. If Jesus Christ, as mediator, is at the centre of God's plan for humankind, the reason is that God placed him there by design. He is the channel through which God comes down to us and we reach up to God; the way God is personally revealed to us and we come to know who God is for us. By the same token, it is also in Jesus Christ that we truly come to know ourselves. Even as Christocentrism and theocentrism call for each other rather than being mutually opposed, so too with Christocentrism and anthropocentrism. This is well stated by the pastoral Constitution *Gaudium et Spes* of the Second Vatican Council. It says:

In reality it is only in the mystery of the Word made flesh that the mystery of man truly becomes clear. For Adam, the first human being, was a type of the one who was to come, Christ the Lord. Christ the new Adam in the very revelation of the mystery of the Father and of his love, fully reveals humankind to itself and brings to light its high calling (22).

"The human person is more than human"; they are called to transcend themselves, although they cannot reach this self-transcendence by their own strength but must receive it from God as a gift. In Jesus Christ we transcend ourselves in God by means of God's self-emptying in humankind. The Incarnation of the Son of God establishes between God and us a "marvellous exchange" by which we become partners with God. Thus we discover what a high value God has set upon us, how precious we are in God's own eyes. "By his Incarnation," says Vatican II, "the Son of God has in a certain way united himself with each person" (GS, 22). Sharing in Jesus Christ's Sonship of God, we find in him the fulfillment of our own openness toward God. Divinization in the God-man brings humanization to its climax. Consequently, no anthropology can claim to be Christian that does not seek humankind's ultimate meaning in Jesus Christ. There is no Christian anthropology without Christology.

A QUESTION OF METHOD

Christology, as every theological discourse, can adopt different methods. The method that predominated until recent times can be called "dogmatic." It took as its point of departure the dogmatic enunciations of the Church Magisterium — here mostly the definition of Chalcedon — of which, as by a movement of retrospection, it endeavoured to verify the component parts in biblical citations chosen and interpreted accordingly. This verification being done, the method delved further into the meaning of the dogmatic definitions of the mystery of Jesus Christ to draw from them ever more precise conclusions.

Such a method was fraught with serious limitations and dangers. The New Testament did not figure here as the soul of the christological project. Being made use of by way of the proof-text method in order to justify dogmatic formulations, the word of God did not constitute the ultimate norm (*norma normans*) by which to interpret those formulations; dogma became the final norm. In the process, Scripture was used uncritically, often with disregard for the exegetical method. In particular, the sayings attributed to Jesus in the Gospels — including that of John — were indiscriminately taken for authentic (*ipsissima verba*). The Chalcedonian model being considered the absolute norm, little account was taken of the plurality of Christologies already present in the New Testament. Much less was room left

for a non-Chalcedonian model of Christology after the council had determined the christological dogma. Briefly, the connection between Sacred
Scripture, Tradition and the Magisterium so aptly expressed by Vatican II
(DV, 10) was deflected in the direction of dogma. There ensued a danger
of dogmatism, a way of absolutizing a certain christological model which,
as history shows, often failed to do full justice to the true humanity of Jesus
and forgot his human "story" to a great extent. The dogmatic method thus
led to an abstract Christology, which, having lost touch with the concrete
life of Jesus, was in danger of lacking relevance to our own.

Recent decades have witnessed the development — in theology in general
and Christology in particular — of another, more adequate method that can
be called genetic or historical-evolutive. It starts from Sacred Scripture,
specifically from the messianic expectation in the Old Testament and its
fulfillment in the person of Jesus according to the New Testament. It goes
on to study the New Testament Christology — that is, the faith reflection by
the apostolic Church on the Christ-event in the light of the Easter experience — without, however, always attending adequately to the plurality of
New Testament Christologies, sometimes in an express attempt to reduce
those diversified Christologies to an artificial synthesis. The method further
follows the development of christological reflection through the postbiblical
tradition, in the Church Fathers. So it arrives at the christological councils,
whose immediate purpose was to refute and condemn the christological
heresies that arose from two opposite directions — Nestorianism on one side
(Ephesus) and Monophysitism on the other (Chalcedon). The method likewise reviews the postconciliar christological developments through more
recent history down to the present time, ending with the christological
questions called to attention in the present state of reflection.

The Decree on Priestly Formation of Vatican II (OT, 16) has recom-
mended the use of the genetic method in theological studies. This method
was developed in preconciliar years characterised by a definite return to
biblical and patristic sources. The main merit of this method, as compared
to the dogmatic, consists in the primary place it assigns to "positive" theology — that is, to the study of the sources — as distinct from "speculative"
theology. Dogmatic development is thus viewed in linear fashion, as a progressive movement leading to an ever deeper comprehension of the christological mystery. It needs, however, to be asked whether the linear concept
of christological development does not simplify the historical data. Did each
and every christological trend in the course of tradition represent an
advance and an authentic gain in the Church's perception of the mystery
of Christ? Has not, perhaps, one christological model — which need not have
been viewed as absolute or unique — acquired a de facto monopoly of christological reflection, displacing other models in the process, with real loss
to the Church's perception of the mystery? We shall have to return to such
questions later.

Meanwhile, it may be said that the genetic method runs the risk of leaving little room for christological pluralism. Where the New Testament is concerned, the prologue of John's Gospel is—rightly—considered the apex and summit of biblical Christology. But is adequate space left for the early Christology of the early kerygma? Similarly, in tradition the Chalcedonian model—with its further determinations in Constantinople III— tends to be absolutized as the only possible, and therefore the universal, model. Just as was the case with its dogmatic counterpart, so too a Christology developed along the genetic method can be overwhelmingly speculative, to the detriment of concrete life and the context in which Christology is done. The more that speculative deductions are drawn from the fundamental christological data, the greater the danger of abstraction and moving away from the real Jesus of history and the concrete content of his Gospel. Generally speaking, the genetic method shows little concern for contextualizing the comprehension of the mystery of Christ.

Both the dogmatic and the genetic methods are deductive; both seek to draw ever more precise conclusions from previous christological data, going from the better known to the less known. Both are also primarily speculative, proceeding from doctrine to its application to reality—often, however, without succeeding in establishing contact with the reality of concrete life. This lack of touch with reality that is characteristic of much traditional theological speculation suggests that a new method be devised, which may be called inductive. The inductive theological method finds its point of departure neither in dogmatic definitions nor even in the biblical data, but in the lived reality of a concrete situation and the problems it raises for faith reflection; that is, from the context. To start from the context—or to be contextual—represents for theology in general and Christology in particular a turn about. In Christology it will mean primarily seeking an answer to the problems the present world raises for individuals and society in the story of Jesus. The Anselmian definition of theology as "faith seeking understanding" (*fides quaerens intellectum*) remains valid for inductive theology, but its meaning is renewed. It is no longer a question of deducing theologoumena from the data of faith; rather it means living the faith in context and confronting contextual reality with Jesus and his Gospel. Where the deductive method sought—often in vain—to apply doctrine to reality, the inductive proceeds from faith lived in context to reflection on the context in the light of faith.

Vatican II has, in the course of its development through various sessions, known such a reversal of perspective. While the Dogmatic Constitution *Lumen Gentium*, following the deductive method, started from the data of revelation to deduce theological conclusions, the Pastoral Constitution *Gaudium et Spes,* inverting the process, adopted an inductive method. It first looked at the present world, listened to its problems with attention and sympathy, discovered in the longings and aspirations of people of our time the working of the Holy Spirit, found in those aspirations "signs of the times" and responded to the problems and expectations of the world of today in the light of the Gospel message. In the process — and not merely by chance — *Gaudium et Spes* has contributed the two main christological developments produced by Vatican II in which the mystery of Christ is viewed as manifesting the mystery of humankind and its destiny (22) and the Lord himself is seen as "the goal of human history, the focal point of the desires of history and civilization, the centre of humankind, the joy of all hearts, and the fulfilment of all aspirations" (45).

THE HERMENEUTICAL PROBLEM

The turn from the deductive method to the inductive raises, however, the hermeneutical problem. Must theology or Christology be done by starting from the data of faith, hoping to reach out to the reality of the context? Or should it start from the lived reality, then seek a direction for a Christian praxis in the revealed data? More succinctly: Is the right process from the data to the context, or vice versa?

The answer to this question has been called the "hermeneutical circle." It consists of a continuous circular movement, first from the context to the revealed data, then back from that data to the context, and so forth. In Christology this means from the questions the context addresses to the life of faith to the person and work of Jesus Christ, *and* vice versa.

There arises, however, a further question. Is the data of faith ever available to us in naked form, as mere objective truth, entirely pure and unadulterated? Is there an uninterpreted Gospel? Or must we admit that the revealed data always reaches us already interpreted? The entire New Testament Christology, that of the apostolic kerygma included, is a hermeneutics of the story of Jesus done from the vantage point of the disciples' paschal experience. It does not witness to a single apostolic hermeneutics of the Jesus story, but to several. The diverse Christologies of the New Testament represent distinct interpretations of the event in the light of Easter, each conditioned by the particular context of a Church to which it is addressed and by the singular personality of the author or editor of the material.

If, then, as seems to be the case, the revealed data is always a faith interpretation of the event, "doing theology" in context will consist of pursuing in today's situation the process of interpretation of the Christ-event already initiated by the apostolic Church. Theology in context is hermeneutical theology.[4] Each Christian generation, as well as each local church, is bound, throughout space and time, to enter into the hermeneutical process.

The hermeneutical circle stands for the dialectical process that obtains in hermeneutical theology between a concrete context and the revealed data; in other words, between text and context. However, to the dialectic of two elements it seems preferable to substitute, for clarity's sake, the mutual action and reaction of three components: the text, the context, and the interpreter. The circular image will be replaced by the graphic representation of a triangle. But each of the three poles in mutual interaction, each of the elements constitutive of the triangle, needs to be viewed in the integrity of its complex reality.

Text means not only the revealed data contained in the Bible, specifically in the New Testament. It comprehends all that goes under the term "Christian memory," the objective tradition. It extends to the various readings and interpretations the ecclesial tradition has made of the revealed message, including official conciliar formulations. The text therefore comprises Scripture, Tradition and the Church's Magisterium (in its objective aspect), between which Vatican II has shown the intimate connection (cf. DV, 10).

Where context is concerned, the elements that constitute it will differ from place to place as well as between distinct periods in history. Yet the context also needs to be taken in its complex reality, including sociopolitical, cultural and religious conditions. In a word, the context comprises the entire surrounding cultural reality.

As for the interpreter, this is not, properly speaking, the individual theologian, but the ecclesial community to which the theologian belongs and at whose service he is placed. This is the local church, a believing people living its faith experience in diachronic communion with the apostolic Church and in synchronic communion with all the local churches — a communion over which the bishop of Rome presides in charity.

The hermeneutical triangle consists in the mutual interaction among text, context and interpreter, as these have just been described. That is, among the Christian memory, the surrounding cultural reality, and the local church. The context acts upon the interpreter by raising specific questions; it influences the precomprehension of faith with which the interpreter reads the text. The text, in turn, acts on the interpreter, whose reading of it will provide a direction for Christian praxis. And thus onwards. As can be seen, the interaction between text and context, or between memory and culture, takes place in the interpreter, that is, in the local church.

DIVERSIFIED CHRISTOLOGIES

We have noted the complexity of the context, the various components of which need to be taken into account by any theology that claims to be contextual. Something needs to be added with regard to the diversity of contexts. To this contextual diversity, more than to any other factor, is to be assigned the need for theology to be plural. Theology understood as contextual interpretation must be local and diversified, since the Christian experience is always conditioned by the context in which it is lived, with its sociopolitical, cultural and religious dimensions. No contextual theology can therefore claim universal relevance; but, conversely, no theology claiming to be universal is truly contextual. This means that no single theology can claim to be valid for all times and places. Universal theology consists in the communion of various local theologies, even as the universal Church is the communion of all the local churches.

There is no need to argue at length the diversity of context in which theology and Christology are to be done. To limit ourselves to geographical areas, it is common knowledge that the present context of the so-called First World is widespread technological progress with the ensuing process of secularization. In such a context, the addressee of theology is more often than not the nonbeliever. By contrast, the Third World continents are characterized by the dehumanizing poverty and underdevelopment of large masses of people and the consequent need for integral liberation. In such a context, the addressee of theology is not the nonbeliever but—in the words of the theology of liberation—the nonperson. More correctly, the nonperson is not merely the addressee but the agent of theologising, together with the believing community in which he is placed and with which he is engaged in a liberating praxis.

The communality of underdevelopment notwithstanding, the context for doing theology differs vastly among the various continents of the Third World, resulting in distinct emphases. While the Latin American continent, made up of vast Christian populations, is overwhelmingly concerned with integral human liberation, the African continent lays heavy stress on the cultural dimension and stands in search, primarily, of inculturation or "African authenticity," as it has come to be called. The context of the Asian continent is heavily marked by the coexistence of tiny Christian minorities with vast majorities of people belonging to other religious traditions, and by the growing interaction among the various traditions. In such a context, a theological evaluation of other religious traditions and the praxis of interreligious dialogue become theological as well as pastoral priorities.

These vast contextual divergences call for many diversified theologies and Christologies. There is need in the affluent West for a Christology for "human come of age" in a secularized world. Such a Christology will be primarily "fundamental" in the sense of laying the foundations for faith in Jesus Christ in the secular city. But there is an equally pressing need in the continents of the Third World for a Christology of liberation, a Christology of inculturation, and a Christology of religious pluralism.

OUTLINING A CONCRETE CHRISTOLOGICAL PROJECT

The present "Introduction to Christology," however, aims at being, insofar as possible, applicable to distinct situations. It will, therefore, not be possible to abide directly and distinctly by any particular context. What is thereby unavoidably lost by way of immediate relevance to a concrete situation will, it is hoped, be made good inasmuch as the primary concerns of the vastly different contexts described above will be kept in mind. Thus, an effort will be made to seek in the liberative praxis of the historical Jesus the foundation for a Christology of liberation. Similarly, the need for inculturating the christological faith will be taken into account and the open-endedness of traditional christological formulations will be argued, thus laying the foundation for a Christology of inculturation. Again, the mystery of Jesus Christ will be seen in the vast context of the plurality of religious traditions, and the relationship of the other traditions to the mystery of Jesus Christ will be shown to pave the way for a Christology of religions.

Our first chapter will review various approaches to Christology characteristic of recent times, with a view to searching for an adequate perspective. A balance sheet is thus drawn of the various christological tendencies existing today, not out of a merely academic concern, but in order to devise a coherent approach that will thereafter be called an "integral Christology," and to situate it in the framework of the christological enterprise of the present time. This first chapter is entitled "Christology and Christologies: A Survey of Recent Approaches."

Chapter 2 asks what ought to be the point of departure of Christology. It is not enough to answer that the New Testament, as the *norma normans*, is also the starting point, for there arises the question of the origin of the New Testament, the history of its composition, and its relationship to the historical person of Jesus of Nazareth. Is Jesus the starting point for doing Christology, or is the point of departure to be sought in the Easter experience of the disciples? But does the faith interpretation of Jesus after the resurrection serve as adequate foundation for the whole christological enterprise? If not, can it be shown that the christological faith of the apostolic Church is based on the Jesus of history, and that between him and the apostolic Church there is no break in continuity? These questions will be dealt with under the title "Jesus at the Source of Christology: From the Pre-Easter Jesus to the Easter Christ."

Based on the Jesus of history, yet starting with the Easter experience of the disciples, the Christology of the apostolic Church is subject to an organic growth and development. Chapter 3, "The Development of New Testament Christology: From the Risen Christ to the Incarnate Son," follows this development. It shows the continuity that exists between the functional Christology of the early kerygma of the apostolic Church and the ontological Christology of later New Testament christological reflection. The plurality of New Testament Christologies cannot, however, be reduced to an amorphous diversity, for between the various stages of New Testament christological reflection there exist at once an organic process of growth and a substantial unity of content.

There has been much discussion in recent years on the value of dogma in general and of christological dogma in particular. The Chalcedonian definition has been accused of being abstract, ahistorical and dualistic, of representing a hellenization, even a corruption and alienation of the Jesus of history. It needs to be asked if the christological dogma constitutes a legitimate development in continuity with the New Testament. What value is to be assigned to it? Is it such as to leave room for other enunciations of the christological faith? The fourth chapter, "Historical Development and Present Relevance of Christological Dogma," attempts to answer these questions. Specifically, it shows what kind of logic is inherent in the elaboration of the christological dogma.

Among the christological problems most dicussed in recent decades are those concerned with the human psychology of Jesus. How was he aware of his personal identity as the Son of God? How did his human knowledge and will function? Did Jesus have authentic human freedom? Was he subject to the ordinary law of human development? Did he have to discover day by day how to respond to his messianic vocation? In sum: How did the human psychology of the Son of God incarnate in kenosis function during his earthly life, prior to his transformation into glory? Chapter 5, "The Problem of the 'Human' Psychology of Jesus," is dedicated to these questions.

The question asked in the sixth chapter has for centuries engaged the attention of Christologists, though a fully adequate answer seems to elude us even today: Why Jesus Christ? *Cur Deus homo?* However, the context in which the question is asked will be broadened here to extend to the present reality of religious pluralism. Was Jesus Christ necessary for the salvation of humankind? If not, why has God chosen to communicate and save in this apparently discriminating fashion? And what of the uniqueness of Jesus Christ, universal Saviour, in a context where an ever-vaster majority of people — more than four billion today — have not heard his message? This last chapter is entitled, "Jesus Christ the Universal Saviour."

It is hoped that at the end of the enquiry some aspects of the mystery of Jesus Christ to which less than justice has sometimes been done will have been recovered. The conclusion will summarise the main traits that need to distinguish an integral Christology. Such a Christology would hold together, in fruitful tension, such complemetary aspects of the mystery as soteriology and Christology or functional and ontological Christology. It would also mark a return to the human story of Jesus often neglected under the pressure of christological speculation. It would further show how the event of Jesus Christ is at once the story of the Triune God, Father, Son and Spirit; how the mystery of the Trinity is immanently present in that of the person Jesus; and how, consequently, reflection can validly ascend from Jesus the Christ to the God revealed in him: from Christology to theology.

NOTES

1. Cf. Leonard Swidler, " 'Jesus' Unsurpassable Uniqueness': Two Responses," *Horizons* 16 (1989) 119.

2. Text in Michael Sharkey (ed.), *International Theological Commission, Texts and Documents 1969-1985,* San Francisco: Ignatius Press, 1989, p. 296.

3. See Karl Rahner, "Theos in the New Testament," *Theological Investigations,* vol.1, London: Darton, Longman and Todd, 1974, pp. 79-148.

4. See Claude Geffré, *The Risk of Interpretation. On Being Faithful to the Christian Tradition in a Non-Christian Age,* New York and Mahwah, N.J.: Paulist Press, 1987.

1

Christology and Christologies

A Survey of Recent Approaches

There has never been, not even in the New Testament, a single Christology. Our own time has witnessed a variety of christological approaches, of which this chapter attempts to give a general survey. The aim is to evaluate the merits and limitations of various christological postures, in order to benefit by the gains they have made and remedy their shortcomings in devising a more comprehensive christological perspective.

With this end in view, the survey does not aim to be exhaustive.[1] Some christological perspectives that were important not long ago have lost some of their relevance today and will not be considered here. For instance, the *Leben-Jesu-Forschung Schule* is somewhat obsolete today, and the *Religions-geschichtliche Schule*'s comparative religion approach is equally out-of-date. On the other hand, greater attention will be given to christological perspectives from the Third World than is customary. The christological approach based on dialogue with other religions will not be limited, as is often done even today, to the Christian-Jewish dialogue, but will extend to other religious traditions as well. We will also include the "Liberation Christology" approach that has spread fast in the Third World continents in response to the dehumanizing socioeconomic conditions of large masses and the "inculturation Christology" perspective that arises from the encounter of the mystery of Christ with various cultures in which it has not as yet struck deep roots.

Mention has already been made, while discussing method, of the traditional dogmatic approach to doing Christology. We showed it to be fraught with dangers, among which we pointed especially to a dogmatically inspired and uncritical use of Scripture and to the attendant tendency to absolutise dogmatic formulations. This material need not be repeated here. However, it may be a good idea to point out the similar dangers inherent in systematic christological treatises that, while using the Bible more critically, sin nonetheless by excess in their attempt to make an overall synthesis of the christological data. Such perfect continuity is then postulated between the historical Jesus and the Christ of faith that the true discontinuity that obtains between them is overshadowed. A double distance tends thus to be overlooked: first, between the pre-Easter Jesus and the post-Easter Christ; second, between Jesus Christ and God his Father. To which must be added a third distance likewise undermined by unwarranted systematic tendencies: that between the messianic hope in the Old Testament and its fulfillment in Jesus Christ according to the New. Here too perfect continuity tends to be presumed, as though the messianic prophecies furnished a circumstantial description of the Messiah which the life of Jesus would be seen to fulfill materially. To postulate this is to impose a priori a Christian meaning on texts whose immediate reference is to the old dispensation, a process by which the thorough newness of the "fulfillment" in Jesus Christ of the messianic hope is obscured. Complete syntheses betray an exaggerated concern for harmony, first between both testaments, then also within the New, between the Jesus of history and the Christ of faith. In both cases, the reality is in fact more complex.

The christological approaches studied here fall under two categories. Some are concerned with biblical Christology; others refer to theological perspectives. After discussing them, some conclusions will be drawn concerning the approach that will be followed hereafter in this book.

BIBLICAL AND THEOLOGICAL APPROACHES TO CHRISTOLOGY

BIBLICAL PERSPECTIVES

Historico-critical Approach

This refers to the use made of the "historico-critical" method of modern exegesis in order to retrieve from the Gospels whatever can be affirmed critically about Jesus. R. Bultmann's extreme scepticism with regard to the possibility of affirming anything with certitude about the historical Jesus is well known. He wrote:

> I am undoubtedly of the opinion that we can no longer know anything on the life and the person of Jesus, since the Christian sources showed no interest in it except in a very fragmentary way and not without a propensity for legend, and because there exist no other sources on Jesus.[2]

But equally known is the fact that Bultmann's successors, while abiding by the same method, have reached different conclusions. E. Käsemann, for instance, has shown that traditional elements exist in the synoptic tradition that the historian must recognize as authentic:

Out of the obscurity of the life story (*Historie*) of Jesus, certain characteristic traits in his preaching stand out in relatively sharp relief,
and . . . primitive Christianity has united its own message with these.
. . . The question of the historical Jesus is, in its legitimate form, the
question of the continuity of the times and within the variation of the
kerygma.[3]

The post-Bultmannians have thus recovered confidence in being able to
retrieve the Jesus of history from the Gospel tradition and to establish a
true continuity between him and the early kerygma, the discontinuity notwithstanding. The Instruction *Sancta Mater Ecclesia* (1964) of the Pontifical
Biblical Commission has recognized the validity of a prudent and balanced
historico-critical method.[4] It distinguished three stages in the formation of
the Gospels: the Jesus of history; the oral and already partly written
traditions that were circulated in the churches after Jesus' resurrection;
and the editorial work of the synoptic writers. (The Constitution on Divine
Revelation of Vatican II took over from the Instruction this threefold stage
for describing the formation of the Gospels [DV, 19].) Through the use of
a threefold method, called *Formgeschichte, Traditiongeschichte* and *Redak-
tiongeschichte* respectively, critical exegesis is able to retrieve the Jesus of
history from the present written form of the Gospels. It becomes possible
to recover, if not his "personal consciousness," at least his fundamental
ways and attitudes—for instance, his healing and wonder-working ministry—and with them the main traits of his personality: the way in which he
spoke of himself, conceived his mission, and was understood by his disciples.
Thus, the explicit Christology of the post-Easter kerygma can once more
be based on the implicit Christology of Jesus himself. Continuity can be
established between one and the other, even while a real discontinuity also
exists between them.

I have spoken of a prudent and balanced use of the historico-critical
method of exegesis. This requires that it never be considered exclusive and
standing in isolation from the ecclesial tradition and the Church's teaching
authority, as is clearly stated in Vatican II's Constitution on Divine Revelation (DV, 10). To apply the historico-critical method of exegesis in isolation from the Church's memory would entail the risk of a christological
reductionism that would fall short of the Church's faith. Such reductionism
may consist of adopting an exclusively functional Christology that intentionally remains silent on the ontology of Jesus Christ or his personal identity as the Son of God. This may happen through a selective choice of
material, as, for instance, when the Gospel of John is left out of consideration because (as it is claimed) while offering a deep meditation, psychological and ontological, on the person of Jesus Christ, it is neither
historically reliable nor can it be trusted for the authenticity of the sayings
it attributes to Jesus. Granting that the fourth Gospel calls for special
critical criteria, such reductionism inevitably results in leaving an unsur-

mountable gap between the Jesus of history and the Christ of faith; the discontinuity leaves no room for continuity.

Existential Approach

We have noted the influence exercised by R. Bultmann on the use in exegesis of the historico-critical method. We have further noted that Bultmann's followers departed from his extreme scepticism as regards the possibility of establishing the Christology of the early Church kerygma on a solid foundation in the historical Jesus. Bultmann himself held this to be neither possible nor necessary. According to his existential interpretation, what matters is not what Jesus may have thought or done. What matters is that through the word that comes to us in the kerygma we are challenged to a decision of faith. God's invitation to us in the kerygma and our existential response in the decision of faith constitute the true revelatory event; that it be founded or not in the historical Jesus is in the last analysis immaterial. As for the New Testament christological formulations, they are coined in the mythological language of the time; they must therefore be demythologised, that is, given an existential interpretation. Bultmann wrote:

> Surely *Jesus* as simple man appeared as a prophet and a rabbi. He did not proffer a doctrine concerning his person but he affirmed that the fact of his activity was the decisive fact. His doctrine is not new where ideas are concerned. Under that aspect it is nothing but pure Judaism, pure prophetism. ... Whether Jesus has had or not the consciousness of being the Messiah, changes nothing. ... It is true that his call to decision implies a Christology; but it is not a Christology conceived as metaphysical speculation on a heavenly being or as a picture of his person with a problematic consciousness. It is a Christology which is proclamation, summoning.[5]

There is no need to expand on the influences and presuppositions on which Bultmann's existential approach to the New Testament and Christology is based. Paramount among these are: a particular Lutheran concept of faith as fideism; the existential philosophy of Heidegger; and a rationalist prejudice that makes him deny a priori the possibility of miraculous divine interventions. More important for our purpose is to evaluate the risks for Christology inherent in Bultmann's position.

For Bultmann, the historical Jesus, his message and activity, cannot be claimed as the source for the Christology of the Church's kerygma. No continuity can be established or sought between the kerygmatic proclamation of Christ and the historical Jesus. Furthermore, the symbolic language used by the New Testament kerygma to express the christological faith is reduced to mythical language. It does not convey any objective truth concerning the person and work of Jesus Christ, but serves only as a challenge for the decision of faith. In the process, Christology is reduced to anthropology. There is no longer question of asserting the significance of the person and the event of Jesus Christ for the salvation of humankind; what matters is the personal decision of faith of the believer in relation to God. In the last analysis, the Christ of Bultmann's Christology has no real foundation in the Jesus of history. Belonging only to the kerygma, he is reduced to a myth without historical substance.

Christological Approach through Titles

Some New Testament Christologies present themselves as title Christologies. The following can be mentioned: O. Cullmann, F. Hahn, V. Taylor, L. Sabourin.[6] The christological titles used in the New Testament fall under different categories. Some are messianic titles, such as "the Christ" (masiah, the anointed one), the "Servant of Yahweh" (Isaiah 42-53), the "Son of Man" (Daniel 7). Others are functional titles referring to the salvific role of Jesus toward humankind—"Prophet," "Saviour," "Lord." Others still may refer to the personal identity of Jesus, and as such are called ontological—"Word of God," "Son of God." The ontological meaning of titles may not, however, be presumed. The overall perspective of New Testament Christology is primarily functional, not ontological. While it is true that the dynamism of faith causes it to rise to the ontological level, it needs to be shown where this happens and cannot be presumed. Where the import of christological titles is concerned, special attention is called for, as different levels of meaning need to be distinguished. To give but one example: the title Son of God has broad meaning in the Old Testament, where it is used of God's chosen people in general, and in particular of the Davidic king as God's representative among the people, or of every just person in Israel. Where it is applied to Jesus in the New Testament, the meaning is primarily functional, in continuity with the original Old Testament meaning; it needs to be shown where it acquires an ontological significance.

The importance of christological titles in New Testament Christology cannot be underestimated; but neither can it be exaggerated. A Christology of titles can never constitute by itself a complete Christology. Morever, keeping in mind the critical and methodological difficulties with which their use in the New Testament is fraught, it would be wise not to assign them more certainty than they are able to support. Some of the critical questions to which they give rise include, Has such or such title been used by Jesus himself, or has it been applied to him by others? If by others, was it by Jesus' hearers during his lifetime, or by the apostolic Church after his resurrection? Was the title used with its original meaning, or did it receive (and if so, where?) a "surplus meaning"? Is it to be understood as exclusively functional, or does it rise—and where—to the ontological level of Jesus' personal identity and relationship to God? Recent discussions on

the Son of Man title[7] are ample evidence of the caution with which christological titles need to be handled.

Incomplete in itself, a Christology of titles has the added inherent draw-
back of saying little about the concrete human story of Jesus; to that extent
it runs the risk of remaining abstract. More importantly, however, not unlike
the other biblical approaches mentioned above, the titles approach to New
Testament Christology also raises the question of the continuity and discontinuity between the Jesus of history and the Christ of faith. Clearly, this
is a major issue that must occupy any biblical treatment of Christology that
would claim to be critical. Jesus himself must be seen to be at the origin
of the New Testament christological faith. How can it be shown that he is?

THEOLOGICAL PERSPECTIVES

A Critico-dogmatic Approach

Speaking earlier of the dogmatic method and approach to Christology,
we have pointed out its inherent danger of absolutizing the value of dogmatic formulations. The christological definition of Chalcedon is considered
the only possible way of enunciating the mystery of Jesus Christ; it is
claimed to be valid for all times and all places. The critico-dogmatic method
is a reaction to such christological dogmatism. The new approach is based
on the understanding that dogmatic enunciations are, of necessity, conditioned in time and space by the surrounding culture in which they have
been framed. They are and remain valid within the parameters of that
culture; indeed, within their historical context, they were often necessary.
They also form part of the Church's memory today. Nevertheless, their
deep intention was to assert the meaning of the mystery through the mediation of concepts capable of conveying it, no matter how inadequately,
though the meaning itself always remains beyond the mediating concepts.
It is this deep meaning, not the formulations themselves, that needs to be
preserved through the centuries. Culture is, however, open to evolution,
and the meaning of the concepts may change. In situations of cultural
evolution — and, even more so, in situations where the Christian message is
to become incarnate in cultures distinct from that in which it was originally
coined — faithfulness to the deep intention and meaning of traditional, even
dogmatic, formulations may require that new ways of expressing that meaning be devised. Dogmatic pluralism appears, therefore, as a distinct possibility, even if it requires a prudential discernment. Nor can this claim be
accused of dogmatic relativism, for to profess the value of dogmatic formulations to be relative and not absolute is not equivalent to relativising
truth and denying it all objectivity.

The relativity of dogmatic formulations has not always been openly recognized by the Church's teaching authority. Suffice it to recall Pius XII's
condemnation of dogmatic relativism with its apparent claim about absolute

value for the Church's dogmatic formulations in the Encyclical *Humani Generis* (1950)[8]; and, closer to our time, Paul VI's Encyclical *Mysterium Fidei* (1965), in which the pope upholds the lasting, unchanging and universal value of dogmatic formulations coined in concepts derived from universal human experience and therefore not liable to cultural change.[9] However, in his inaugural speech at the first session of Vatican Council II (1962), Pope John XXIII made in this regard an important pronouncement which needs to be quoted. The pope said:

> In fact, the deposit itself of the faith, that is, the truths contained in our doctrine is one thing, another is the form in which they are enunciated, while however keeping the same meaning and the same sense.[10]

This important text, which implicitly recognized the possibility of a plurality of dogmatic formulations, has been substantially adopted and made its own by Vatican II. The Constitution *Gaudium et Spes* declared:

> The deposit and the truths of faith are one thing, the manner of expressing them is quite another, the meaning and the sense remaining, however, always the same (GS, 62; cf. GS, 42; UR, 4,6).

To which must be added the Declaration *Mysterium Ecclesiae* (1973) of the Congregation for the Doctrine of the Faith.[11] This declaration distinguishes the meaning of the dogmatic formulations, which abides, from the formulations themselves which, being subject to historical conditioning, remain open to deeper enunciations or eventually to new expression.

The critico-dogmatic approach to Christology is based on the recognition of the possibility of dogmatic plurality, as well as of the eventual need, in situations of cultural change, of having recourse to new formulations in order to preserve the meaning unaltered. A recent Christologist put the question as follows:

> What does a real, creative loyalty to our faith in Jesus as the Christ demand? How can this faith be professed today without foreshortening or distortion, but also without holding on to patterns of thought which no longer express what was formerly intended?[12]

This is not the place to enter into a dicussion of the merits or demerits of concrete attempts in this direction, but only to offer some critical remarks. A first observation is that the leading concern that prompts such christological proposals is that of the inculturation of faith in Jesus Christ in the context of cultural evolution or the encounter with alien cultures. This concern is not only welcome but binding. Yet in the vast field of the incarnation of Christianity in different cultures, doctrinal inculturation is, no doubt, the most problematic aspect. It raises delicate hermeneutical questions as to the possible modality of "transculturation." Awareness of such problems is needed both for the practice of doctrinal inculturation and the evaluation of its results. A second observation has direct relevance to the purpose of the present survey. It will be seen that the fundamental challenge to Christology is that of holding fast to both continuity and discontinuity in the profession of christological faith: continuity in the sameness of meaning; discontinuity in the mediation of concepts. Once more it becomes clear that the continuity-discontinuity dialectic is an important aspect of christological discourse.

Salvation History Approach

This approach consists in situating the event of Jesus Christ in the overall economy of God's dealings with humankind throughout history in self-revelation and self-gift. The history of salvation is coextensive with the history of the world; it extends from the protology of creation to the eschatology of the parousia in the end-time. It is, however, distinct from profane history, insofar as its formal object is the dialogue of salvation initiated by God with humankind and pursued through the entirety of world history. The salvation history approach to Christology shows the central place the event of Jesus Christ occupies in the linear unfolding of the history of salvation. According to O. Cullmann,[13] the Christ event—from the incarnation of the Son of God down to the paschal mystery of his death and resurrection—is not only the real centre of history but also the dynamic principle of intelligibility of the entire historical process. What precedes it is oriented toward it as "evangelical preparation"; what follows after belongs to the unfolding of the potentialities of the event in the "time of the Church."

The centrality of the Christ-event notwithstanding, there remains a tension in salvation history, to which the New Testament testifies, between the "already" and the "not yet"; between what has already been achieved in Jesus Christ and what still remains to be realized in the eschatological future. This abiding tension between the "already" and the "not yet" gives rise to distinct emphases on the one or the other among salvation history Christologists. Thus we distinguish "realized eschatology," which bears the name of C. H. Dodd, with its emphasis on the "already" and "consequent eschatology," with the name of A. Schweitzer, which places the stress on the "not yet." While O. Cullmann clearly belongs to the first group, J. Moltmann[14] inserts himself unambiguously in the second. For Moltmann, the whole of human history aims toward the realization of a divine promise of an eschatological salvation, of which the death and resurrection of Jesus is the proleptic model. The irreplaceable role of Jesus Christ notwithstanding, the focal point and pivot of the entire process of salvation history is the eschaton.

Different emphases notwithstanding, the two forms of the salvation history approach have the merit of situating the Christ-event within the entire framework of God's dealings with humankind in history. They show how God's saving design for humankind in Jesus Christ unfolds progressively in history, which is also centred on Jesus Christ. At the same time, they show the ambivalence in Christian theology of such concepts as eschatology and the Reign of God. While the Old Testament was oriented toward a decisive intervention of God in an indefinite future that was called "the last times," eschatology in the New Testament is split into two distinct moments — the already accomplished and the still to come. As for the establishment of the Reign of God on earth, a threefold distinction needs to be made. God inaugurates his Kingdom in Jesus Christ in two moments. First, the Kingdom begins to dawn on earth in Jesus' lifetime and ministry; second, it is truly inaugurated in the paschal mystery of his death and resurrection. But the Kingdom still needs to grow to its eschatological fulness in the end of times. Until then, the tension between the "already" and the "not yet" will endure; we may never do without the "eschatological remainder." From this it may be seen once again that the dialectic of continuity and discontinuity is intrinsic to Christology. It will have to be shown how this dialectic applies to the distinction between the history that went before the Christ-event and that which follows after it, as also between what has been accomplished by God in the Christ-event and the "eschatological remainder" that stands in the future.

The Anthropological Approach

It has been observed earlier that in the mystery of Jesus Christ, the mystery of humankind is fully revealed. That in Jesus Christ God enters into a "marvellous exchange" with humankind supposes a capacity and openness for such an exchange on the part of humanity. The anthropological approach to Christology is so called because it endeavours to show the stepping-stones of the mystery of Jesus Christ in humankind or, inversely, the place and role of Jesus Christ in the pilgrimage of humankind toward God. Here Christology begins with anthropology; not, it should be clear, with anthropology in the sociological sense, but in the theological.

An anthropological approach to Christology can take two distinct forms. One consists in situating humankind in the evolutive process of the cosmos that positive science postulates as an axiom. In such a perspective, Jesus Christ will be seen — in the word of P. Teilhard de Chardin, the protagonist of this anthropologico-christological vision — as the "motor" of the evolutive process. Teilhard called him "the evolutive Christ." The other approach considers humanity philosophically open to self-transcendence in God and capable of receiving the free gift of God's self-communication. It further sees humanity theologically as being created by God with such a destiny, existentially ordained to, and on the lookout for, the eventuality of God's highest possible self-communication in the mystery of the incarnation. K. Rahner, whose name is attached to this type of anthropologico-christological vision, speaks of a "transcendental Christology" ending up in a "searching Christology."

Neither of the two visions can be developed at length here; a few indications and critical observations must suffice. P. Teilhard de Chardin seeks, in the context of an alleged contradiction between faith and science, to reconcile what he calls his two "faiths": his scientific faith in the evolutive process of the world, and his theological faith in the cosmic Christ of whom St. Paul speaks. Between the one and the other, there exists, as he sees it, not a contradiction but rather a "marvellous convergence." Jesus Christ is the Omega point of the world's evolutive process, the final cause that sets the entire process into motion by drawing it to itself. The cosmic Christ of St. Paul is the "evolutive Christ." To stress the cosmic character of Christ-the-Omega-point, Teilhard speaks of his "cosmic nature."

Two observations are in order here. First, it would be wrong to suppose that in the mind of Teilhard a scientific axiom such as that of the evolutive process can by its own resources arrive at, or even postulate, the mystery of the incarnation as necessary. The event of the incarnation is and can only be known through revelation, and only Christian faith in the mystery of Christ can make us discover the "marvellous convergence" that exists between the world's evolutive process and "Christo-genesis." Second, the Christ-Omega, with his "cosmic nature," cannot be reduced, in Teilhard's mind, to an abstract principle. He is identically Jesus of Nazareth, dead and risen, who has been constituted "Lord" by the God who raised him. The Jesus of history is personally the Christ of faith. Teilhard insists that only if the cosmic Christ has inserted himself personally into the "phylum" of humankind can he act as the final cause that draws the cosmos to itself in the process of evolution. Similarly he wrote:

> To suppress the historicity of Christ, i.e., the divinity of the historical Christ would immediately result in reducing to nought all the mystical experience of 2000 years of Christianity. Christ born of a virgin and the risen Christ: both are inseparable.[15]

K. Rahner's "transcendental Christology"[16] is founded on a philosophico-theological analysis of humankind in the concrete historical condition in which it is created by God and destined to union with God. The "supernatural existential" inherent in concrete historical man is not to be identified with an "obediential potency" or "natural desire" for the vision of God inherent in human nature as such, metaphysically considered. In the concrete, supernatural order of reality, we carry in us more than a passive potency for self-transcendence in God. We are concretely and actively oriented toward the realization of such a self-transcendence. Even more, existentially, we are awaiting in anticipation the mystery of the incarnation.

The supernatural existential inherent in us in our concrete historical condition thus constitutes the a priori condition for the possibility of the incarnation. Or, to put it the other way round, the mystery of Christ is what happens if God freely brings to realization in its deepest possible form the capacity for union that in the concrete order of reality inheres in humankind through the supernatural existential. Historical humanity is on the lookout for the mystery of the incarnation. Thus, Christology becomes the perfect realization, the absolute fulfillment, of anthropology. Jesus Christ, in whom the absolute mode of divine-human union is actualized, is the absolute Saviour of humankind, the centre of salvation history, because in him the openness to God inscribed in transcendental human experience finds its total realization.

Here too some observations are in order. First, it would be wrong to attribute to K. Rahner the claim that the mystery of the incarnation can be deduced from our open nature to transcendence, or even from our historical condition as called to union with God. The incarnation can only become reality through God's free choice and gratuitous initiative. Only the Christian revelation can, and does, tell us that in Jesus of Nazareth our openness to God has come to a climax in what is its highest possible realization, and that he is indeed God's Son made human. Secondly, K. Rahner's transcendental Christology and searching Christology—as well as, in another perspective, that of Teilhard de Chardin—can be viewed as distinct forms of the "from below" or "upward" Christology. Not in the sense that it takes its point of departure in the human existence of the man Jesus, or even in the glorified state of his manhood, but in a philosophico-theological analysis of human nature in the present order of creation. Such upward Christology does not, however, represent the only christological perspective of K. Rahner. The from above or downward perspective is also found in his writings. It is conspicuously present where Rahner follows the schema of christological refection of the Johannine prologue: The Word became flesh (Jn 1:14).[17] The coexistence of both perspectives raises the question of their relationship, to which we shall have to return at a later stage. Meanwhile, it needs to be remarked that Rahner's transcendental Christology—and anthropological Christology in general—rests on a limited biblical foundation and tends to lose touch with the concrete life and story of Jesus in his historical cultural circumstances. K. Rahner himself was sensitive to this lack and advocated a return to the story of Jesus and his "historical mysteries." Lastly, it can be seen that anthropological Christology raises once more, even though in a distinctive manner, the issue of continuity-in-discontinuity; this time, between our openness to the mystery of Jesus Christ and God's realization of it in history.

The Approach of Liberation Christology

It has been shown earlier that R. Bultmann thought it practically impossible to retrieve the Jesus of history from the faith interpretation of the

New Testament kerygma. It has been added that the post-Bultmannians have regained confidence in being able to recover the Jesus of history to a theologically significant extent. They have expressed their conviction that Christology, if it is to have a valid foundation, needs to be based in Jesus Christ. There ensued in recent christological studies what must be seen as a massive "return" to the Jesus of history, to "Jesuology."[18]

However, the return to the Jesus of history is variously motivated and takes on distinct significance and meaning in different contexts. In the context of Western hermeneutics, it is determined primarily by the need to retrieve the historical Jesus as the necessary foundation for a valid Christology. The intention is to provide the christological faith with an adequate critical basis in what Jesus taught and did, in his words and in his works. The process belongs primarily to what can be called "fundamental Christology," which, dealing with the foundations of faith, is directed to the would-be believer.

By contrast, the return of liberation Christology to the historical Jesus is marked by a vastly different intention and significance. It is not meant to retrieve historical data critically in order that the christological faith may have a valid historical foundation. It is rather ordained to the recovery of the praxis of the historical Jesus as the hermeneutical principle for the liberative praxis of the Christian Church. Jesus' praxis has a paradigmatic value for Christian praxis. This is especially true in the context of masses of people subject to a dehumanizing poverty arising from unjust sociopolitical structures and the consequent crying need for the integral liberation of the poor. Liberation Christology returns to the historical Jesus, not in search of a valid foundation for the christological faith of the Church, but for his own sake and as a criterion of discernment for Christian praxis. The christological dogma is not denied; it is taken for granted by a believing people, even if a critique of its formulations is considered necessary. But faith does not primarily consist of an assent to the truth of christological enunciations, but in discipleship of the historical Jesus, without which there is no access to the Christ of faith. Furthermore, in a liberation context, the Jesus of history has special immediate relevance, because the context in which he exercised his liberating action was in many regards strikingly similar to that in which today's poor are struggling for liberation.

So Jesus' historical praxis becomes the privileged theme of liberation Christology: his actions, that is, as well as his message, his attitudes, his choices and options, his social involvement and the political implications of his life and death. In a word, liberation Christology revalues Jesus' human story—without claiming thereby to rewrite a history of Jesus—as the medium of God's liberating and saving action in history. Such a Christology is resolutely a Christology from below, which does not, however, prescind from Jesus' personal identity as the Son of God. There is no break between the Jesus of history and the Christ of faith, even while orthopraxy precedes orthodoxy. But in the human story of the Son of God, liberation

Christology seeks the "project" which God has accomplished in him of integral human liberation.

One of the possible dangers for a theology of liberation — one directly relevant to Christology — would be the risk of christological reductionism. To remedy this, the Church's teaching authority, while recognizing the legitimacy of the liberation christological project, has warned against distortions of the person of Jesus at variance with the Church's faith and laid stress on the need to profess the integral truth about Jesus Christ.[19] To hold the full truth about Jesus Christ and his work must mean, on the one hand, to profess that the human story of Jesus is that of one who is personally the Son of God and, on the other, that the liberation God has accomplished in him is not only horizontal but vertical, not only human but divine. To say this is to show that the fundamental problem for a Christology of liberation is that of accounting for true continuity in discontinuity. In order that continuity with the Christ of faith may be shown, the full truth about the Jesus of history first needs to be taken into consideration.

The Feminist Liberation Approach to Christology

Liberation theology turns to the historical Jesus as the hermeneutical principle for a Christian liberation praxis in the context of the dehumanizing poverty of the masses and the struggle of the poor for integral liberation. However, unjust sociopolitical structures do not consist merely of classism but comprise, among other aspects, racism and sexism. Liberation theology, which in its original concern for the liberation of the poor masses has spread rapidly to the three continents of the Third World, has also taken on distinctive forms in the First World and elsewhere, as it addresses itself to the struggle for liberation of entire peoples discriminated against through racism and apartheid[20] or to the plight of women striving to liberate themselves from discrimination through sexism. The feminist liberation theological movement calls for explicit mention here, both for the momentum it has gained and the approach to Christology it has initiated.[21]

That the present feminist movement responds to a pressing need is borne out by U.N. statistics that show that, while forming one-half of the world population, women do three-fourths of the world's work, receive one-tenth of the world's salary, and own one-one-hundredth of the world's land. Two-thirds of illiterate adults are women. Over three-fourths of starving people are women and their dependent children. Added to this dark picture is the bodily and sexual exploitation of women. Sexism in its many forms is pervasive on a global scale.

The new awareness on the part of women — primarily in the First World — of their massive exploitation through sexism has given rise to two distinct forms of feminist theology. The first, called Revolutionary Feminist Theology, chooses to opt out of Christianity and the Church, which it considers irremediably aligned to a sexist view of society and Church, based on patriarchy and androcentrism. It advocates a return to some kind of goddess religion. The other—the only one with which we are concerned here—calls itself reformist. It stigmatises all manifestations of sexism as structural evil militating against God's will in creation as well as the ideal of equality in partnership and mutuality that characterised the sisterhood and brotherhood of disciples in the Jesus movement.

Liberation from the prevailing patriarchy and androcentrism of the Jewish tradition was an essential part of the social revolution implied in the irruption of God's Reign that God was bringing about in Jesus; even though—as the New Testament testifies—it found its way back in societal Church structures in apostolic times, only to be further restored thereafter. Feminist reformist theology sets itself the task of developing a feminist hermeneutic of God, of Jesus himself and of the movement initiated by him. With this in view, it unmasks the sexist bias of the critical exegesis of the Bible and the New Testament as propounded by Western scholarship and the naiveté of its claim to neutrality and objectivity. Here, as in all situations of oppression, neutrality is at best an illusion. To claim it is to betray one's covert option for the status quo through the maintenance of the structures of oppression. Liberation theology in general considers opting for the poor as the only appropriate response in keeping with God and Jesus' own bias in their favour. The rich are called to conversion through the practice of institutional justice toward the dispossessed. Feminist reformist theology does not aim to institute a gynocentric or matriarchal order of society, which could turn out to be equally, though inversely, oppressive. By unmasking the oppression of women implied in the prevailing structures and engaging in liberation activities, it seeks to restore the equality in partnership and mutuality between the sexes that characterised the social order of the Jesus movement.

The hermeneutical task that feminist reformist theology sets itself is no easy one. Only some aspects of its approach to Christology, and in particular its way of retrieving the historical Jesus and the movement launched by him, can be indicated here. The maleness of Jesus has often been interpreted as the only way in which a God presumed to be male could be revealed. Jesus, it is further claimed, can only be fully represented by males. Yet the Old Testament witnesses to the use of feminine metaphors as well as masculine ones with reference to God. As for interpreting Jesus himself, the New Testament Christology, Paul and John in particular, have developed a Wisdom (*Sophia*: feminine) Christology of great depth that shows that Jesus' divine identity can be confessed in a nonandrocentric framework. Far from laying a foundation for patriarchal attitudes in the community of Jesus' disciples, his "Abba" guarantees a rapport of equality, mutuality and reciprocity among its female and male members. The Reign of God breaking in through Jesus marks the end of sexist discrimination, as of every other discrimination; Jesus' partiality in favour of the marginalized includes women. He called them to discipleship; they were present under the cross and became the first recipients of resurrection appearances. In fact, both during his earthly life and after his resurrection, Jesus included women in his community of disciples, made up as it was of sisters and brothers on a basis of equality. The Church, in its earliest days, knew women as missionaries and leaders of house churches. The forces and influences that brought about the decrease in later apostolic times of the public ministry of women are complex and remain the subject of intense debate and study. The fact, however, is that patriarchy and androcentrism did return to the Church structures, even as they endured and continued to prevail to a great extent in society.

The feminist liberation Christology discovers Jesus the Liberator not in a generic way as the Liberator of the poor, but specifically as the Liberator of women from the discrimination, supported by sexism, of which they are the victims in both the Church and society. That the charge in its globality is founded, must be admitted squarely. Nor will justice be done by simply paying lip-service to the principle of their equal dignity as human persons created in God's image, saved and made "one in Christ" and co-members of the People of God which is the Church, if effective participation in Church and society continues to be denied them. Not all theological problems are, however, solved thereby. While the difference between the sexes, if it is explained in terms of "complementarity," runs the risk of leading to woman's subordination, effective partnership in mutuality and reciprocity does not imply identity of roles, whether in society or the Church. As the U.S. bishops wrote: "A notion of equality which eliminates distinctive differences in women and men does not do justice to the challenges sexism poses."[22] To the difference between the sexes there correspond distinct endowments and tasks in society, as in the Church a variety of charisms flourish in diversified services, functions and ministries—all of which are to be gratefully acknowledged as manifesting, in their differences, the diversity of divine gifts.

The New Testament testifies to the association of women with men as co-disciples of Jesus. It also bears witness to the extraordinary influence women exercised, according to their own gifts and charisms, in spreading the Gospel of the Risen Lord, whereby they shared as partners in the mission of the Church. This inheritance from apostolic times must be gracefully recognized and implemented. It need not, however, contradict the Church's unbroken tradition—also based on apostolic practice—of discerning God's call to the ordained priesthood only among men. Eligibility of men only to priestly ordination—which it would be wrong to assign simplistically to sexist discrimination—remains a controverted issue in the Church today. Where Christology is concerned, the problem consists in discerning rightly and interpreting correctly the continuity-in-discontinuity that obtains between the mind of the historical Jesus and the praxis of the Church, apostolic and postapostolic.

Christology in Interreligious Perspective

This approach to Christology, which is only beginning to arise in today's context of religious pluralism, has little to do with the former *Religionsges-chichtliche Schule* approach. That approach relied on the science of comparative religion; this one takes its point of departure in the praxis of interreligious dialogue. In this, its method resembles *mutatis mutandis* that of liberation Christology; it is initially inductive. Not unlike liberation Christology which, being based in a liberative praxis of faith, finds its hermeneutical principle in the historical Jesus, so too a Christology of religions relies on a praxis of interreligious encounter and seeks to discover in this broad context the specificity of Christian faith and the uniqueness of Jesus Christ. Needless to say, the praxis of interreligious dialogue is always particular, depending on a concrete context. Furthermore, it has to do not with religious traditions in an abstract, impersonal manner, but with concrete religious people. This means that, while it is legitimate to write a Christology of religions that seeks to situate the mystery of Jesus Christ in the context of religious pluralism in general,[23] other christological studies are also required that directly situate themselves in the context of the encounter with a particular religious tradition. The tradition in question will belong either to the so-called monotheistic or prophetic religions (Judaism, Christianity, Islam) or those called "mystical" or oriental (Hinduism, Buddhism, and others) or even to one of the traditional religions.

Christology in dialogue has been developed in recent years in the context of the Jewish-Christian encounter. Christological studies by Jewish scholars such as P. Lapide, D. Flusser, G. Vermes, J. Neusner and others[24] have placed in evidence the authentic Jewishness of Jesus of Nazareth; they have shown how deeply Jesus was inserted into the culture and religious ethos of his people. While falling short of the Christian faith in Jesus, such works are of considerable help to the Christologist in his bid to rediscover the historical roots of Jesus. They will, moreover, assist him greatly in approaching the "First" Testament more objectively than he is often inclined to do. The texts dealing with God's covenant with Israel, those related to the messianic expectation in particular, must first be read within the historical context of God's dealings with the chosen people.[25] A Christian interpretation cannot a priori be superimposed on them; rather, such an interpretation needs to be shown to result from a "re-reading" done in the light of the Christian experience and by which "surplus meaning" is added to the texts.

His deep roots in Judaism notwithstanding, the Christologist will also have to show the originality of Jesus, the difference he makes, the distinctiveness of his personality, and finally the uniqueness of his person. He will have to put evidence forward to the effect that, while assuming Jewish culture and religion, Jesus also transformed it deeply, to such extent that a new reality came to birth in him. The expectation of the First Testament is not only fulfilled in him, it is fulfilled in a thoroughly unexpected manner. Jesus is a prophet, but not only a prophet; nor only a charismatic healer and thaumaturgist; nor only a Palestinian rabbi. While recognizing the commonalities, the divergences must also be noted, nay more, the contradictions; for Jesus is different. It will be seen that we encounter once more, though under a different angle, the problem of continuity-in-discontinuity — this time between the historical roots of Jesus Christ in Judaism and the significance of his mystery according to christological faith. Christology cannot overlook this aspect.

Christology of religions cannot, however, be limited to the Jewish-Christian dialogue. It must also meet the distinct religious traditions the Christian faith encounters concretely in various contexts, be it Islam, Hinduism, Buddhism, or whatever other religious tradition. Here the Christologist will have to discover the stepping-stones for the mystery of Jesus Christ not only in humanity understood as open to God's self-gift ("transcendental" Christology), nor only in the subjective religious life of individual persons in whom God's grace in Jesus Christ is already operative through the Holy Spirit (GS, 22), but also in the objective elements that together constitute the religious traditions of the world (NA, 2; LG, 16; AG, 9,11,15). To identify the "elements of truth and grace" (AG, 9) present in those traditions is a difficult task requiring keen discernment, but it is one that cannot be dispensed with if the mystery of Christ is to be inculturated in a context of religious pluralism. To identify in the other religious traditions the stepping-stones for the mystery of Jesus Christ or the "seeds of the Word," and to interpret those seeds not merely as expressions of our aspiration toward God but as traces of an initial approach of God to us, is to build a searching Christology of a new kind. For it brings to light not only our existential waiting for God, but God's historical waiting for us. While the first finds in Jesus Christ the realization of a hope and aspiration, the other reaches its climax and fulness in him. Such a Christology of God's search for people in their own religious traditions brings out once more the problem of continuity-in-discontinuity, but it asks the question in a new, original fashion. This is the discontinuity of the absolute newness of the mystery of Jesus Christ in the continuity of the first steps and approaches made by God to people in anticipation of God's coming.

TOWARD AN "INTEGRAL APPROACH" TO CHRISTOLOGY

The expression *integral Christology* is borrowed from the Pontifical Biblical Commission;[26] however, integral approach receives a more ample meaning here, where it refers to a comprehensive perspective. Integral Christology is understood by the Biblical Commission to be one that takes into account the entire biblical witness. In his commentary to the document of the Biblical Commission, J. A. Fitzmyer explains it in this direction:

In the study of Christology one has to listen to the whole biblical tradition, the Old Testament as well as the New Testament, since it is all given to us as the norm of Christian faith. Indeed, the literary development of the canonical unity of the Bible reflects the progressive revelation of God and his salvation offered to human beings. One must trace, then, the promises made to the patriarchs and subsequently expanded through the prophets, the expectations of God's Kingdom and Messiah that these have both introduced, and finally the realization of them in Jesus of Nazareth as the Messiah and the Son of God. . . .[27]

This is very true; however, an integral approach in Christology, while it must have the revealed message as its soul, must also benefit from the insights that distinct theological approaches have brought to the fore. The foregoing survey of christological approaches allows us to draw some preliminary conclusions as to what an integral approach to Christology would necessarily involve. This is done here by enunciating various principles.

THE PRINCIPLE OF DIALECTICAL TENSION

We have seen dialectical tension at work in many different ways and under different aspects where we pointed out the continuity-in-discontinuity between, for instance, the Old Testament messianic expectation and its fulfillment in the New; between Jesus' Jewishness and his transformation of Judaism; between the Christology of the historical Jesus and the Christology of the early Church; between the Christology of the apostolic kerygma and the more mature christological reflections of the New Testament; between the early postbiblical enunciations and the later christological developments. The same principle is operative in the continuity-in-discontinuity between the searching Christology of man's supernatural existential and the historical event of Jesus Christ; or again between the searching Christology of the world religious traditions and God's finding of religious humanity in Jesus Christ. In all these and other instances of the principle of dialectical tension, the rapport between continuous and discontinuous elements will have to be ascertained. That rapport may involve a "thorough newness" (St. Irenaeus), as between "evangelical preparations" (in humanity, in religions, or even in Judaism) and the historical event of Jesus Christ. It may, on the contrary, imply sameness of meaning in divergence of expression, as between the New Testament Christology and that of the postbiblical tradition. One same principle has, therefore, many different applications, each of which needs to be evaluated in its own right.

THE PRINCIPLE OF TOTALITY

By this is meant that a well-poised Christology must avoid all danger of reductionism or of unilateralism, in whatever direction. The christological mystery is made up of complementary aspects, often at first sight mutually opposed, yet which must be held together, even if often in tension. All false dualisms and apparent contradictions must be overcome, such as, for instance: between the Jesus of history and the Christ of faith; between Jesus' own implicit Christology and the Church's explicit Christology; between functional and ontological Christology; between soteriology and Christology; between salvation and human liberation; between horizontal and vertical liberation; between the historical ("already") and the eschatological ("not yet"). Or again: between anthropology and Christology; Christocentrism and theocentrism, and so forth. The Chalcedonian model of union "without confusion or change, without division or separation"[28] may serve here as a useful paradigm. Distinctions need to be made, but unity must be preserved.

THE PRINCIPLE OF PLURALITY

We have observed that the New Testament testifies to a plurality of Christologies to be held together in substantial unity. The principle of plurality applies even more where the postbiblical christological tradition and recent christological developments are concerned. Wherever it has arisen, such plurality has throughout the Christian tradition been guided by the concern to inculturate and to contextualise the christological faith. It could easily be shown that in the New Testament a concern for inculturation and the will to contextualise are at the root of the variety of approaches to the mystery of Jesus Christ witnessed to in the kerygmatic preaching,[29] as when from a prevalently Jewish cultural setting it passes over to a Jewish-Hellenistic and further on to a resolutely Hellenistic context.[30] Vatican II recognized as much when in the Constitution *Dei Verbum* it referred to the *Sitz im Leben* of the Gospels, that is, to the way they were written "with an eye to the situation of the Churches" (DV, 19).

The same concern to contextualise and inculturate has been at work in the development of the christological dogmas in the postbiblical tradition, as will be shown later when discussing hellenization and de-hellenization. The same remains operative in recent christological approaches and perspectives. To give some examples among those mentioned above, the critico-dogmatic approach to Christology is inspired by the concern for the inculturation of the christological faith in a context of cultural change. The problem it raises is how to maintain and express the traditional faith in Jesus Christ in the context of a changing culture where, due to an evolution in the meaning of concepts, the traditional formulations run the risk of betraying the sense they were meant to convey. The same preoccupation governs the anthropological approach to Christology, whether in the form of a christological evolutionism that attempts to reconcile Christian faith and scientific culture, or in the form of a transcendental Christology directed to humanity "come of age" in a secularized world. The same is true of the various Christologies — that of liberation as well as that of religions — that have arisen in the Third World continents in response to the challenge of human liberation and religious pluralism.

THE PRINCIPLE OF HISTORICAL CONTINUITY

Cultural diversity has given rise to distinct expressions of christological faith through the centuries. These notwithstanding, there exists a large degree of historical continuity between the various christological approaches, as well as between various christological reductions and heresies, at different stages of the tradition. The permanence of fundamental attitudes to the mystery of Jesus Christ is basically due to the ontological structure of the mystery made up, inseparably and unalterably, of duality and unity. This structure opens the way to two basic ways of approach: "from above" and "from below." That is, from the person of the Son of God who becomes human, or from the human Jesus who is personally the Son of God. Later, the question will have to be asked as to which of these two fundamental approaches to the christological mystery has had historical priority in biblical and postbiblical traditions. While we set aside this consideration for the time being, the constancy through the centuries of the logic inherent in each of the two ways of approach can be taken note of.

On one side is the downward or from above approach, which starts from the person of the Son of God. The kind of reductionism to which this approach can eventually give rise consists in undermining the reality or the authentic human character of Jesus' humanity. In the early tradition, this tendency gave rise to various christological heresies such as docetism, gnosticism, apollinarianism, monophysitism and others. In scholastic Christology the same showed up again under various forms, such as the principle of "absolute perfections" of Jesus' humanity, the theory of the beatific vision during his earthly life, or the Jesus of baroque spirituality pictured as a theophany of the "good God" showing up in human form or appearance. The same tendency remains a distinct possibility today. It has been observed that monophysitism is the continual temptation of pious but less-informed people (E. Masure), and K. Rahner has spoken of the "crypto monophysitism" of many Christians of our own time. The same tendency is at work, though in a covert, more subtle manner, in the existential Christology of R. Bultmann, which in some way evokes the early gnostic and docetist currents. As we have seen earlier, that nothing significant can be safely recovered from the human story of Jesus is for Bultmann finally immaterial, the only significant event being that of the word proclaimed in the kerygma, by which humanity is challenged to a faith decision. What finally matters for Bultmann is not the meaning attached to a historical Jesus-event, but the "event of the word" that exists in itself and is in no need of a foundation in the historical Jesus. The earthly life of Jesus, the mysteries of his flesh, have neither relevance nor value for salvation. Bultmann's christological stand amounts to a new version, in a vastly different cultural context, of the ancient docetism and gnosticism. His Christ of faith without the Jesus of history ends up in a myth.

On the other side is the upward or from below approach, which takes its point of departure in the person of Jesus. The reductionism to which this movement is liable is the exact reverse of that issuing from the opposite direction. It would consist in undermining the divine condition of Jesus or in falling short of the assertion of his personal identity as the Son of God. In the ancient tradition, reductionism in this direction showed up in various ways, as when Jesus was reduced by the ebionists to being a Jewish prophet among others, or in the christological heresies of adoptionism, arianism and nestorianism. In scholastic Christology, the same model appeared in an extreme form of the Christology of the "man assumed" (*homo assumptus*), which would have the man Jesus existing prior to being indwelt by the Son of God; and again in the Spanish "adoptionism," which assigned to Jesus as human an adoptive sonship of God. The same tendency is widespread today in the context of the modern, secularized Western world, where rationalism and truth derived from scientific observation often prevail. No matter how valid is the upward advance toward the christological mystery, more often than not, Christologists following it fail to reach out adequately to Jesus-the-Son-of-God. Christology then becomes a "degree Christology," in which Jesus is reduced to an ordinary man in whom God is present in an extraordinary degree. In such cases, Christology from below ends up in a "low Christology."[31]

In sum, the structure of the christological mystery opens the way to two opposite christological approaches — the downward and the upward — both of which are legitimate and should complete each other. But both have their connatural dangers which, unless guarded against, can eventually lead to opposite heresies. On the one hand, the approach from above, characteristic of the Alexandrian school, which has developed a Christology of the "Son incarnate," is liable to monophysite tendencies. The from below approach, typical of the Antiochian school, which has given rise to the Christology of the "man assumed," can lead toward Nestorianism. Any Christology desirous of maintaining the integrity of the christological mystery will have to hold together both ends in unity beyond any form of reductionism.

The Principle of Integration

An integral Christology must hold together complementary, though apparently contradictory, component elements of the mystery of Jesus Christ. It must likewise recover and reintegrate into a comprehensive presentation some aspects of the mystery which, in the course of tradition or even in recent times, have fallen by the wayside or been to a considerable extent neglected.

We have asserted the validity and the mutual complementarity of the christological approaches from above and from below. An integral Christology needs to combine both; how both call for each other in the dynamic of faith will be shown later. Similarly, soteriology and Christology also complement each other and mutually call for each other; how this is, will also be shown hereafter. In both these cases, a complete circle is in order: from Christology from below to Christology from above, and vice versa; and, in a similar way, from soteriology to Christology and back. Such a complete circular movement would best show the dialectic that obtains between the complementary approaches from opposite ends.

Christology has often sinned by impersonalism. To remedy such a shortcoming, the personal and trinitarian dimension of the mystery must be present everywhere. A Christology of the God-man is an abstraction; the only Christology that is real is that of the Son-of-God-made-man-in-history. The personal intratrinitarian relations must, therefore, be shown to inform every aspect of the christological mystery; this is especially true where the human psychology of Jesus is concerned. Part of the trinitarian dimension of the christological mystery is its pneumatological aspect. Christology must include a "pneumatic Christology," which will lay emphasis on the universal, operative presence of the Spirit of God in the Christ-event.

The historical dimension of the mystery of Jesus Christ, as well as the true human "story" of Jesus, must also be brought out once again, against the "de-historising" and abstracting tendency of much Christology of the past. Christian faith is in Jesus-the-Christ, that is, in the Jesus of history who has been constituted as the Christ by God in his resurrection from the dead. It is neither faith in a Jesus without Christ, nor in a Christ without Jesus. "Jesuology" and "Christology" must, therefore, be held together, for while a Jesus without Christ is empty, a Christ without Jesus is a myth.

Finally, the universal significance of the Christ-event and the cosmic dimension of the mystery of Christ must also be upheld, the historical particularity of the man Jesus notwithstanding. It needs to be shown that the mystery of Jesus Christ is the "concrete universal" in which universal meaning and historical particularity coincide. In Jesus of Nazareth, the Son of God has become humanized, and his human story is that of God.

NOTES

1. In 1984, the Pontifical Biblical Commission published an important volume entitled *Bible et Christologie* (Paris: Cerf, 1984). The volume contains "A Survey of Methodologies Used Today in Christology" (pp. 14-69), followed by an account of "The Global Testimony of Sacred Scripture about Christ" (pp. 71-109). The survey coincides partly with the one proposed here. An English translation with a commentary of those two parts of the volume has been published by Joseph A. Fitzmyer, *Scripture and Christology. A Statement of the Biblical Commission with a Commentary,* New York/Mahwah: Paulist Press, 1986.

2. Rudolf Bultmann, *Jesus*, Tübingen: Mohr, 1958, p. 11.

3. Ernst Käsemann, "The Problem of the Historical Jesus," in Id., *Essays on New Testament Themes*, London: SCM Press, 1964, p. 46.

4. See Josef Neuner and Jacques Dupuis (eds.), *The Christian Faith in the Doctrinal Documents of the Catholic Church*, London: Harper-Collins, 1992, nn.240-245.

5. See Rudolf Bultmann, *Glauben und Verstehen*, Band I, Tübingen: Mohr, 1933, pp. 245-267; see pp. 265-266. Also Rudolf Bultmann, *Jesus Christ and Mythology*, London: SCM Press, 1958.

6. Oscar Cullmann, *The Christology of the New Testament*, London: SCM Press, 1963; Ferdinand Hahn, *The Titles of Jesus in Christology. Their History in Early Christianity*, London: Lutterworth Press, 1969; Vincent Taylor, *The Names of Jesus*, London: Macmillan, 1954; Leopold Sabourin, *The Names and Titles of Jesus. Themes of Biblical Theology*, New York: Macmillan, 1967.

7. See, for instance, Maurice Casey, *Son of Man. The Interpretation and Influence of Daniel 7*, London: SPCK, 1979; also Barnabas Lindars, *Jesus Son of Man*, London: SPCK, 1983; Douglas R. A. Hare, *The Son of Man Tradition*, Minneapolis: Fortress Press, 1990.

8. AAS 42 (1950) 561-578; Neuner and Dupuis (eds.), *The Christian Faith*, nn. 147-148.

9. AAS 57 (1965) 753-774.

10. AAS 54 (1962) 792. This official text is an expanded version of the Italian text published in *L'Osservatore Romano*, Oct. 12, 1962, p. 3 and in *La Civiltà Cattolica* 113 (1962/4) 214, which in English translation would read: "The substance of the ancient doctrine of the deposit of faith is one thing, and the way in which it is presented is another." Alberto Mellosi has shown that the Italian version of this sentence is faithful to the manuscript that John XXIII had prepared for his opening address. See Alberto Mellosi, "Sinossi critica dell'allocuzione di apertura del Concilio Vaticano II *Gaudet Mater Ecclesia* di Giovanni XXIII," in Giuseppe Alberigo et al., *Fede, tradizione, profezia*, Brescia: Paideia, 1984, p. 269.

11. AAS 65 (1973) 396-408. See the commentary by Karl Rahner, "Mysterium Ecclesiae," *Theological Investigations*, vol. 17, London: Darton, Longman and Todd, 1981, pp. 139-155.

12. Piet Schoonenberg, *The Christ*, London: Sheed and Ward, 1971, p. 50.

13. Oscar Cullmann, *Christ and Time*, London: SCM Press, 1965.

14. Cf. mostly his recent work, Jürgen Moltmann, *The Way of Jesus Christ. Christology in Messianic Dimensions*, London: SCM Press, 1990.

15. Pierre Teilhard de Chardin, *Letters from a Traveller*, London: Collins, 1962, pp. 42-43.

16. See especially Karl Rahner, *Foundations of Christian Faith. An Introduction to the Idea of Christianity*, London: Darton, Longman and Todd, 1978.

17. See Karl Rahner, "On the Theology of the Incarnation," *Theological Investigations*, vol. 4, London: Darton, Longman and Todd, 1974, pp. 105-120.

18. See, among other important "Jesus Books," the following: Charles Harold Dodd, *The Founder of Christianity*, London: Macmillan, 1970; Günther Bornkamm, *Jesus of Nazareth*, London: Hodder & Stoughton, 1960; Eduard Schweizer, *Jesus*, London: SCM Press, 1978; Hans Conzelmann, *Jesus*, Philadelphia: Fortress Press, 1973; Xavier Léon-Dufour, *Les évangiles et l'histoire de Jésus*, Paris: Seuil, 1963;

Joachim Jeremias, *New Testament Theology*, vol. 1, London: SCM Press, 1971; Charles Perrot, *Jésus et l'histoire*, Paris: Desclée, 1979.

19. See Pope John Paul II's inaugural speech at the Puebla Conference of Latin American Bishops (1979) in AAS 71 (1979) 187-205; also the Final Document of the Puebla Conference, nn.175-181, in John Eagleson and Philip Scharper (eds), *Puebla and Beyond*, Maryknoll, N.Y.: Orbis Books, 1979, p. 145.

20. See, among others, James Cone, *A Black Theology of Liberation*, Philadelphia: Lippincott, 1970; Albert Nolan, *Jesus Before Christianity*, Maryknoll, New York: Orbis Books, 1978.

21. See mostly Elisabeth Schüssler Fiorenza, *In Memory of Her. A Feminist Theological Reconstruction of Christian Origins*, New York: Crossroad, 1983; Id., *Bread Not Stone. Feminist Biblical Interpretation*, Boston: Beacon Press, 1984. Also Elisabeth A. Johnson, *Consider Jesus. Waves of Renewal in Christology*, New York: Crossroad, 1990; Id., *She Who Is. The Mystery of God in Feminist Theological Discourse*, New York: Crossroad; Elisabeth Moltmann-Wendel, *The Women Around Jesus*, New York: Crossroad, 1982.

22. "One in Christ," by the U.S. Bishops' Ad Hoc Committee for a Pastoral Response to Women's Concerns, *Origins* 22 (1992) 489-508; see n.51, p. 495.

23. See Jacques Dupuis, *Jesus Christ at the Encounter of World Religions*, Maryknoll, N.Y.: Orbis Books, 1991.

24. Pinchas Lapide and Hans Küng, *Jesus im Widerstreit. Ein Jüdisch-Christlicher Dialog*, München: Kösel, 1976. David Flusser, *Jesus*, New York: Herder and Herder, 1969; Geza Vermes, *Jesus the Jew*, London: Collins, 1973; Id., *Jesus and the World of Judaism*, London: SCM Press, 1983; Id., *The Religion of Jesus the Jew*, London: SCM Press, 1993; Jacob Neusner, *Le judaïsme à l'aube du christianisme*, Paris: Cerf, 1986; James H. Charlesworth (ed.), *Jesus' Jewishness: Exploring the Place of Jesus in Early Judaism*, New York: Crossroad, 1991.

25. See "Orientations and Recommendations for the Application of the Conciliar Declaration *Nostra Aetate*, no. 4," published by the Commission for Religious Relations with Judaism (1975), *Origins* 4 (1974-1975) 463-464; also "Notes for a Correct Presentation and Catechesis of the Catholic Church," published by the same commission (1985), *Origins* 15 (1985-1986) 102-107.

26. Joseph A. Fitzmyer, *Scripture and Christology*, p. 32.

27. Fitzmyer, *Scripture and Christology*, p. 92.

28. Neuner and Dupuis, *The Christian Faith*, n.615.

29. See Albert Vanhoye, "Nuovo Testamento e inculturazione," *La Civiltà Cattolica* 135 (1984/4) 119-136; George Soares-Prabhu, "The New Testament as a Model of Inculturation," *Jeevadhara* 6 (1976) 268-282.

30. See Reginald H. Fuller, *The Foundations of New Testament Christology*, London: Collins, 1969.

31. For instance, John A. T. Robinson, *The Human Face of God*, London: SCM Press, 1972, who expressly professes a "low," "degree" Christology. See also John Macquarrie, *Jesus Christ in Modern Thought*, London: SCM Press, 1990, who also explicitly professes a degree Christology.

2

Jesus at the Source of Christology

From the Pre-Easter Jesus to the Easter Christ

We have observed above that, being the *norma normans,* the New Testament must also be the foundation of Christology. We have further indicated that, considering the various stages of composition of the New Testament, the question of the fundamental reference of Christology to the New Testament needs to be asked more precisely. Is the point of departure the post-Easter Christology of the apostolic Church? Or is the resurrection of Jesus and the disciples' Easter experience the point of departure? Or, again, is it the pre-Easter Jesus himself? The introduction to this chapter must show the articulation among those various elements; it must indicate in what sense and how the earthly Jesus is at the source of the Church's Christology.

The decisive role the resurrection of Jesus and the Easter experience of the disciples occupy in the genesis of the christological faith must be fully recognized. These events gave rise to Christology and, in that sense, mark its point of departure. Before the resurrection of Jesus, the disciples had not perceived the true significance of the master's person and work. They had, no doubt, had some glimpse of his mystery and seen in him the eschatological prophet of the Reign of God, but without grasping the exact bearing of what Jesus had declared to them. Witness to the lack of comprehension of the disciples during Jesus' earthly life are: their complete loss of courage at Jesus' ignominious death ("we had hoped," Lk 24:21); their slowness to believe and understand after the resurrection, dramatically exemplified by Thomas's obstinate refusal to believe and his exemplary profession of faith ("My Lord and my God," Jn 20:28). Acts tells us that even after the resurrection, their expectation was that of a political kingdom and the restoration through Jesus of Israel's supremacy (Acts 1:6). Caution is, therefore, needed in interpreting Peter's profession of faith in Mt 16:16: "You are the Christ, the Son of the living God," followed by Jesus' promise of building his Church on Peter's faith. Mark's version of Peter's profession of faith — which is closer to the event — is more sober: "You are the Christ" (Mk 8:29). Characteristically, Jesus' reaction consists of announcing that he must fulfill his messianic vocation as the suffering Servant of God. Matthew's narrative, the exegetes tell us, has undergone a strong redactional influence and reflects a post-Easter christological understanding. A similar remark is called for concerning Mt 14:33, the other Matthean text containing a pre-Easter profession of mature faith on the part of the disciples: "Truly you are the Son of God." Symptomatically, Mark's parallel text includes no such profession of faith and is content to report the disciples' wondering (Mk 6:51). R. Schnackenburg has shown clearly the difference between the disciples' faith before and after the resurrection of Jesus. He writes:

> To recognize that the disciples did not reach a true christological faith before Easter is not to deny them any faith whatever in Jesus during their earthly pilgrimage with him. For why then would they have followed him and remained with him? But it remains difficult to determine more closely the content of their faith at that time. The question of the sons of Zebedee (Mk 10:37; cf. Mt 20:21) and other indications allow us to conclude that they were still caught up in earthly messianic hopes of this world. Luke describes them as maintaining that attitude until the ascension of Jesus (cf. Lk 19:11; 22:38; 24:21; Acts 1:6); for him only the mission of the Spirit at Pentecost marks the change of attitude. From then on they announce unanimously, as Peter, their spokesman, does forcefully in his discourse on the day of Pentecost, "that God has made him both Lord and Christ, this Jesus whom you crucified" (Acts 2:36). What Luke puts in evidence in his theological vision constitutes substantially the conviction of all the evangelists: only after the resurrection of Jesus have the disciples reached full faith in Jesus as Messiah and the Son of God.[1]

It could, perhaps, be said that from disciples Jesus' followers became "believers" in the full biblical and theological sense through the Easter experience.

Jesus' resurrection cannot, however, be reduced to an Easter experience understood as "conversion" on the part of the disciples. Undoubtedly the disciples knew the subjective experience of conversion, but if they were transformed, it was because they met the risen Jesus who manifested himself and "made himself seen" by them in his glorified state. The transformation of the resurrection affects Jesus himself in the first instance; objective in him, it is subjective in the disciples. This real transformation of Jesus as he passed from death to risen life, from kenosis to glory, could only be perceived by the faith of the disciples in relation to Israel's eschatological expectation, that is, as reaching beyond death to eschatological fulness.

That Jesus' resurrection and the Easter experience of the disciples marked the beginning of their christological faith does not mean that the resurrection of Jesus sufficed by itself to prove or testify to the personal identity of the Risen one as the Son of God. Jesus' personal identity is an object of faith; it is not open to any proof. The appearances of the Risen one to the disciples were signs capable, no doubt, of arousing and helping faith. Without them, the disciples would probably not have been able to perceive the real transformation that had intervened in Jesus' humanity. Yet faith in the resurrection could not be arrived at on the sole premise of the appearances, as though these were able to prove it.[2]

How then did the disciples arrive at faith in Jesus Christ through the resurrection? The appearances of the Risen one "signified" that Jesus had reached, beyond death, to the eschatological state. The fulness awaited in the eschatological time had been accomplished in him; or, conversely, eschatology had intruded into time. This entirely new condition of Jesus' humanity, never experienced before, aroused questions as to the identity of the Risen one. The disciples were thus sent back to the testimony of Jesus during his earthly life. Prompted by the Spirit, they recalled the things the pre-Easter Jesus had done and said, which had gone mostly misunderstood at that time. This memory of the historical Jesus played a decisive role in the genesis of the christological faith of the disciples. It supplied the link between Jesus himself and the disciples' faith interpretation of him after the resurrection. Through it the Church's christological faith truly goes back to, and can be based on, the Jesus of history, thus finding in him its historical foundation.

It will be the task of this chapter to show that Jesus is truly at the source of the Church's christological faith or that there is continuity in discontinuity between Jesus' implicit Christology and the explicit Christology of the apostolic Church. Continuity in discontinuity applies here to Jesus himself as he passes from his kenotic state to his glorified condition through the real transformation of his person in the resurrection; it applies to the disciples as they pass from mere discipleship to Christian faith through their Easter experience.

Such continuity cannot be presumed, but it needs to be shown. It has often been denied. It has been said, for instance, that while Jesus preached the Reign of God, the apostolic Church preached Christ instead. The announcer of the Kingdom had thus become the object of the kerygma — a change that amounted to a falsification of Jesus' message. Jesus' own mind had been entirely centred on God and the impending Kingdom; never did he make his own person the object of his message. The apostolic Church, however, turned him into the object of her proclamation. At her hands by a process of divinization of the man Jesus, Christ was substituted for the Kingdom of God as the object of Christian faith. The God-centredness of Jesus himself was replaced by the Christ-centredness of the early Church.

Again it has been suggested that while Jesus preached the impending Kingdom of God, it was the Church that came about. By which is meant that Jesus, concerned as he was with the impending establishment of God's final rule, gave no thought to an intermediary period of time during which the Kingdom of God, already present in the world, would have to grow through history to its perfection and completion. Jesus never meant to found a Church. The Church was founded by his disciples when they were faced with the delay in the establishment of God's final rule after his death.

These partial constructions of Jesus' mind show how important it is to discover his true message if the christological faith of the apostolic Church is to find its foundation in him. It needs to be shown that between him and her there is no unbridgeable gap, but true continuity, the discontinuities notwithstanding.

It will be noted that the order of reality or the historical order being followed here is the reverse of the epistemological order. Since all the documents of the New Testament, the synoptic Gospels included, convey a faith interpretation of the story of Jesus in the light of the Easter experience of the disciples, we have no access to the historical Jesus except through the Christ of faith. When the historical Jesus is retrieved through the use of the critico-historical method of exegesis, the real, historical movement can be followed anew, or the journey traveled again that leads from the rediscovery of the Jesus of history to the discovery of the christological faith.

This journey has been traveled by Jesus' followers as they passed from mere discipleship to faith, or equivalently from a "Jesuology" to a "Christology." The same has been traveled by later disciples through the centuries and needs to be traveled today by disciples desirous of reaching a mature, reflective faith in Jesus Christ. The route leads from a personal encounter with the earthly Jesus to the discovery of him as the Christ; that is, from below upwards. Each disciple is thus faced with a decisive question: When, where, how have I made the experience of Jesus? When, where, how have I discovered him as the Christ?

The task of this chapter consists in showing that Jesus' works and words, his self-consciousness and self-revelation, his choices and options, his attitude to life and death — his entire mission and human existence — are at the origin of Christology. The treatment will by necessity be brief, though it must account for the "whole" Jesus of history, in his "vertical" as well as his "horizontal" dimension, his personal relation to God as well as his way of relating to people. To do less would amount to betrayal and ruin the continuity between Jesus and Christ. The matter will be divided into four sections: the mission of Jesus; the personal identity of Jesus; Jesus facing his imminent death; Jesus' resurrection and the Easter experience.

THE MISSION OF JESUS

The Kingdom of God and its coming is the central theme of Jesus' preaching. The theme was known before him and was conceived differently by various preachers in contemporary Judaism. The latest among these was John the Baptizer, at whose hands Jesus himself was baptized (Mk 1:9-11), for whom the Kingdom of God was imminent divine judgment. Jesus' concept of God's Kingdom was, however, new and original. For Jesus, the Kingdom was symbolic of the new "rule" God will bring about in the world, renewing all things and restoring all relationships between God and human beings as well as among people. For Jesus, too, the Reign of God was impending; indeed, it was not only at hand but had already begun to break through in his own mission. Jesus announced it as the irruption of God's rule among people, by which God manifests God's glory. This is why the arrival of the Kingdom is Good News.

The ambivalence of the texts regarding the imminence or the already installed presence of the Kingdom must be taken note of. The Gospel of Mark begins the narrative of Jesus' ministry with a programmatic summary of his early preaching of the Gospel of God: "The time is fulfilled, and the Kingdom of God is at hand; repent, and believe in the Gospel" (Mk 1:15). The coming of the Kingdom is God's own doing, though it calls humans to repentance, conversion (*metanoia*) and faith. The Kingdom is conceived here as impending and imminent. In other texts, however, Jesus is reported to affirm that it is already being inaugurated, indeed that it is already present and operative. Such is the case in another programmatic sample of Jesus' early preaching as presented in the Gospel of Luke. Having read in the synagogue of Nazareth from Isaiah's announcement of the preaching of the Good News (Is 61:1-2), Jesus commented: "Today this scripture has been fulfilled in your hearing" (Lk 4:21), indicating that God's Reign was already breaking through in him. More clearly still, in the controversy with the pharisees about the way in which he cast out demons, Jesus declared: "If it is by the Spirit of God that I cast out demons, then the Kingdom of God has come upon you" (Mt 12:28). God's Kingdom is already present.

For Jesus, it is in the events that make up his own life and mission that the Reign of God begins to break in and is already present and operative; yet it is present as a seed that must continually grow and for whose growth we must pray: "Thy Kingdom come" (Mt 6:10; Lk 11:2). Jesus exulted with joy at the sudden irruption of God's Reign, of which he was not only the witness or the herald, but the instrument. In the "already" of the sudden breaking through of the Kingdom of God in him, he saw the promise of its full accomplishment in the "not yet."

The theme of the Reign of God undoubtedly places God at the source and at the heart of Jesus' action. The Reign of God really stands for God's beginning to act in the world in a decisive manner, becoming manifest and putting order in creation. This is done through Jesus' human actions. Jesus' early mission is accompanied by miracles that it would be wrong to treat as merely establishing the credentials of God's prophet of the Kingdom. The miracles of healing and the exorcisms (akin to healings) that generally figure among the unassailable historical data of Jesus' early ministry — the "miracles of nature" as well as the resurrections from the dead — all are signs and symbols that through Jesus, God is bringing about God's rule on earth, overcoming the destructive power of death and sin. They are the firstfruits of the operative presence of the Kingdom of God among people.

The significance of Jesus' miracles as a constitutive part of the inauguration of God's Kingdom is clearly marked by the evangelists. Suffice it to recall Jesus' programmatic preaching in the synagogue of Nazareth, where healings figure among the signs, foretold by Isaiah 61:1-2, which are part of the Kingdom of God's already effective presence (Lk 4:18-21). More clearly, with the disciples whom John the Baptizer sent to inquire from Jesus, "Are you he who is to come, or shall we look for another?" (Mt 11:3), Jesus' answer points to his healing miracles as signs and symbols of the Kingdom already operative through him (Mt 11:4-6). The same role in relation to the presence of the Kingdom is assigned to the exorcisms of Jesus in the controversy with the pharisees referred to above (Mt 12:28).

The Kingdom of God is God's rule among people. It requires a complete reorientation of human relationships and an ordering of human society according to God's mind. The values which, in accordance with God's Reign, must characterise human relationships, can be summed up in a few words: freedom, brotherhood, peace, justice. Accordingly, throughout his missionary action, Jesus denounces whatever in the society of his time offends against those values. This sets him in opposition to various categories of his own people: he chastises the oppressive legalism of the scribes, the exploitation of people by the priestly caste, the arrogant self-righteousness of the pharisees. Jesus is not a conformist, but a subversive on behalf of the rule of God. He refuses to abide by the stereotyped unjust structures of the society in which he lives; he associates preferentially with sinners and tax-collectors, with Samaritans and prostitutes, with all the despised sections of the society of his time. To all of them he announces that the Reign of God has come about; he invites them all to enter into it through conversion and an ordering of their life.

The Kingdom of God that is coming about through Jesus' life and action is predominantly addressed to the poor, the *anawim* of God, that is, all the despised categories of people, the oppressed and the downtrodden. For all these, Jesus manifests a preferential option that amounts to a declaration of God's own mind in their favour. Biblical exegesis has shown that the poor to whom the Kingdom of God, according to Jesus, is preferentially destined are the economically poor, to whom the despised, the oppressed and emarginated classes are assimilated — all those who suffer disability under the pressure of unjust structures.[3] This is not to say that economic and social dehumanizing poverty constitutes for Jesus an object of choice for its own sake. Jesus is on the side of the poor, not of poverty; conversely, what Jesus challenges is riches, not the rich.[4] What counts for him is readiness to enter into the Kingdom by practising its values. The poor are those predisposed to it, who place their trust in God, not in themselves, and among whom the values of the Kingdom are seen present and operative.

"Blessed are you poor, for yours is the Kingdom of God" (Lk 6:20). The Lukan form of the first beatitude clearly states that the Kingdom of God is primarily destined to the poor. The direct speech ("you poor") indicates that this version is closer to Jesus' speech than is the Matthean version: "Blessed are the poor in spirit, for theirs is the Kingdom of heaven" (Mt 5:3). Is there, however, a change in orientation from one to the other? Must it be thought that Jesus' preference for the poor, because of its apparently scandalous character, was toned down after him to be reduced to a "spiritual poverty" or "openness" to God within the reach of all? It does not seem so. It may, on the contrary, be thought that there is continuity between both versions: the real poor are also those who are "single-minded," open to God and to his Kingdom.

Clearly affirmed in the first beatitude, proclaimed in the sermon on the mountain (Mt 5) or in the plain (Lk 6:17ff), the destination of the Kingdom of God for the poor is also made manifest in the programmatic passages referred to above. In the episode at the synagogue of Nazareth, the Good News preached to the poor is what is being fulfilled in the hearing of Jesus' listeners through his action and ministry (Lk 4:18-21). The Reign of God, already present and operative in the person and action of Jesus, is destined to the poor. Similarly, in Jesus' response to the Baptist's envoys, the fact that "the poor have the Good News preached to them" is sign of Jesus' mission in relation to the Kingdom (Mt 11:5); it is to them that the Kingdom belongs.

From the above it should have become clear that Jesus' attitude to justice and poverty goes beyond the message of the Old Testament prophets on the subject. The prophets had spoken in favour of the poor and the oppressed and in defense of their rights. Their prophetic discourse was clearly indicative of God's mind on their behalf: God's predilection for the poor and divine wrath at the injustice inflicted upon them. Jesus, however, does not only manifest a preferential option for the poor; he is not merely "in their favour." He identifies with them personally and associates with them preferentially. He is not only *for* the poor; he belongs *to* and *with* them. In this belonging and association of Jesus with the poor, God's preferential love for them comes to a climax. Jesus' attitude is not only indicative of God's mind for the poor; it embodies God's commitment to and involvement with them.

Jesus is the "eschatological prophet" of the Kingdom of God in whom the Kingdom is not only announced but brought about. His entire mission is centred on the Reign of God, that is, on God as God is establishing God's rule on earth in God's messenger. Centred on the Reign of God, Jesus is by that very fact centred on God. There is no distance in him between the one and the other: regnocentrism and theocentrism coincide. The God whom Jesus calls Father is at the centre of his message, of his life and of his person. Jesus did not primarily speak about himself; he came to announce God and the coming of God's Reign, and to be at God's service. God is at the centre, not the messenger.

THE PERSONAL IDENTITY OF JESUS

Yet Jesus is not only a prophet, not even merely the "eschatological prophet" who announces that God's Reign is finally being established on earth. As we have already insinuated, he situates himself in a radically new way in relation to God and God's Reign: It is in his life and in his person that God is intervening in history in a decisive manner with the inauguration of God's Kingdom. What then does he say about himself? How much of his own identity does he declare?

Apparently little. In spite of appearances to the contrary, Jesus seems to lay no definite claim at being the Messiah, the Christ, the descendant of David (the "Davidic King") in whom the messianic expectation of Israel was to be fulfilled (2 Sam 7:4-17). It is true that the synoptic tradition has preserved at least two scenes in which the messianic question is explicitly raised with regard to Jesus: the confession of Peter at Caesarea Philippi (Mk 8:29) and Jesus' trial before the Sanhedrin (Mk 14:61-62). Without denying all historical foundation to these events, modern exegesis — as has already been recalled earlier with regard to the episode in Caesarea Philippi — inclines to see them coloured by the Easter faith. The first is a christological profession of faith that coincides with that of the post-Easter apostolic kerygma; the other is a post factum foretelling — prophecy *ex eventu* — which, after the Son of Man prophecy of Daniel (Dan 7:13), describes in anticipation the glorious appearance before God of the Risen one. However this may be, it is certain that Jesus himself, unless enticed by others to accept the messianic title, consistently abstained from using it spontaneously. The political overtones of the title in the minds of his hearers would have been sufficient reason for this. Jesus, to be sure, did not claim to be a political Messiah.

Nor does Jesus seem to have attempted to legitimise his mission by reference to other titles that had nourished the Jewish expectation of the last era and would later be applied to him by the New Testament Christology. He did not introduce himself as the prophet announced by Moses. He seems rather, at least implicitly, to have identified himself with the mysterious suffering "Servant of God" of the Deutero-Isaian prophecy (Is 42-53), as will appear later when we study Jesus' attitude to his impending death. This title, however, besides having remained relatively obscure, ranked low in the people's estimation, being at the antipodes from a triumphant Messiah! As to the expression "Son of Man," it remains, even today, a disputed question among exegetes[5] whether Jesus used it of himself with explicit reference to the exalted figure of the prophecy of Daniel (Dan 7:13-14). Some think that he did. They point to the fact that in the synoptic tradition the expression "Son of Man" is exclusively found in Jesus' sayings about himself; they see in this a strong indication that Jesus did speak of himself in this manner. The explicit reference to the prophecy of Daniel is, however, even more problematic, and other exegetes suspect that, where the reference seems evident (Mk 14:62), the Easter faith has influenced the way in which the Gospel narrative relates the events. In itself, the expression Son of Man — a typical Hebraism — could simply be a redundant manner of speaking about oneself: Everyone is a "son of man." Jesus could have used it to arouse questions in his hearers' minds about his true identity. There is, moreover, the question whether in Jesus' sayings the Son of Man referred to himself or to another. Bultmann's position in this regard — admittedly an arbitrary one — consisted in considering as authentic those sayings attributed to Jesus by the synoptic tradition in which the Son of Man could be understood as referring to "another," while denying the authenticity of those where grammatically the expression would have to be understood as referring to Jesus himself!

However this may be, caution is in order where the use of messianic titles by Jesus himself is concerned. In the case of the title Son of God, it is certain that, at the level of the historical event of the pre-Easter Jesus, it is never used with the fulness of meaning that New Testament Christology will give to it. In the mind of Jesus' hearers, the title evoked the kind of metaphorical sonship of God the Old Testament had attributed to the Davidic King (cf. 2 Sam 7:14; Ps 2:7). In the Old Testament the title Son of God received, moreover, a very broad meaning and was put to many different uses. It applied to Israel as God's chosen people and to those persons in Israel who were just before God, specifically to the Davidic King in his special relationship with God. But in no case did it connote anything beyond a metaphorical sonship. In its traditional meaning, the title was unable to express Jesus' true identity. To convey it, it would have to take on a surplus meaning that would amount to the totally new significance of Jesus' "natural" Sonship of God.

That this surplus meaning is already contained in the synoptic tradition is testified by several instances. One is Jesus' "hymn of jubilation" (Mt 11:27; Lk 10:21-22) — often referred to as a Johannine "meteor" fallen into the synoptic material — in which Jesus in thanking the Father refers as Son to their mutual knowledge: "No one knows the Son except the Father, and no one knows the Father except the Son and anyone to whom the Son chooses to reveal him" (Mt 11:27). Another is, in Mk 13:32 (cf. Mt 24:36), Jesus' admittance that "no one, not even . . . the Son but only the Father" knows the day of judgment. A third, less explicit, is the parable of the wicked tenants found in each of the synoptic Gospels (Mt 21:37; Mk 12:6; Lk 20:13), in which the owner of the vineyard sends his son to the tenants, thinking that "they will respect my son."

All these instances convey Jesus' natural sonship of God, but each clearly goes beyond what the Old Testament title Son of God was able to convey.

The conclusion imposes itself that by revealing himself as the Son of God, his Father, Jesus was going beyond every Old Testament foreknowledge of a filial relationship with God. Moreover, the way Jesus conveyed the mystery of his person was destined to remain the privileged manner in which the apostolic Church formulated her faith in the mystery of his person. The continuity of expression between Jesus' self-revelation as the Son of God and the christological faith of the apostolic Church is well noted by J. Guillet when he writes:

> If "Son of God" is probably a Christian creation, the content which it encompasses comes not from its previous history but from the object which it designates; and if the expression as such has probably never been pronounced by Jesus, it is the echo of a word certainly authentic by which Jesus allowed its deepest secret to come through in some decisive moments: he is the Son. Such moments are rare: the synoptics mention but two, the "hymn of jubilation": "No one knows the Son except the Father and no one knows the Father except the Son" (Mt 11:27; Lk 10:22), and the admittance to not knowing at the end of the eschatological discourse: "But of the day and hour no one knows, not even the angels in heaven, nor the Son, but the Father only" (Mt 24:36; Mk 13:32). Two texts the authenticity of which seems well assured both by the unique character of their content, hard to imagine, and their inimitable style.[6]

But let us not anticipate. To conclude with regard to the messianic titles, our enquiry seems to yield mostly negative results. But in spite of differences of opinion about different titles, exegetes today are largely agreed that the messianic titles occupy but a secondary place in Jesus' testimony about himself. His self-consciousness need not be made dependent on ready-made categories that are both too precise and too narrow and, therefore, in the long run inadequate. There is another side to the question.

Beyond all titles and in spite of Jesus' apparent reluctance to declare himself, an astonishing self-awareness emerges from his words and actions. While it may be said that we have no direct access to the subjective consciousness of Jesus or his human psychology, it is nonetheless certain that through his works and words we reach them indirectly, for in his speech and actions, Jesus' self-awareness shows forth. In fact, his attitudes and his demeanour altogether exceed, in the most natural fashion, all accepted norms. No received categories could ever encompass him. His thorough originality and the difference he makes manifest themselves in many ways.

A first way in which Jesus' novelty stands out consists in the transcendent manner in which he fulfils the Old Testament promises. Jesus transforms what he accomplishes. In particular, the Old Testament messianic expectation finds completion in him in a manner never awaited or suspected. While there exists true continuity between the ancient promises and their fresh realization, the discontinuity between them is even greater, for the event brings something entirely new: *omnem novitatem attulit seipsum afferens*, St. Irenaeus wrote.[7]

We have already noted the surprising way in which Jesus situates himself in relation to the Reign of God. Not only does he herald the coming of the Kingdom as the eschatological prophet. He further claims that the Reign of God—God's self—is breaking through to people in him, in his life and mission, in his preaching and action. His ministry is God's decisive intervention in the world; in it God is making the cause of human beings God's own. The time of preparation is over; God's Reign has now irrupted in the world through and in Jesus' human life. The miracles of Jesus are part and parcel of this irruption of God's Kingdom on earth.

Jesus presents himself as a *rabbi*, but his teaching arouses astonishment, for he teaches with a singular authority, not like the scribes who merely interpret the Law (Mk 1:22). Jesus makes the enormous claim that his authority surpasses that of Moses (Mt 5:21-22; Mk 10:1-9). What is the source of this astounding authority? Jesus declares God's ultimate purpose, not as a lesson he has learned from the Scriptures, not even as a message he has received from God and has been commissioned to announce, but out of his own ineffable familiarity with God's mind. Jesus simply knows the mind of God, which he proclaims. His way of speaking implies that he perceives it in an immediate intuition, and he declares it in his own name: "I say to you." The strength of this personal authority and self-assurance is further reinforced by the singular usage of the term, "Amen"—"Truly I say to you," in which the authentic echo of Jesus' manner of speech has been preserved. It testifies to Jesus' awareness of teaching, with a personal authority received directly from God, a doctrine fully reliable—solid like rock—because it embodies God's own consistency (*èmèt*).

Jesus taught in parables. Apparently the parables of Jesus say nothing that concerns him directly. They explain the way in which God inaugurates God's Reign on earth, the way in which it grows, and the conditions to enter it. Yet, at the same time, they also manifest Jesus' awareness of being the "beloved son" in whom the Kingdom of God and the end-time are being established (Mk 12:6). In particular, the parables of mercy witness to Jesus' awareness of reflecting in his own attitude toward sinners the merciful attitude of God. He knows and declares how God deals with the lost sheep, with the prodigal son and the vine-dressers of the last hour. This knowledge entitles him personally to declare God's pardon: "Your sins are forgiven" (Mk 2:5).

At the source of Jesus' personal authority is a surprising nearness to God, of which the Gospel narrative has preserved striking indications. The clearest one consists in Jesus' unprecedented manner of invoking God as his Father, with the term *Abba*. J. Jeremias—among other exegetes, such as F. Hahn, B. Van Iersel—has shown convincingly that his way of addressing God in prayer was unknown to contemporary Judaism.[8] The evidence put forward to the contrary by G. Vermes and D. Flusser[9] does not stand up to examination, for if the use of the term Abba with reference to God was not altogether unknown to rabbis in Palestinian Judaism, the fact remains that Jesus alone is known to have addressed God directly in prayer with the term Abba (Mk 14:36). The term represented the familiar, intimate manner in which a Jewish child addressed his earthly father: "Daddy." Jesus, however, conversed with God in this intimate fashion, and the novelty involved in his way of addressing God in prayer was so great that the original aramaic term has been preserved in the Gospel tradition (Mk 14:36). It conveyed the unprecedented intimacy of Jesus' relationship to God his Father; nay more, the consciousness of a singular nearness such as needed to be rendered in unheard-of language. Taken by itself and in isolation, the term would not suffice to account theologically for a "natural" sonship of God, yet it testifies beyond doubt to Jesus' consciousness being essentially filial: Jesus was aware of being the Son.

This awareness expressed eminently by the term Abba is supported by the complementary evidence referred to above, in which Jesus manifestly relates to God as his Father in a unique, unprecedented manner (Mt 11:27; Mt 24:36). There is, moreover, no dearth of exegetes who think that in the Lukan form of the Lord's Prayer, the short form "Father" stands for the original Abba (Lk 11:2). The prayer would then directly echo Jesus' own prayer. It would explain on what ground, following the example of their Master, the early Christians dared to address God as Father with the same intimacy as Jesus himself had used (Gal 4:6; Rom 8:15): they were conscious of being "sons in the Son."

If it is true to say that Jesus' whole life and mission is centred on God, not on himself, it is no less true that, by the very fact, his entire posture, his mind and actions, his attitudes and demeanour, carry a Christology which, if it remains implicit, is in clear possession. It would be wrong to expect Jesus to declare his identity in terms not yet accessible to his hearers. In particular, the term *God* was totally inaccessible. For Jesus himself, as for his hearers, "God" (*theos*) referred to Yahweh, whom Jesus addressed as Father and to whom he related as Son. Had Jesus said that he was God, he would only have provoked inextricable confusion and made his own self-revelation unintelligible. The mysterious nature of the Father-Son relationship between God and Jesus, its thorough newness and lack of precomprehension in the religious experience of Israel, as well as the shortage of terms available in the surrounding culture to carry the new meaning, all explain abundantly the unavoidable slowness of Jesus' self-revelation. A divine pedagogy was needed if Jesus was to convey his message in an intelligible manner. The slowness required by the divine revelation that takes place in him probably has something to do with the much-spoken-of "messianic secret" of the Gospel of Mark; it is part of God's personal insertion in the history of humankind and of God's people. Revelation is at once "unveiling" and "concealing."

However, Jesus did better than simply declare his mystery in partly intelligible terms. His life and mission spoke for himself, and in them God had
already begun to reveal God's Son. We say begun, for the full disclosure
by God of Jesus' identity would and could only consist in God's action of
raising him from the dead. It is not by mere accident but by a natural
necessity that explicit Christology was a post-Easter development. But
Jesus' death was first to intervene.

JESUS FACING HIS IMMINENT DEATH

How did Jesus face his impending death? What meaning did he attach
to it? It must be admitted that the experience of his ministry and the tide
of opposition it aroused taught Jesus to look on a violent death not only
as a distinct possibility, but an unavoidable fate. It is no less certain that
he gave it a definite meaning in the perspective of his mission. This is not
to say that Jesus explained explicitly the significance of his forthcoming
death in the terms that will be used after him by New Testament soteriology. As Jesus' own Christology was implicit, so too was his soteriology;
both were destined to pass from implicit to explicit in the light of the Easter
faith. What foundation was there in his own understanding to justify the
later developments of New Testament soteriology? Exegetical discernment
is again required here. If the Gospel tradition has preserved several pre-
dictions by Jesus of his own death, with clear indications of its redemptive
meaning (Mk 10:45), the manner in which these are formulated reflects the
post-Easter understanding of the event in early Christian communities.[10]

Speaking of Jesus himself and avoiding throwing back on him later developments that arose from the Easter experience, what can be said with
certainty as to the way Jesus understood his death? Generally speaking, it
may be said that Jesus' fundamental attitude of self-giving led him from an
awareness that through his preaching, actions and personal presence he
was establishing God's final salvation, to a subsequent acceptance of his
victim role. The Jesus who began by proclaiming the eschatological Reign
of God ended by obediently accepting his role as the victim whose death
and vindication would bring salvation.[11]

Two extreme positions, both unwarranted, must be avoided here. Sinning
by excess is the position according to which Jesus would have foreseen and
foretold all about his death, indeed that he would have premeditated it
from the beginning of his ministry and offered it as a sacrifice in explicit
terms such as will be used by New Testament soteriology (cf. Heb 10:5 and
Ps 40:7-9, Septuagint). On the other extreme, sinning by defect, is the
position according to which Jesus would merely have suffered his death
passively, having neither foreseen nor offered it in any way. The middle
course between these two extreme positions consists in recovering Jesus'
implicit soteriology. Jesus did look upon his impending death as the cul-

minating point of his mission, of which he explained the salvific meaning
to his disciples at the Last Supper.

How can this be shown? Mk 10:45 can hardly be thought to have preserved the very words of Jesus (*ipsissima verba Jesu*). While Jesus may well
have identified himself with the Servant of God who was to offer his life
for the salvation of others (cf. the fourth song of the Servant in Deutero-
Isaiah 52-53), the theological concept of ransom belongs to later New Testament soteriology and can hardly be attributed to Jesus himself. Where
the Last Supper narrative is concerned—of which the New Testament has
preserved four versions: Mt 26:26-29; Mk 14:22-25; Lk 22:17-19; 1 Cor
11:23-26—the question arises of the influence exercised on the narrative
by the post-Easter liturgical practice, specifically on the words of Jesus,
such as those over the cup: "This is my blood of the covenant, which is
poured out for many" (Mk 14:24). However, if the "very words" of Jesus
escape us to no small extent, his "very intention" (*ipsissima intentio*) can be
safely ascertained. What then was Jesus' intention as he found himself faced
with his impending death?

We have already mentioned that Jesus could not but envisage the prob-
ability (not merely the possibility) of a violent death, once the conflict and
confrontation with the pharisees, the saducees and other groups began to
gain momentum. By the end of his ministry, a showdown seemed unavoidable. When Jesus entered Jerusalem and expelled the profaners of his
Father's house from the temple, he knew that his faithfulness to his mission
was putting his life in the balance, indeed leading him to his death. How
did he react to the prospect of a violent death? How did he look upon it?

Jesus' attitude throughout his ministry had been one of service and love,
of "pro-existence." The violent death he now foresaw clearly he would have
accepted not merely as the unavoidable consequence of his prophetic mission, but as the ultimate embodiment of his loving service, as the culmination and climax of his pro-existence: He would be, to the end, the "man-
for-others."

Moreover, Jesus had identified himself, at least implicitly, with the Servant of God. He would now fulfil the role of the Servant in suffering and
death. He knew, therefore, at the Last Supper, that his imminent death
would be unto the remission of sins, even if he did not conceive it as ransom.
He would, moreover, have linked it with the establishment of the Kingdom
of God, as is seen in the Markan narrative (Mk 14:25). In sum: The advent
of the Reign of God and his own redemptive death to which it is linked
together make up Jesus' "very intention" at the end of his earthly ministry.
They constitute his implicit soteriology, the source of the explicit soteriology
of the apostolic Church.

What more can be added? First, the Gospel tradition of the "agony" at
Gethsemane shows an anguished Jesus faced with the prospect of an ine-
luctably violent death. It also shows him submitting in blind obedience to
the will of his Father (Mk 14:36). The same twofold reaction of anguish

and self-commitment to the hands of the Father is expressed in Jesus' last cry on the cross: "My God, my God, why have you forsaken me?" (Mk 15:34). This cry is not one of despair, nor need it be thought that Jesus was abandoned on the cross by his Father, though the sense of being abandoned was indeed real. It was no doubt a cry of distress but, at the same time, as the last verse of Ps 22 from which it is quoted indicates, an expression of trust and hope in the God in whose hands he abandoned himself and committed his spirit. The driving force of Jesus' entire life had been faithfulness to his mission and absolute trust in God his Father. This double disposition found its supreme expression in the face of death.

Second, the Gospel tradition of the Last Supper—the influence of post-Easter liturgical practice on the narrative notwithstanding—has preserved decisive actions and words of the Master, which later will appear as particularly loaded with meaning and become the core of the Church's Eucharist. These reveal better than any other data Jesus' attitude in the face of death. Having, as was customary, said the blessing (*berakah*) over the bread and wine, Jesus unexpectedly added, in substance: "Take, this is my body"; "this is my blood of the covenant which is poured out for many" (Mk 14:22-24). With these words, previously unheard of, the sharing of bread and wine acquired a new meaning. It referred to Jesus' imminent death. It symbolized and effectively carried the offering that Jesus was making of his life. The eucharistic rite of the Supper is the living parable of what Jesus will accomplish on the cross, the gift of his life as the fulfillment of his mission and the seal of God's new covenant with the people. It expresses the meaning that Jesus is giving to his death. He does not submit to it passively; he does not even merely consent to it with absolute trust in God, who is able to vindicate the Servant. He gives it in full conformity with God's loving plan for human beings, of which it is part. The last word will belong to God.

JESUS' RESURRECTION AND THE EASTER EXPERIENCE

To complete the journey from the pre-Easter Jesus to the post-Easter Christ, that is, from implicit to explicit Christology, we must speak of the resurrection of Jesus and the Easter experience of the disciples. Here is where the transition takes place from mere discipleship to faith—more exactly, where discipleship becomes faith.

The death of Jesus on the cross was a shattering experience for his followers. The Gospels, however, witness to distinct ways in which they reacted to the event. Typical is the reaction of the disciples on their way to Emmaus: "We had hoped that he was the one to redeem Israel" (Lk 24:21). All hope being lost, what meaning could be given to the life of the dead master? More positive is the reaction of some holy women who rush to the tomb on Easter Sunday to anoint the body. They remain faithful to

Jesus and wish to keep his memory alive. Indeed, humanly speaking, nothing more could be done! Had Jesus not risen from the dead, Christianity could only have consisted in a group of Jesus' friends keeping alive the memory of his teaching and reproducing as best they could his example. Jesus would still be one of the great religious geniuses of humankind, but he would not be the Lord. Christianity would be a lofty moralism; it would not be Good News today for all men and women.

The resurrection of Jesus, however, makes the whole difference; it marks the starting point of Christian faith and stands at its centre. Its significance for us has often been underestimated, as though it concerned Jesus only. Was it not right that he should receive from God his reward for a work well done and accomplished in his death? As for its meaning for us, it has often been reduced to a last proof, given by God, of the credentials of God's messenger.

Yet being a Christian does not consist in venerating a dead master or merely keeping his memory alive and putting his doctrine into practice. It means to believe that Jesus is alive today because he was raised from the dead by the Father: "Why do you seek the living among the dead?" (Lk 24:5). It means likewise to believe that Jesus is present among us and active in the world through his Spirit. To open oneself to this event and to welcome this new light is to gain access to Christian faith. To become a Christian, then, is to meet, in one way or another — in the word of God, in the Eucharist, in the "sacrament of the other," in the poor — the Risen Christ and, in the light of Easter, to discover with new eyes Jesus himself, God, the human person, and the world. For the disciples of Jesus it meant meeting him in the foundational experience of Easter and, thereby, having unmasked for them his true identity and the real significance of his life and death.

It is therefore essential that something be said at this point about the foundational experience of the disciples, without which there would have been no Christian faith. We shall not insist on the stories of the appearances which, according to the Gospel testimony, brought about the experience and set the process of faith into motion. The appearances of the Risen Lord were signs given to the disciples to arouse faith. They believed *because* they saw Jesus alive. They were indeed transformed by this newly acquired faith — and one can legitimately speak of a conversion experience — but, it must be added, it is the Risen Lord who brought about in them this transformation by manifesting himself as being alive: He "made himself seen" (*òphtè*: 1 Cor 15:5). A study of the appearances of the Risen Christ in the Gospels would show how Jesus made himself recognized as alive and present. The narratives are made up of a threefold moment: the manifestation of Jesus as alive; the recognition of him by the disciples; the mission given to them by Christ.

The resurrection affects Jesus himself before it transforms the disciples. Jesus is alive, but not with the life he had before. He is really transformed, for the resurrection is not the resuscitation or revivification of the corpse that lay in the tomb—as in the case of Lazarus, who was raised only to die again! Jesus, on the contrary, is alive to a new life; he has entered into an entirely new condition, having been transformed into it by God. Humans had never had any experience of this new human condition, though it could only be understood by the disciples as the anticipated realization in Jesus of the resurrection on the last day that the Jewish faith had hoped for, not without hesitation. In sum, as far as Jesus is concerned, the resurrection consists in his reaching the eschatological condition. As for us, it means the irruption of eschatology in our history.

Transformed into this new state, Jesus was no longer subject to death. The sign of his new life given to his disciples in the appearances may pass away, but he is alive forever and ever present to those who believe in him. Such is the foundation of the Christian faith and the point of departure of New Testament Christology. Our task in the next chapter will consist in showing how, in the light of the foundational experience, the apostolic Church expressed its newly acquired faith in the person of Jesus and the meaning of his life, death and resurrection. Explicit Christology begins with Easter.

NOTES

1. Rudolf Schnackenburg, "Christologie des Neuen Testaments," in Johannes Feiner and Magnus Löhrer (eds.), *Mysterium Salutis,* III, 1: *Das Christusereignis,* Einsiedeln, Benziger Verlag, 1970, p. 232.

2. See Gerald O'Collins, *Jesus Risen,* Mahwah, N.J.: Paulist Press, 1987, pp. 128-147.

3. See Jacques Dupont, "The Poor and Poverty in the Gospels and Acts," in Augustin George, et al., *Gospel Poverty,* Chicago: Franciscan Herald Press, 1977, pp. 25-52; Id., *Les béatitudes,* 3 vols, Louvain: Nauwelaerts, 1958-1973.

4. See George Soares-Prabhu, "The Kingdom of God: Jesus' Vision of a New Society," in Duraisamy S. Amalorpavadass (ed.), *The Indian Church in the Struggle for a New Society,* Bangalore: NBCLC, 1981, pp. 579-608; Id., "Good News to the Poor," ibid., pp. 609-626; Id., "Class in the Bible: The Biblical Poor a Social Class?" in R. S. Sugirtharajah (ed.), *Voices from the Margin: Interpreting the Bible in the Third World,* Maryknoll, New York: Orbis Books, 1991, pp. 147-171; Norbert F. Lohfink, *Option for the Poor,* Berkeley: Bibal Press, 1987; Jorge Pixley and Clodovis Boff, *Opzione per i poveri,* Assisi: Cittadella, 1986.

5. See, for instance, the works of Maurice Casey and Barnabas Lindars mentioned in note 7 of Chapter 1.

6. Jacques Guillet, *Jésus devant sa vie et sa mort,* Paris: Aubier, 1971, pp. 228-229 (= *The Consciousness of Jesus,* Paramus, New Jersey: Newman Press, 1972).

7. *Adv. Haer.,* 4.34.1.

8. See Joachim Jeremias, *Abba,* Gottingen: Vanderhoeck & Ruprecht, 1966; Id., *Neutestamentliche Theologie,* Gottingen: Mohr, 1971. Also Witold Marchel, *Abba, Père. La prière du Christ et des chrétiens,* Rome: PIB, 1963.

9. See Gerza Vermes, *Jesus the Jew,* London: Collins, 1973, pp. 210-211; Id., *Jesus and the World of Judaism,* London: SCM Press, 1983, pp. 41-42; David Flusser, *Jesus in Selbstzeugnissen und Bilddokumenten,* Hamburg: Rowohlt, 1971.

10. On Jesus' understanding of his death, see Jacques Guillet, *Jésus devant sa vie et sa mort,* Paris: Aubier, 1971; Xavier Léon-Dufour, *Face à la mort, Jésus et Paul,* Paris: Seuil, 1979; Heinz Schürmann, *Jesu ureigener Tod,* Freiburg: Herder, 1975.

11. See Gerald O'Collins, *What Are They Saying about Jesus?,* Mahwah, N.J.: Paulist Press, 1983, p. 72.

3

The Development of New Testament Christology

From the Risen Christ to the Incarnate Son

Explicit Christology begins with Easter. Yet, the Christology of the New Testament passed through a process of development as the early Christians deepened their faith reflection in Jesus who is the Christ. We must now follow this process in its main stages. As will be seen, between the earliest Christian kerygmatic preaching and the last stage of apostolic writing, a movement of reflection on the mystery of Christ is at work, that begins with a Christology "from below" and progressively passes over to a Christology "from above." Starting with the glorified state and the "divine condition" of the Risen one, Jesus' personal identity and divine Sonship will be gradually deepened through a process of "retro-projection," first through the "mysteries" of his life down to his human birth, and then beyond this to the "preexistence" in the mystery of God.

The first Palestinian Christology was one of the parousia (*marana tha*). Exegetes are not, however, agreed as to how this primitive Christology was intended and understood. According to some, this parousia Christology would have existed independently of a Christology of Jesus' exaltation in resurrection. Jesus would have been destined to become the glorified Messiah in his eschatological return; he had not been made such by a resurrection event. Such an opinion does not correspond to the historical data of the New Testament. Palestinian Christology has from the outset combined Jesus' glorification in resurrection and his eschatological return in the parousia. Never has the eschatological "not yet" of the parousia stood, in the apostolic christological faith, without the "already" of the Resurrection. He who must return is he who beyond death has been raised and glorified. R. Schnackenburg writes pointedly:

A first stage in which a Christian (Judaic-Palestinian) community would have entertained the idea of awaiting the parousia without the idea of exaltation, certainly never existed.[1]

But the reverse is also true: Never has there been a Christology of the Risen one that did not expect his future return in the parousia. The already of the resurrection is the promise of the not yet of the eschatological fulfillment in the parousia. The primitive Church, from the outset, combined the already and the not yet and held them in fruitful tension. R. Schnackenburg is right in remarking:

> The primitive community had first of all to show in front of Judaism that the *crucified* Jesus was nonetheless the Messiah who through the *resurrection* had already been confirmed as such. The return in glory is then the consequence, and in this conception the *necessary* consequence, in order that Jesus be shown in relation to the whole world as redeemer or judge. The complex saying of Mk 14:62 which puts together the exaltation of Jesus with his future coming on the clouds of heaven, contains therefore in reality the most ancient comprehension accessible to us of the Church of the origins with regard to the position and the function exercised by the Risen one: exaltation and parousia. There never was a faith in a parousia of Jesus without exaltation; but there never was either a faith in a pure and simple exaltation, on the contrary the parousia was also awaited of the one who had been exalted with God.[2]

As for the exaltation and resurrection, they coincide in one event in the early Christology of the New Testament: Jesus is glorified and exalted in and through his resurrection from the dead by the Father. This again has been well observed by R. Schnackenburg, who writes:

> The circle of ideas which must be invoked with the Christology of the "exaltation" is centred on the conviction that God has bestowed on Jesus after, or rather with the resurrection (in the most strict connection with it), dignity and power. That is why to that Christology belong also all the passages in which there is question of Christ sitting or being seated "at the right hand" of God, an image for the kingly enthronement in the divine power and office.[3]

The process of development of New Testament Christology will be followed here through two main stages: the proclamation of the Risen Christ in the early kerygma, and from the proclamation of the Risen Christ to the confession of the Son of God.

THE PROCLAMATION OF THE RISEN CHRIST IN THE EARLY KERYGMA

We have no direct access to the earliest Christology of the apostolic Church for the simple reason that the earliest writings of the New Testament come from the fifties, more than twenty years after the death and resurrection of Jesus. Yet exegetes are agreed that a fairly accurate picture of the Christology of the early apostolic kerygma can be drawn from our present documents.

WHERE IS THE EARLY APOSTOLIC KERYGMA FOUND?

Some passages of St. Paul's early letters, or even of the pastoral letters, testify in some way to the Church's early kerygma. The following passages are often mentioned: 1 Cor:15:3-7 on Paul's "paradosis" of Jesus' resurrection and appearances; the formula of faith of Rom 1:3-4, which, however, already includes a more elaborate Christology in which the "flesh" and the "spirit" refer to the two stages of the Christ-event; and a piece of primitive hymnology preserved in 1 Tim 3:16, in which "flesh" and "spirit" again stand for Jesus' self-emptying and glorification. Other passages can be added to the list, such as: 1 Thes 1:10; Gal 1:3-5; 3:1-2; 4:6: Rom 2:16; 8:34; 10: 8-9; Heb 6:1. From such passages, important characteristics of the early kerygma can be ascertained: the paschal mystery of Jesus' death and resurrection constitutes the core of the kerygma; the stress is where the primacy belongs, that is, on the resurrection, though it can never be separated from the death that preceded it; the resurrection means the entry of Jesus in the eschatological state, as well as his exaltation as Lord. All this is being announced as Good News; for, having been joined to God in his entire being, Jesus has opened the way for us.[4]

However, rather than witnessing directly to the early kerygma, the passages mentioned above are reflections of it in Paul's — and other — letters. But there exists another way by which the Christology of the early kerygma can be more directly (and more safely) recovered: the missionary speeches of Peter and Paul recorded in the Acts of the Apostles (Acts 2:14-39; 3:13-26; 4:10-12; 5:30-32; 10:34-43; 13: 17-47) by way of kerygmatic proclamation, mostly to the Jews (Peter's speech to Cornelius's household in 10:34-43 is similar in content).[5] Paul's preaching to the Gentiles at Lystra (Acts 14:15-18) and before the Areopagus at Athens (Acts 17:22-31) is left out of consideration here, for it witnesses to a distinct approach adapted to non-Jewish audiences. The earliest kerygma is, by contrast, addressed to the Jews and makes abundant reference to Israel's faith and messianic expectation.

It cannot, of course, be thought (nor is it neccesary to think) that Luke recorded in his book of Acts the exact wording of early kerygmatic discourses, somewhat as a stenographer might have done. What he meant to do was to show in general, and under a somewhat stereotyped form, how Jesus was being preached by the apostles at the time of the first generation of Christians. From this we can gather a clear enough view of how Christian faith in Jesus came first to be expressed. We can also discover some specific features of this earliest faith and the characteristic approach it followed.

Here then is to be found the first specifically Christian way of presenting Jesus and his mystery.

A study of the apostolic speeches of Peter and Paul referred to above summarises the content of the early kerygma in the following seven points:

1. You are now witnesses and have the experience of the action of the Holy Spirit; 2. If the Holy Spirit has been poured in such abundance over Israel, this signifies that the "last days" foretold by the prophets have come; 3. This has been verified in the birth, the life, and the miracles of Jesus of Nazareth, whom the Jews have killed, but whom God has raised from the death — of which we are witnesses; 4. This Jesus, God has constituted Lord and Christ, making him ascend into heaven and placing him at his right hand; 5. All this has happened in conformity with the Scriptures; it is part of the plan of God for salvation "from our sins," and is conformed to the faith of our fathers; 6. The Risen Jesus is the new Moses, who will come on the clouds of heaven as the Son of Man to lead the eschatological Israel to final redemption; 7. If you believe the word which has been preached to you, if you repent and are baptized, you will be saved.[6]

Peter's speech on the day of Pentecost (Acts 2:14-39) may serve as model of the apostolic kerygma. Not only is it presented by Luke as the first Christian preaching, he seems to propose it as paradigmatic of how the mystery of Jesus was proclaimed to the Jews — Palestinian and Hellenistic (Acts 2:5-13) — in the early days of the apostolic Church. We are, moreover, informed that Peter spoke in the name of the eleven (Acts 2:14). The christological core of Peter's proclamation — easily identifiable in other speeches as well — holds in the following verses:

[22]Men of Israel, hear these words: Jesus of Nazareth, a man attested to you by God with mighty works and wonders and signs which God did through him in your midst, as you yourselves know— [23]this Jesus, delivered up according to the definite plan and foreknowledge of God, you crucified and killed by the hands of lawless men.[24] But God raised him up, having loosed the pangs of death, because it was not possible for him to be held by it. . . .

[32]This Jesus God raised up, and of that we all are witnesses. [33]Being therefore exalted at the right hand of God, and having received from the Father the promise of the Holy Spirit, he has poured out this which you see and hear.[34] For David did not ascend into the heavens; but he himself says: "The Lord said to my Lord: Sit at my right hand,[35] till I make thy enemies a stool for thy feet" (Ps 110:1).[36] Let all the house of Israel therefore know assuredly that God has made him both Lord and Christ, this Jesus whom you crucified.

This fundamental text would deserve a close exegesis. It contains the most fundamental assertions of the early christological kerygma and shows clearly the perspective in which the mystery of Jesus Christ is being proposed. Following it, it becomes possible to indicate the main characteristics of the Christology of the early kerygma.

THE CHRISTOLOGY OF THE EARLY KERYGMA

The distinct characteristics of the Christology of the early kerygma that stand out from Peter's speech can be summed up in a few words. It is an Easter Christology, centred on the resurrection and glorification of Jesus by the Father. His exaltation is an *action of God, upon Jesus, for our sake.* It is God who raises Jesus from the dead, who glorifies him and exalts him, who makes him Lord and the Christ, Leader and Saviour (Acts 5:31). Jesus is the receiver of the divine action of raising, establishing or constituting, but he is made Lord and Christ for our sake. Hence, after the kerygmatic proclamation there follows the invitation to repentance, conversion and baptism (Acts 2:37-39). Something has happened *to Jesus, from God, for us.* Let us resume these three elements.

From God: The divine action referred to consists essentially in raising Jesus from the dead. This action is presented as God's decisive intervention in the history of salvation. If the God of the Old Testament was essentially the God who saved the chosen people from Egypt through the Exodus, this former event is now understood as a type or foreshadowing of the new event of salvation.The resurrection of Jesus from the dead is the final saving event of God. Notwithstanding the fact that God acted throughout history and continues to act today, yet the core of the Christian message, as it stands out in the early kerygma, is that by the Easter event God has brought God's saving action to a climax. All that will follow thereafter depends on this event. In it, God has triumphed over sin and death and manifested God's self fully as a saving God. The resurrection of Jesus is in that sense the fulness of divine revelation.

To Jesus: The resurrection is, for Jesus, the inauguration of an entirely new state. He enters into the end-time and the world of God. The eschatological hope is already fulfilled, in his case, in the totality of his human reality — body and soul. The entirely new condition to which Jesus has passed is expressed in relation to his previous earthly existence and is defined in terms of the eschatological expectation: Jesus has entered into final glory. It is important to note that in this early stage of Christology it is not said that through his resurrection Jesus returns to the glory that he had with God before his earthly life (cf. Jn 17:5). No thought has yet been given to the preexistence of Jesus and to the incarnation of the eternal Son of God. This question has not yet been raised and therefore not yet been answered.

Between the earthly existence of Jesus and his risen condition as Christ and Lord, the early kerygma affirms a true discontinuity. Jesus has been really transformed, and his transformation measures the distance between the Jesus of history and the Christ of faith. By his resurrection Jesus has become fully what he is now; he has reached his own perfection (*teleiòsis*) (Heb 5:9). Christian faith is belief in Jesus *as* made perfect by God. Yet, at the same time, continuity remains between the Jesus of history and the Christ of faith: He is one and the same. Christian faith is belief in *Jesus*, who has been made perfect by God. This continuity in discontinuity is well expressed in the earliest professions of Christian faith, as they can be reconstituted from the New Testament: "Jesus *is* the Christ"; "Jesus *is* the Lord."[7] In the mind of the early Christians, the divine act of raising Jesus from the dead, far from cancelling his earthly existence, ratifies and authenticates his life and mission. Thereby God signifies that God was already at work in Jesus' earthly career, in his teaching and miracles, in his life and death, in his person. All that has gone on during Jesus' earthly life is taken up into his risen condition and receives in it its true significance. The Easter event founds the personal identity and the qualitative difference, the continuity in discontinuity between the Jesus of history and the Christ of faith: The Risen one is he who was crucified (Mk 16:6).

For us: What God has done to Jesus is for us. All the titles by which the newly acquired dignity of the risen Jesus is expressed view him in relation to us. God has made him the Christ (that is, the Messiah promised to Israel); the Lord of all (Acts 10:36); Leader and Saviour (Acts 5:31). To him alone has the supreme name been given in view of people's salvation (Acts 4:12). He alone has been appointed by God to judge the living and the dead (Acts 10:42). The resurrection of Jesus thus inaugurates the decisive advent of salvation.

Here, too, the newness and discontinuity is clearly affirmed. It is the risen Lord who saves, and to the resurrection that salvific significance is assigned, but the Easter event does not cancel out what has preceded, though the saving value of the death of Jesus on the cross is not clearly brought out at this stage. Responsibility for the death on the cross is assigned to the Jews who had him killed (Acts 2:23,36). Attention is drawn to Jesus' kingly investiture, to his enthronement (Acts 2:32-36, with the citation from the enthronement Psalm, Ps 110:1) and the inauguration of his messianic and saving function. With it the earthly mission of Jesus has reached its God-appointed end; Jesus has been established in the fulness and universality of his saving power. At the same time, continuity remains between Jesus' earthly life and his post-Easter saving action. His earthly existence is perceived in a new light, as endowed with messianic and saving power. Looking back on the events of Jesus' life, the early Christians discover their true significance. The healing ministry of Jesus, his attitude toward the Law, his mercy toward sinners, his option for the poor, his openness to all people, all appear now as prefigurations of the salvific action of the Risen one (Acts 2:22). They prepared it and led to it. If Jesus has become Messiah, Lord and Saviour by his resurrection, he had been prepared for this function during his earthly existence.

According to the early kerygma, therefore, Easter is God's action, in Jesus, for us. With this Easter Christology, what we earlier called explicit Christology has been born, for here we find the initial stage of a reflex and organized discourse on the significance of Jesus Christ for Christian faith. This early christocentric discourse seems, no doubt, in contrast with the God-centredness of Jesus himself, which we recalled earlier. The one who had announced God and God's Reign has now become the object of proclamation; the herald of the Kingdom is now being preached by the Church. Yet, the contrast is but apparent, for the one who had put God at the centre of his message has now been placed by God at the centre of God's saving design and action. Such is the import of the resurrection for Christology.

Jesus had been reluctant to apply messianic titles to himself. In particular, he had kept aloof from Davidic messianism and identified himself with the Suffering Servant of God. Now that he had been transformed by God into the Risen one, the Old Testament messianic titles became the channel through which the early Christians first attempted to express his function and significance. He is the Christ, the Lord. By so doing, they were making use of the only categories at their disposal in their Jewish culture, while at the same time being aware of the transcendent manner in which Jesus was fulfilling the ancient messianic promise.

The discontinuity is therefore striking, yet the continuity remains, and the explicit Christology of the early kerygma had its root in the implicit Christology of Jesus himself. In particular, if Jesus has become the centre, inasmuch as God placed him there through the resurrection, never does he substitute for God or take God's place. God has given Jesus to humankind that, once exalted, he might draw all to him (Jn 12:32). Jesus Christ is the Mediator (1 Tim 2:5), he is the way; God remains the goal and the end (Jn 14:6).

That the Christology of the early kerygma is an Easter Christology means that the point of departure of its discourse about Jesus is the Easter event. It implies a projection into the eschatological future, by which Jesus' significance is explained in relation to the end-time of salvation. The personal origin of Jesus himself has not been touched. Only further developments will lead to the consideration of his preexistence and consequently to a Christology of the incarnation. In this sense, the earliest Christology may be termed a Christology from below, for it starts from the human reality of Jesus transformed through the resurrection, not from the preexistence of the Son of God become man.

This is not to say that the early Christology fails to account for the divine condition of Jesus Christ nor, on the contrary, that his divine condition is a Christian affirmation superimposed on Jesus by Christian faith by a process of deification, of which the early kerygma would be the first witness.

Neither is true. On the one hand, the divine condition of the Risen Lord is affirmed by the Christology of the early kerygma. In particular, the term *Lord* is applied to him to signify that God's own Lordship of the people now extends to Jesus himself. On the other hand, Jesus has not been deified by the early Christians. Rather, his true identity has been manifested by God in his resurrection and acknowledged in faith by the early Church. What is true, however, is that the real identity of Jesus Christ has first been manifested and, consequently, also encountered and discovered, in his risen and glorified human reality. It was therefore natural that it be first affirmed at that level, resulting in an Easter Christology.

Finally, the Christology of the early kerygma is essentially soteriological. By this is meant that its discourse about Jesus Christ is centred on his significance for the salvation of people. We have shown that all the titles applied to Jesus at this early stage of christological reflection express his meaning for us as intended by God and realized fully through the resurrection. In other words, early Christology is decidedly functional, Jesus' identity being defined by the functions he exercises toward us in his glorified state. What is being enunciated is what God made Jesus to be for us. The mystery of his person, his own deepest identity, still remains veiled, and will only be brought out through further reflection.

In particular, in the early kerygma, the title Son of God is not yet applied to Jesus with the fulness of meaning it was destined to take on later. Earlier we have noted the Old Testament roots of this title and the broad meaning ascribed to it when applied to the Davidic King. In this sense it could be used of Jesus and, characteristically, referred to his messianic investiture by God in his resurrection. Paul's speech at Antioch, as recorded by the Acts, is a clear witness to this use. Paul explicitly quotes the enthronement Psalm (2:7), which he sees fulfilled in God's action of raising Jesus from the dead (Acts 13:32-33; cf. also Heb 1:5). In this context, the title remains messianic and functional. Only later would it be filled with new meaning, to become one of the privileged expressions of Jesus' true identity in relation to God.

The Christology of the early kerygma may be called primitive in the sense that it reflects the earliest Christian understanding of Jesus. Later developments, however, will neither cancel it out nor abrogate its significance and validity for us today. Those developments will only bring out the implications of what has already been said about Jesus in the early kerygma. Between the early kerygmatic presentation of Jesus and the subsequent deeper insights into the mystery of his person there is continuity and homogeneous development. The same faith is expressed in both; it only becomes progressively more reflexive and articulate. The essential, decisive message has been announced from the start, for in what God has made Jesus to be for us, the true identity of his person is already involved, even if it remains hidden and will need to be unveiled. The Christology of the early kerygma was functional; it was a reflection on Jesus in the functions he exercises toward us. Later, through an organic process, this will develop into an ontological Christology where the reflection will extend to Jesus as he is in himself, to his person in his relationship to God.

FROM THE PROCLAMATION OF THE RISEN ONE TO THE CONFESSION OF THE SON OF GOD

The original Easter faith proclamation gave a coherent picture of Jesus, yet its presentation of Jesus was but a first step in the development of New Testament Christology. From the Christology of the Risen Lord seated at God's right hand, established by God as Saviour and calling people to reconciliation with God and among themselves in justice and love, to the Christology of the divine Sonship of Jesus, of his origin in God and preexistence with him, the distance is indeed great. The New Testament, however, testifies to a progressive but massively significant advance toward such a Christology. Such an advance is verified not only in the letters of St. Paul, the Gospel of John and the Book of Revelation; it is found as well in the Letter to the Hebrews and the Synoptic Gospels. All these writings draw attention to the person of Jesus, no longer merely to the unique role assigned to him by God in the plan of salvation.

They do it in different ways, each author with personal insight and theological intent. Our intention here is not to review the specific Christology of each New Testament writer.[8] A broad sketch of the Christology of each of the synoptics would show that each author has a specific approach to the mystery of Jesus' person. As for the Gospel of John, it delves into the mystery with such unprecedented depth as will in fact remain unsurpassed. The Christologies of Paul, of the Letter to the Hebrews — and others — are also rich in personal insights and would need a distinct treatment. This we cannot attempt here. What we can do is sketch out in general terms the organic development of New Testament Christology as it stands out from the New Testament corpus considered as a whole. It is possible to indicate some landmarks in this development that point to a progressive elucidation of the personal identity of him whom God has established as the Christ and the Lord. They witness, among other things, to various stages of development of a Christology of the Son of God.

A HOMOGENEOUS DEVELOPMENT TOWARD "PREEXISTENCE"

The task of showing this progressive elucidation is a delicate one. It requires, if distinct stages of comprehension are to be distinguished, that each author and each text be read in its context and with its original meaning. It would be wrong to level up all the evidence by reading everywhere a depth of meaning which will only be reached at a later stage. Speaking of the title Son of God, we have recalled its metaphorical meaning in the

Old Testament and its messianic significance when applied to Jesus in the early kerygma. The same title will now progressively acquire a surplus meaning. At the end of this development, it will unambiguously refer to the unique, ontological, divine Sonship of Jesus. But this must not be read where it is not yet intended. It is clear, for instance, that the Christology of the Son of God in the infancy narrative (Lk 1:32) only says that the child born of Mary comes from God; he will be called "Son of the most High." It does not yet make reference to Jesus' eternal Sonship of God in his preexistence, but to the fact that Jesus is from God from his very birth.

Everything looks as if the divine condition of Jesus that the early kerygma first perceived in his glorified state through the resurrection is progressively thrown back toward the past by a process of retroprojection. But this happens through various stages. The virginal birth of the infancy narratives is presented as a God-given sign that Jesus is from God from the very beginning of his earthly existence. It remains silent on the further question of his eternal origin from God as Son. The question of the preexistence of Jesus, of the mystery of his person prior to his earthly life and independently of it, is not yet raised, and therefore not yet answered. Where and when considered, it will lead in Paul and his environment to new christological insights (Phil 2:6-11; Col 1:15-20; Eph 1:3-13) and, above all, in John's Gospel, to the heights of the prologue (1:1-18) in which, from that angle, can rightly be found the summit of New Testament Christology.

It was indeed unavoidable that, having perceived in the glorified human existence of Jesus his divine condition and his God-given status as the Saviour of all, Christian faith should further reflect on the mystery of his person by asking the question of the origin of his exalted dignity. A first way of doing this consisted in showing that the pre-Easter Jesus was, throughout his earthly life from its very beginning, from God, and destined to the glory finally manifested in his resurrection. The Synoptic Gospels witness to this reflection: the baptism of Jesus in the Jordan at the beginning of his public mission is accompanied with a theophany testifying to his divine origin (Mk 1:11, with the double quotation from Ps 2:7 and Is 42:1); the theophany at the scene of the transfiguration is a further indication of the same (Mk 9:7, with the quotation from Is 42:1). Turning back to the very beginning of Jesus' earthly life led the Synoptic Gospels to the affirmation of the divine origin of his human birth (Lk 1:32). But no further! The threshold of Jesus' preexistence has not yet been crossed.

Yet crossing the threshold of preexistence was as unavoidable as it was pregnant with christological significance. It would introduce the decisive step in the inquiry about Jesus' true identity and lead to the deepest insights into the mystery of his person. If, as God had manifested and faith perceived, his condition as the Risen Lord was divine, if further this divine condition, manifested in his glory, had been latent in him throughout his earthly life, starting from its very origin from God, then beyond his human origin from God he was and is already with God. He preexisted; he was with God and in God in an eternal beginning, independently of and prior to his manifestation in the flesh. For humans do not become God, nor can they be made God, even by God. The divine condition of Jesus that God caused to shine forth through the glorified state of his human existence was but (and could only be) a reflection, in his humanity, of the divine identity that was his in his preexistence with God.

Humans cannot become God, but God can become human, and did in Jesus Christ. This is the unheard-of affirmation to which the faith reflection of the early Christians was inescapably leading, if only the implications of the Christology of the early kerygma were fully developed. This they discovered with awe and wonder and proclaimed with joy as Good News for the whole world. So it was that gradually a Christology developed in the New Testament, the scope of which was no longer limited to affirming Jesus' divine condition as expressed in his glorified state, nor even the divine origin of his human existence, but extended to his preexistence in God, from whom he came and by whom he was sent.

Such a Christology will unfold itself in two complementary parts, characterised as it is by a double movement — downward and upward, descent and ascent — insofar as such graphic images can be used, and comprising the entire salvific event of Jesus Christ. He came from God, with whom he preexisted from all eternity, and through the paschal mystery of his death and resurrection, he returned to the glory of his Father. In this perspective, the glory of the resurrection no longer merely appeared as given to Christ by God when God raised him from the dead; it was also a return to the glory he had in God before he was sent by the Father on his earthly mission, indeed "before the world was made" (Jn 17:5).

An early witness to the way in which — going beyond the limits of the human birth of Jesus — christological reflection crosses the threshold of preexistence is found in Romans 1:3-4. The Gospel of God, according to Paul, is about "Jesus Christ, our Lord," "his Son who was descended from David according to the flesh and constituted Son of God in power according to the Spirit of holiness by his resurrection from the dead." Descent from David and the constitution in power by the resurrection express the two moments, downward and upward, of the Christ-event. One is symbolized by the flesh, the other by the Spirit. One is the entry into the world of one who is the preexistent "Son" of God ("his Son"); the other, his being constituted Son of God in his glorification from the Father. A Christology of preexistence and descent has been prefixed to the Easter, or ascent, Christology of the early kerygma. The process of retroprojection beyond the human birth to the preexistence has resulted, paradoxically, in a Christology of the "Son" of God made human who becomes "Son of God" in his resurrection.

A clear instance of a comprehensive christological development made up of descent and ascent is found in the liturgical hymn quoted by St. Paul in his Letter to the Philippians (2:6-11). Paul founded the church at Philippi in the year 49 and wrote his Letter to the Philippians in 56. If, however, we reckon that he is quoting a liturgical hymn he communicated to them at the time of the foundation of their church, we may conclude that this "apotheosis of the crucified" existed in the forties. The importance of this fact for the development of New Testament Christology has not escaped the notice of M. Hengel, who wrote:

> One would be tempted to say that within the course of less than two decades christology has undergone a development the proportions of which are greater than anything that has happened thereafter in seven successive centuries, till the completion of the dogma of the ancient Church.[9]

The hymn to the Philippians is a well-balanced composition that may be divided into two parts, each with three stanzas, developing the descending and ascending movements, respectively, of which the Christ-event is made up in its totality, and a clear transition between the two parts: therefore (*dio*). It is being quoted here, following this metric composition:[10]

> [6] Who, being in the form of God (*en morphè tou theou*),
> did not count equality with God
> something to be grasped (*arpagmos*).

> [7] But he emptied (*ekenòsen*) himself,
> taking the form of a slave (*morphè doulou*),
> becoming as human beings are;
> and being in every way like a human being,
> [8] he was humbler yet,
> even to accepting death, death on a cross.

> [9] And for this (*dio*) God raised him high,
> and gave him the name
> which is above all other names;

> [10] so that all beings
> in the heavens, on earth and in the underworld,
> should bend the knee at the name of Jesus
> [11] and that every tongue should acknowledge
> Jesus Christ as Lord (*Kurios*),
> to the glory of God the Father. (NJB)

We cannot enter into the details of the exegesis of this text. Suffice it to note a few salient points. The double movement, downward and upward, is obvious, each comprising three of the six stanzas of which the hymn is made up. Jesus came from God, in whose glory (*morphè theou*) he dwelt (*huparkòn*) prior to his human life; he returned to him with his glorified human existence through the resurrection. The human life of Jesus and his death on the cross are seen as self-emptying (*kenòsis*); they verify the Deutero-Isaian figure of the Servant of God (*morphè doulou*) in terms of which Jesus himself had understood his death. Conversely, but in parallel fashion, the exaltation of the resurrection is coined in terms strongly reminiscent of the early kerygma: The name above every name which Jesus received in his resurrection is the name Lord (*Kurios*). Clearly, the Christology developed here does not cancel out the earlier one; it nevertheless enters more deeply into the mystery of the person of Jesus by raising and beginning to answer the question of his preexistence with God. But the new question has arisen out of the Easter proclamation of the Risen Lord, and the more evolved Christology to which it gives rise enunciates what was latent in the early kerygma: Who really is the Risen Jesus, since God has made him the Lord? Implied in *what* he is *for us* is *who* he is *in himself.* Functional Christology naturally ends with questions concerning the person of Jesus Christ, and the answer to these necessarily marks the advent of a Christology which rises from the functional to the ontological level. The inner dynamism of the Easter faith leads from one to the other.

The hymn to the Philippians should not, however, be taken in isolation. The captivity and the pastoral letters quote other christological hymns, also rich with christological doctrine. They too witness to the direction in which Pauline Christology—and the Christology of the apostolic Church—gradually evolved, from functional to ontological. We may mention, among others, Ephesians 2:14-16; Colossians 1:15-20; 1 Timothy 3:16; Hebrews 1:3; 1 Peter 3:18-22. The importance of the early hymnology for New Testament Christology has not escaped the notice of theologians. G. Segalla, for instance, wrote:

> As far as the christological content is concerned, one notes immediately the extreme importance of the hymns in the development of Christology, both as regards the understanding of the person of Christ, in particular his pre-existence in God, and his redemptive mission, universal in space and time.[11]

FROM PREEXISTENCE TO DIVINE SONSHIP

That an ontological Christology was latent in the functional Christology of the early kerygma does not, however, mean that the one could be (or would in fact be) deduced from the other by way of a merely logical process. We must account not only for the fact that the preexistence and divine identity of Jesus came to be progressively enunciated, but also that it was precisely understood in terms of divine Sonship. The title Son of God, with the definite ontological meaning it will gradually take on when applied to Jesus, will become the privileged and decisive way in which to express his true personal identity. This cannot be explained unless, beyond the Easter experience of the first believers, we return to Jesus himself via the memory of his earthly life as it was preserved in the early Christian communities. Isolated from Jesus' witness about himself, the Easter experience would not by itself suffice to explain the Church's christological faith. Jesus, however, had lived his divine Sonship in all his attitudes and actions, above all in his prayer to the God whom he called Abba. He had done so under the astonished eyes of the disciples who shared his daily existence. His human consciousness was essentially filial. No doubt, the novelty of addressing God in prayer with the term Abba notwithstanding, the disciples had not fathomed the depth of the relationship of Jesus to his God. Now that God had allowed Jesus' divine condition to be manifested in the resurrection, however, the full significance of Jesus' Sonship of his Father was becoming clear.

The elaborate New Testament Christology of Jesus' ontological Sonship of God gives objective expression to the filial consciousness that had been at the centre of Jesus' subjective experience of God during his earthly life. A glimpse into this had been given to the disciples, but its full significance had become manifest only now. In the last analysis, the Christology of Jesus' Sonship of God has, and could only have, as its last foundation the filial consciousness of Jesus himself. Such is its ultimate source. Only by going back in remembrance to what Jesus had said about himself could the mystery of his oneness with God be finally perceived. "When he was raised from the dead, his disciples remembered" what he had said, writes John in his Gospel (Jn 2:22), indicating the process of remembering through which, after Easter, the disciples came to understand who Jesus was. John further indicates that this process of remembrance and understanding could only happen under the guidance of the Holy Spirit. He it was who would "teach you all things and bring to your remembrance all that I have said to you" (Jn 14:26; cf. 16:12-13).

At the stage of New Testament Christology we have reached, there took place, therefore, a continuous going and coming between the questions Christian reflection raised about Jesus and the testimony of Jesus himself as it had been entrusted to Christian memory. Here we find the hermeneutical circle at work in the New Testament interpretation of Jesus. From this process, the answers of faith evolved, leading to the confession of Jesus as the Son of God. The Jesus of history, as critical exegesis is able to discover him today through the Gospel tradition, had done and said enough to warrant the faith interpretation of his person which, in the light of the Easter experience, the apostolic Church built gradually.

Let it suffice to recall some of the elements pointed out in the previous chapter: the authority with which Jesus declared the plan and the mind of God as though he read it in God's own heart; his certitude that the Reign of God was not only close at hand but being inaugurated through his own life and action, in his own person; his assurance that his attitude to people and institutions and his miracles conveyed God's own attitude and action; his conviction that being open to him and his preaching was to respond, in conversion and repentance, to God's offer of salvation, that to become his disciples was to enter the Kingdom of God; above all, his unprecedented nearness to God in prayer. The questions that the life and preaching of Jesus raised were finally being answered in a decisive manner: Jesus is the Son of God. The traditional biblical expression was being resumed but, being now applied to Jesus after long years of reflection on the mystery of his person carried on in the light of the Easter experience, it became so loaded with new meaning as to refer in proper terms to a singular Son-to-Father relationship. It now conveyed, still inadequately, no doubt, yet truly, the properly unique and ineffable mystery of the communion of Jesus, the crucified one who had been raised, with God.

The depth of Jesus' divine Sonship having been discovered, a new approach lay open for the discourse of faith which no longer would start, as the early kerygma had done, from the Lordship of the Risen one, but, inverting the perspective, would resolutely take as its point of departure the togetherness of Father and Son in an ineffable communion of life prior to and independently of the Son's mission from the Father. The preexistence of Jesus before his earthly life that the divine condition of his risen state postulated was, in fact, existence in the eternity of God. It therefore became possible to invert the whole christological discourse and start from the contemplation of the ineffable mystery of the communion of Father and Son in the inner life of God. W. Kasper has shown well the enormous import of the reversal of perspective brought about in Christology and theology by the consideration of the preexistence in God of Jesus Christ. He writes:

> What the pre-existence statements of the New Testament really do is to express in a new and more profound way the eschatological character of the person and work of Jesus of Nazareth. Since in Jesus Christ God himself has definitively, unreservedly and unsurpassably revealed and communicated himself, Jesus is part of the definition of God's eternal nature. It follows therefore from the eschatological character of the Christ-event that Jesus is Son of God from eternity and God from eternity is the "Father of our Lord Jesus Christ." The history and fate of Jesus are thus rooted in the nature of God: God's nature proves to be an event. Thus the New Testament pre-existence statements lead to a new, comprehensive interpretation of the term God.[12]

This approach, in fact, leads the New Testament Christology to a climax. It finds its best expression in the Prologue of the Johannine Gospel (1:1-18), which may be considered as the culmination of the New Testament christological reflection.

¹ In the beginning was the Word (*logos*):
the Word was with God (*ho theos*)
and the Word was God (*theos*).
² He was with God in the beginning.
³ Through him all things came into being,
and of all that has come to be
not one thing had its being except through him.
⁴ In him was life,
and that life was the light of men;
⁵ and light shines in darkness,
and darkness could not overpower it. . . .
¹⁴ The Word became (*egeneto*) flesh (*sarx*),
he dwelt (*eskènòsen*) among us,
and we saw his glory (*doxa*),
the glory that he has as the one-begotten
(*monogenès*) from the Father,
full of grace (*charis*) and truth (*alètheia*). . . .
¹⁶ From his fulness we have all received —
one gift (*charis*) replaced another;
¹⁷ for the Law was given through Moses,
grace (*hè charis*) and truth (*hè alètheia*) have come
through Jesus Christ.
¹⁸ No one has ever seen God;
it is the only-begotten (*monogenès*) Son who is
close to the Father's heart
who has made him known (*exègèsato*). (based on JB)

Without entering into an elaborate exegesis of the text, a few remarks may be made. The writer applies to the preexistent Son the concept of the "Word" (*dabar*) of God, borrowed from the sapiential literature of the Old Testament. God the Father (*ho theos*) is distinguished from the Word who is "God" (*theos*).[13] "The Word became flesh" (*sarx egeneto*) expresses the personal human becoming of the Word; the "flesh" indicates the feeble human condition he shares with human beings. "He dwelt (*eskènòsen*) among us" recalls the Old Testament theology of the *shekinah* in virtue of which Wisdom "pitched her tent" to dwell among people. The weakness of the "flesh" notwithstanding, according to John, the glory (*doxa*) of God shines through the human existence of Jesus from the beginning; the manifestation of his glory is not delayed, as for Paul, till the time of his resurrection and exaltation. Jesus Christ, the Word made flesh, is the "only-begotten" (*monogenès*) "Son of God." By this his eternal begetting from the Father is expressed — distinct from the functional title of "first born" (*pròtotokos*) from the dead, attributed to Jesus in his resurrection (cf. Col 1:18). That the Word incarnate is "full of grace and truth" signifies that in his person he is the culmination of God's loving kindness (*hèsèd, charis*) and faithfulness (*èmèt, alètheia*) toward people. For, while the Law given by God through Moses was already a grace (*charis*), Jesus Christ is God's supreme grace (*hè charis*) and the supreme manifestation of God's faithfulness to God's saving purpose (*hè alètheia*).

If, starting from the Prologue, we take a rapid overview of the entire Gospel of John, it is clear that the Christ-event stands out in its fulness, from "exodos" to "eisodos." The Son eternally with the Father, the incarnation of the Son, the beholding of his glory in his human condition, which culminates in the cross-resurrection, the effusion of the Spirit: Such is the mystery of Jesus Christ and the Christ-event in its full amplitude.

The similarities between the christological hymn to the Philippians and the Johannine Prologue notwithstanding, the route Christology has traveled from one to the other needs to be fully appreciated. It has been well observed by R. Schnackenburg, who wrote pointedly:

> The Christology of the exaltation and the glorification notwithstanding, for John the incarnation has nevertheless become another knot of the whole question. While the hymn to Christ in Phil 2:6-11 is still entirely oriented to the enthronement of Christ as having dominion over the world and considers the pre-existence only as point of departure of the life of Christ, to make intelligible the unheard of fact of his "self-emptying" and "abasement," for John the first change from the heavenly world to the earthly dwelling becomes also supremely important. The entire road travelled by Christ is henceforth seen as a whole, as a descent and ascent of the Son of man (3:13,31; 6:62), as the coming of the "Son of God" into the world to return to the Father (13:1; 16:28) and reach again to the original glory which was his even before the foundation of the world (17:5, 24).[14]

With this a climax has been reached that will remain unsurpassed. We have made a complete circle from the divine condition of the Risen one to the mystery of the eternal communion of the Son with the Father. The divine economy of salvation has yielded the theology of God's inner life, the seeds of which it had been carrying in itself. Functional Christology has, through the impulse of the inner dynamism of faith, fructified into ontological Christology. The answer given by faith, in the light of the Easter experience, to the question "What is Jesus for us?" has led to the final answer that faith can and must give to the question, "Who is Jesus?" The Christology of John's Prologue is, we may say, the decisive Christian answer to the question put by Jesus to Peter: "Who do you say I am?" (Mt 16:15). But this answer only became possible at the end of a long process of christological reflection.

The Christology with which the New Testament comes to its close is a downward Christology. We have explained earlier in what sense the Christology of the early kerygma could be called upward, insofar as the divine condition of Jesus had first been perceived and affirmed in the glorified state of his human existence. We have followed the process of questioning that this first perception set in motion and the progressive reversal of perspective that ensued as the root of this divine condition was sought at ever-deeper levels, to be finally placed in the secret of God's inner life prior to and independently of Jesus' human existence on earth. The Christology that flows from this complete reversal of perspective becomes, of necessity, a downward one. It starts from the eternal being of the Son with the Father, to proceed to his becoming man in his earthly mission from God, and, through his paschal mystery, to his return to the glory of the Father.

The Son of God has known a human becoming, and a human history has been his own. Is the sequence, to which the development of the New Testament faith testifies, from an upward Christology to a downward one, purely fortuitous? Or must we, on the contrary, think that this development was bound to take place, impelled as it was by an intense dynamism? The second is the correct answer. In the last analysis, the divine condition of Jesus Christ first perceived in faith through its manifestation in his glorified humanity could not, as faith became reflexive, continue to be placed in his humanity only. The glorified humanity was just a pale reflection of his divine condition. The reversal of perspective was as unavoidable and necessary as it was fruitful, for only thus could reflection on the mystery of Jesus Christ reach a mature stage and find adequate expression. Upward Christology led to downward Christology, carried by the dynamism of faith.

This is not to say that downward Christology supersedes upward Christology and renders it obsolete. The Christology of St. John's Prologue and Gospel did not cancel out that of the kerygma in the early Church; nor must we choose between the two even today, nor, for that matter, between the distinct Christologies of the various New Testament writers. They remain distinct, fragmentary and mutually complementary approaches to the mystery of Jesus Christ which in itself stands beyond them all and will forever defy full comprehension. Today, as in the early Church, the distinct New Testament Christologies need to be kept in fruitful tension and dialogue, lest, choosing one at the expense of the other, we should fail to embrace in our vision the fulness of the mystery and perhaps lose sight of either the authentic humanhood of Jesus or of his true divine Sonship.

This is why, though in a certain sense the Christology of the Gospel of John, and particularly the Prologue, represents the climax of New Testament Christology, it can never be made into an absolute and exclusive model, leaving no room for the more ancient Christology of the early kerygma. Yet this happened to no small extent, not without serious dangers and negative results, in the history of Christology after the Council of Chalcedon — though not in direct connection with the council. Much of recent christological literature, on the contrary, presents itself as a massive reaction against the centuries-old monopoly and the unilateral predominance of the christological model from above.

Conversely, the question will also need to be asked whether the Christology from below, through which recent christological reflection links up again with the Christology of the early kerygma, can ever suffice by itself and be fully adequate without the complement of a Christology from above. Judging from the plurality of Christologies in the unity of faith to which the New Testament testifies, it may be surmised that, to avoid becoming unilateral in one direction or the other, christological reflection will ever need to follow a twofold path, from below and from above, and to integrate both. Starting from below, it will continue from above, and back again; or equivalently, from soteriology to Christology and vice-versa. To make a complete circle by traveling the road twice over: this, perhaps, is what an integral approach to Christology should mean.

Such an integral Christology will assign to the approach from below its lawful and necessary role, mindful of the way in which the early kerygma presented the person and work of Jesus: "Jesus of Nazareth, a man attested to you by God with mighty works and wonders and signs which God did through him in our midst ... " (Acts 2:22). Peter's Christology on the day of Pentecost was one of God's presence and working in the man Jesus; a Christology of "God-in-man," not of a "God-man." What does this mean for us today?

Finally, in the ongoing reflection of the Church on the mystery of Jesus Christ, the New Testament occupies a privileged position as the necessary frame of reference for every further elaboration. It is and must remain for all times the final norm (*norma normans*). New Testament Christology represents the authentic interpretation of the mystery by the foundational apostolic community, inspired by the Holy Spirit and recognized by the Church as the word of God. But it must be remembered that this testimony is not monolithic. Rather, it is made up of a plurality of witnesses in the unity of faith. The tension in unity of the distinct Christologies of the New Testament guarantees the legitimacy and necessity of plural Christologies even today.

NOTES

1. Rudolf Schnackenburg, "Christologie des Neuen Testaments," in Johannes Feiner and Magnus Löhrer (eds.), *Mysterium Salutis* III,1: *Das Christusereignis*, Einsiedeln, Benziger Verlag, 1970, p. 254.

2. Op. cit., p. 256.

3. Op. cit., p. 257.

4. For an analysis of the texts, see Mario Serenthà, *Gesù Cristo ieri, oggi e sempre*, Torino: Elle Di Ci, 1986, pp. 24s; Rudolf Schnackenburg, op. cit., pp. 248s.

5. For the texts, see Charles Harold Dodd, *The Apostolic Preaching and Its Developments*, New York: Harper, 1951.

6. See Giuseppe Segalla, Raniero Cantalamessa, and Giovanni Moioli, *Il problema cristologico oggi*, Assisi: Cittadella, 1973, pp. 74-75.

7. See Oscar Cullmann, *Les premières confessions de foi chrétienne*, Paris: Presses Universitaires de France, 1948.

8. For the Christology of the different New Testament writers, see for instance, Rudolf Schnackenburg, op. cit., pp. 272-383.

9. Martin Hengel, *Der Sohn Gottes*, Tübingen: Mohr, 1975, p. 11.

10. For other opinions on the composition of the hymn, and the additions made by Paul to its original text, cf. Rudolf Schnackenburg, op. cit., pp. 309-322.

11. See *Il problema cristologico oggi*, Assisi: Cittadella, 1973, p. 71.

12. Walter Kasper, *Jesus the Christ,* London: Burns & Oates, 1976, p. 175.

13. This seems to be the first instance where the use of the term *theos* with reference to Jesus is certain in the New Testament. Other instances of the same usage in John's Gospel are: the profession of faith of Thomas after the resurrection (20:28), and 1:18 according to the reading of some manuscripts (*monogenès theos*); the same usage is probable in 1 Jn 5:20. There exist other texts in the New Testament which some exegetes interpret as using the term *theos* about Jesus. These are: Romans 9:5; Colossians 2:2; Titus 2:10; Titus 2:13-14; Acts 20:28; 2 Peter 1:1. All these can, however, be understood—often understood better—as referring the term *theos* to the Father. According to Paul's usage established in 1 Cor 8:6, God (*theos*) refers to the Father while Jesus is called the Lord (*Kurios*). The conclusion would seem to be that John is the first New Testament author to have made use of the term "God" (*theos*)—distinct from *ho theos* = the Father—for Jesus. The meaning of the term is thus being broadened to refer to the "Godhead" common to Father and Son. The "ontic" terminology of the New Testament is beginning to evolve toward an ontological terminology. In Heb 1:8, *theos* is part of a quotation from Ps 45:7. On this question, see, among others, Raymond E. Brown, *Jesus God and Man*, Milwaukee: Bruce Publishing, 1967, pp. 1-38.

14. Rudolf Schnackenburg, op. cit., pp. 339-340.

4

Historical Development and Present Relevance of Christological Dogma

The original perspective of New Testament Christology was functional; it asked and stated *what* Jesus is for us. Through the dynamism of faith, however, this perspective evolved into an ontological one in which the question became *who* Jesus is in himself and in relation to God. This further perspective, which developed progressively in the New Testament, was expressed in "ontic" language and made use of such terms as: *theos, patèr, logos, huios, sarx,* and *anthròpos.* The previous chapter has shown the homogeneous nature of this process of development. The present one intends to follow the development of postbiblical Christology, of christological dogma through the councils of the patristic age. The intention is to show the continuity in sense and content that exists between the Christology of the New Testament and the Church's christological dogma, a real linguistic discontinuity notwithstanding. As the historical development of christological dogma is being reviewed, it is also proposed to point to the inner logic of its genesis, the dialectic, as it may be called, of its evolving process. The question of the abiding value and actuality of the christological dogma today will also be asked. A critical appraisal will be made and perspectives will be opened for a renewal of Christology following an integral approach.

Basic to the New Testament was the assertion that in Jesus Christ, through his death and resurrection, humans have been saved. His personal identity as the Son of God came to be progressively discovered as the foundation in being without which his saving function would have been without ground. This soteriological approach to Christology remained the fundamental perspective in postbiblical christological reflection. Jesus' saving function continued to act as the springboard for the discovery of his person. Function and ontology went hand in hand. This coincidence of two dimensions is well expressed in what became fundamental axioms for the early Church Fathers: "He became man that we might be divinized"; "He took on himself what is ours to share with us what is his." The Fathers thus spoke of a "marvelous exchange" (*mirabile commercium*) that took place between the Son of God incarnate and humankind, as the very raison d'être of the incarnation. He shared with us his Sonship, and the salvation of the human race consists in this, for "whatever has not been assumed (by him) has not been saved."

In its original form, the axiom of the marvelous exchange has a strong personalist and trinitarian character: the Son of God became human to share with us his divine Sonship; we become "sons in the Son" as we partake of his own immortality and incorruptibility. Thus wrote Irenaeus in the second century:

> To this end did the Word of God become man and the Son of God the Son of Man, that man might enter into communion with the Word of God and, receiving the adoption, might become son of God. In fact, we could not otherwise have received eternity and immortality ... unless the Eternal and the Immortal One had first become what we are.[1]

Later, however, the personal trait of sharing in the Sonship of the Son will sometimes be overshadowed and the stress laid on an exchange of natures between the divine and the human. As early as the fourth century, Athanasius wrote, quoting the axiom in the form mentioned above:

> Being God, he became man to divinize us.[2]
> He [the Word] became man that we might be divinized.[3]

From one form to the other, the marvelous exchange that takes place in Jesus Christ undergoes a shift of accent. From a sharing of sonship between sons, it becomes a share in the nature of God on the part of humanity. The second perspective ran the risk of obscuring the personal and historical aspects of the mystery and eventually could deflect the christological and soteriological reflection toward abstract, static considerations.[4]

The christological dogma developed in the early centuries in the context of the encounter between the Christian mystery and the surrounding hellenistic philosophy. Such an encounter offered both an opportunity and a danger; it was both a grace and a task. The opportunity consisted in the way that lay open to express the mystery of Jesus Christ in terms of the prevalent culture of the hellenistic world; it was a grace of inculturation. The challenge was to preserve intact the meaning, and to convey the integrity of the revealed mystery, while transposing it from the linguistic register of the New Testament to that of hellenistic philosophy. The danger — not a fictitious one, as the history of the early Christian "heresies" shows — consisted in all possible forms of reductionism by which the mystery of Jesus Christ would be so cut to size as to fit into the existing framework of hellenistic speculation. It cannot be presumed that the christological heresies always formally intended such reductionism. Often their protagonists, even though mistaken, were moved by a sincere desire to transpose the mystery into their culture. But that the early heresies did in fact imply such reductionism is certain, and this is the reason the Church invested all her energy in refuting them.

A brief survey of christological speculation in the early centuries would suffice to substantiate this abundantly.[5] To uphold the integrity of the mystery of Jesus Christ revealed in the New Testament meant to affirm simultaneously the authentic human existence of the Jesus who died and was raised from the dead by God, and his divine condition and personal identity as God's Son. Against all short-circuiting which, while holding fast to one end of the complex mystery would compromise the other, the Church had to choose the *lectio difficilior* by holding both together in fruitful tension. The earliest threat to the integrity of the mystery of Christ — one known in apostolic times and against which New Testament Christology, especially St. John's, strongly reacts (cf. 1 Jn 1:1-2) — was that of docetism. It tended to reduce the human existence of Jesus to a mere appearance or theophany in human form. Reductionism prompted by hellenistic philosophical speculation was clearly at work here. For hellenistic philosophy — as for the ancient Greek philosophers — it was inconceivable that God might become personally and really involved in human reality. Such a commitment to creation and history was unworthy of the Infinite. The human existence of Jesus as divine manifestation could therefore be no more than a mere appearance. Against the docetic heresy that would have emptied the Christian message, the Fathers of the Church reacted by stressing the personal entry of the Son of God in human history and the authenticity of his commitment to human flesh. In Jesus Christ, they insisted, human flesh had become the pivot of salvation: *Caro, cardo salutis* (Tertullian). The first battle that needed to be fought against christological reductionism issuing from hellenistic speculation had, therefore, to do with the reality of Jesus' human existence. Heresies started from below.

Speaking in general terms, the development of christological dogma in the early centuries can be divided into three periods that correspond to three distinct forms of christological reductionism to which the Church responded with new elucidations and further articulations of the complex mystery. Reductionism concerned first the reality and the integrity of the human existence of Jesus Christ. The response to docetism came from the New Testament itself and from the early Church Fathers, Irenaeus and Tertullian, among others. In its second form, christological reductionism addressed itself to the divine condition of Jesus Christ, producing such heresies as adoptionism, Sabellianism, Arianism, and others. Against all such tendencies, the first two ecumenical councils of Nicaea (325) and Constantinople I (381) (which are at once trinitarian and christological) affirmed both the true divinity of the Son of God, equal to the Father, and the integrity of his human existence. The third form of christological reductionism had to do with the modality of the mysterious union that took place in Jesus Christ between his divine and human condition. This mystery of union in distinction gave rise to opposite heresies. Some upheld the distinction while sacrificing the unity, such as Nestorianism. Others affirmed the unity in such a manner as to deny the distinction, as in the case of monophysitism. Both these heresies fell short of the Son of God made human; they were condemned by the Councils of Ephesus (431) and Chalcedon (451), respectively. It is important to observe from the outset that all forms of christological reductionism proceeded from the same source: the tendency—which will have its equivalent much later, even in modern times, for instance in idealist philosophy—to cut down the mystery of Jesus Christ to the size of human-made speculations. Against all such tendencies the Church elucidated progressively the ontology of the person of Jesus Christ in such a way as to distinguish him clearly from all reductionist pictures, and to preserve intact the originality and the apparently scandalous character of the Gospel message: "Christ crucified, a stumbling block to Jews and folly to Gentiles" (1 Cor 1:23). In the process, the Church made use of the conceptual tools available in the surrounding hellenistic culture.

Chapters 2 and 3 have shown that the New Testament witnesses to a development of Christology moving from functional to ontological. To this development corresponded a certain evolution in terminology. We have noted that the term *theos* came only progressively—and probably not before John's writings[6]—to be used with reference to the person of Jesus Christ. With this new usage, the term tended to convey the divine condition that the Son made human shared with the Father. The development of christological dogma in the postbiblical tradition witnesses to a progressive adoption of an ontological terminology derived from hellenistic philosophy.

It would, however, be wrong to believe that the surrounding hellenistic culture offered ready-made terms capable of conveying the meaning of the christological—or, for that matter, of the trinitarian—mystery. The terms in existence remained in effect ambiguous in their meaning and were used loosely in different senses. In particular, Greek and hellenistic philosophy had never distinguished clearly between nature and person—a distinction that both the trinitarian and the christological mysteries would make imperative for the reflection of the Church Fathers. Consequently, no one term referred unambiguously to one concept as distinct from the other. The confusion was greatest where the Greek term *hupostasis* was concerned. Materially translated into Latin as *substantia*, it was nevertheless used by the Greeks and the Latins in opposite directions. Thus, regarding the trinitarian mystery, the Greeks referred to *treis hupostaseis* in God, meaning three persons, while the Latins spoke of *una substantia* with reference to the divine nature. There ensued mutual misunderstandings and accusations of "tritheism" directed to the Greeks by the Latins and, in the opposite direction, of "modalism" leveled against the Latins by the Greeks. The

same ambiguity of the concepts and the terms obtained with the christological mystery, where in fact it endured even longer. The ambiguity of the
language and the misunderstandings it had provoked were decisively overcome by a canon of the Council of Constantinople II (553), in which the
equivalence of the terms referring to person and nature in both the Greek
and Latin traditions came to be clearly distinguished. In Greek *phusis* and
ousia refer to nature, *hupostasis* and *prosòpon* to person; in Latin *natura*
and *substantia* (and *essentia*) to nature, *persona* and *subsistentia* to person.[7]

Another instance of terminological ambiguity and progressive clarifica-
tion of meaning regards the term *homoousios* (consubstantial), which came
to be used at the Council of Nicaea (325) as the key term to convey the
equality of the Son with the Father in divinity. The same term had previously been condemned by a particular council of Antioch (269) in the
apparently modalist sense (denying the distinction of persons in the unity
of nature) in which it was suspected of having been used by Paul of Samo-
sata. Trinitarian and christological reflection, while making use of terms
existing in or derived from hellenistic philosophy, forced on them a new
surplus meaning, without which they would have remained unequal to the
task of expressing the Christian message.

The use by the postbiblical tradition of hellenistic terminology has often
been accused of corruption of the Christian message by way of hellenization,[8] or, even worse, in more recent years, as amounting to an alienation
of the Jesus of history.[9] To refute the accusation of alienation, Christology
has the task of showing the continuity in content and meaning that obtains
between the Christology of the New Testament and the christological
dogma of the Church, as it has had previously to show the continuity
between the Jesus of history and the Christ of faith of the apostolic Church.
As regards hellenization, however, a clear distinction is to be made between
the legitimate and, in the historical context, necessary use of ontological
terminology to convey the same, unaltered meaning, and the reduction of
the content of the mystery to Greek speculation expressed in hellenistic
terms. The first process amounts to that of inculturation of the Christian
message; the other to its corruption by reductionism to philosophical speculation. Authors have shown[10] that the first process is at work in the development of the christological dogma, not the other; nay more, that
hellenization as inculturation was practised by the early tradition in coun-
teraction against the heretical tendencies toward hellenization as reductionism. In this last sense it must be said that the Christian tradition has
dehellenized the mystery of Jesus Christ rather than hellenized it; or, better,
that the christological dogma represents a dehellenization of content in a
hellenization of terminology. Thus, A. Grillmeier writes pointedly:

> Nicaea is not the hellenization but the de-hellenization or the freeing
> of the Christian image of God from the impasse and the divisions
> towards which hellenism was leading it. It is not the Greeks who have

produced Nicaea; rather Nicaea has got over the Greek philosophers.[11]

In effect, what took place was not the hellenization of Christianity but the Christianization of hellenism. The process of inculturation of Christianity in a particular culture always and necessarily involves a movement toward the Christianization of the surrounding culture, whose concepts acquire a surplus meaning as they are made use of to convey the Christian mystery. M. Bordoni describes well the complex interaction between faith and culture that is operative in the development of the christological dogma leading up to the Chalcedonian definition. He writes:

> Each culture is a legitimate horizon of expansion and penetration for the message; that is why the word of God forces us to overcome a biblical fundamentalism that would limit itself to the fixed letter, to respond to the permanent requirement of actualizing it in an ever renewed understanding of the selfsame Word. In the necessary process of "inculturation," which corresponds to the continuous incarnation of the eternal word, in virtue of the newness and originality derived from its tradition of faith, Christian language must of necessity allow itself adequate space, by making use of, and modifying, where necessary, the categories and linguistic structures in order to make them capable of expressing the mystery of salvation which it announces. . . . An authentic process of hellenization which respects the necessary historical inculturation of the faith, must be conjoined with a corresponding process of de-hellenization. . . . It is in fact the heterodox movements of thought which have promoted a hellenization of the faith by imposing rigidly the conceptual schemes of the culture upon the kerygmatic language. The orthodox thought of patristic theology, on the contrary, while it incarnated the christological faith in the context of the Greek world, in coherence with the tradition of the Church, was preparing actively the new linguistic interpretation which Chalcedon sanctioned solemnly and through which the way was open at the same time, by way of correction (de-hellenization) and of indication (interpretation), for the ulterior development of the tradition of the faith.[12]

We have shown the existence in the New Testament of two distinct approaches to Christology, from below and from above, and the progressive evolution that took place from one approach to the other. Though a definite shift is everywhere visible in postbiblical tradition from functional to ontological, the two distinct approaches continue in existence. Christology from below will now consist in starting from the man Jesus, that is, from the human state or nature of Jesus, to ascend to his divinity as Son of God. This approach, characteristic of the Antiochian tradition, is often referred to as the Christology of the *homo assumptus*, called by A. Grillmeier the Christology of the *Logos-anthròpos*. It corresponds, in an ontological key, to the christological movement from below of the early apostolic kerygma. The danger is in its not reaching out adequately to the divine nature of Jesus Christ, Son of God. This connatural danger did lead historically to the Nestorian heresy, which was decisively condemned by the Council of Ephesus (431).

In the opposite direction, there developed a Christology from above, which took as its point of departure the oneness in divinity of the Son of God with the Father, and from there proceeded to affirm the true humanity Jesus assumed in the mystery of the incarnation. This approach, proper to the Alexandrian tradition, is called the Christology of the *Logos-sarx* and corresponds to the later stage of christological reflection in the New Testament, of which the apex is the incarnation Christology of the Prologue of St. John's Gospel. It has its own possible danger and shortcomings which would consist in falling short of the reality and authenticity of Jesus' human condition. This danger culminated historically in the heresy of monophysitism, which was condemned by the Council of Chalcedon (451).

The two approaches were legitimate in themselves. Both were founded on different strata of New Testament Christology. Both, however, were fraught with danger whenever, starting from one end, christological thinking failed to reach to the other. The following pages aim at describing the going to and fro, the oscillations of the pendulum from one perspective to the other, as through the historical development of the christological dogma the Church responded to all christological reductions with ever more articulated enunciations of the mystery of Jesus Christ. The intention is to show the logic of this development, the dialectic that is at work in it, and at the same time the permanent actuality and abiding value of the dogmatic christological formulations.[13]

THE CHRISTOLOGICAL COUNCILS: CONTEXT AND RESPONSE

The exposition will be limited to the main christological councils, from Nicaea (325) to Constantinople III (681), which have influenced significantly the evolution of the christological dogma. For each, the historical context, the significance of the Church's formulation of faith, and the abiding actuality today of both questions and responses, will be briefly exposed.

THE COUNCIL OF NICAEA

The Problematic of Nicaea

The context of the Council of Nicaea is that of the Alexandrian school of Christology, and especially of the denial by Arius, a priest in Alexandria

(+336), of the equality in divinity of the Son of God with the Father. The Christology of the New Testament and the symbols of faith that followed had based their affirmation of the divine Sonship of Jesus Christ on the glorified state of his risen humanity. In the early symbols, divine condition was attributed to the man Jesus, dead and risen, of whom the faith professed that he preexisted as Son of God. How was this preexisting Sonship of God to be understood? It may be noted that the perspective in which the question was being asked was that of an ascending, from below Christology; the movement and direction followed that which had been characteristic of the Christology of the early kerygma. An affirmation of the divinity of the preexistent Son in proper terms seemed to contradict both biblical monotheism and the philosophical concept of God's absolute unicity. Arius based his argumentation on both, appealing on the one hand to Old Testament texts, specifically to Proverbs 8:22, and on the other hand to the divine "monarchy," to Neoplatonism and the stoic philosophy of the logos-creator. He held that the Son of God was "begotten" (*gennètos*), which term, however, he affirmed in the generic sense of "produced" (*genètos*), but understood in the specific sense of "made," "created." The Son was therefore inferior to the Father, being created in time by God and becoming in turn the instrument in God's action of creating the world. He was in effect an intermediary being between God and the world; not, however, the mediator between God and humankind, uniting both in his person. Not truly God or equal with God, the Son, for Arius, was not truly man, either, for the flesh (*sarx*) that the Word (*logos*) had united with did not (nor could it) constitute a true, complete humanity. It appears that the *Logos-sarx* perspective led Arius to a reductionist Christology that fell short of the revealed mystery of Jesus Christ on both counts—the divinity as well as the humanity. On both counts, Arius's reductionist Christology was principally based on philosophical considerations, tending to a hellenization of content.

The Meaning of Nicaea

In response to the Arian crisis, the Council of Nicaea (325) affirmed that the Sonship of God, which the New Testament attributes to Jesus Christ, must be understood in the strict sense. What it did was interpret the confession of faith of the New Testament in the context of the Arian crisis by providing further explanations, for which use is made of hellenistic categories.

The trinitarian structure of the Nicaean profession of faith notwithstanding,[14] its second article on Jesus Christ adopted—as did the question posed by Arius—a perspective from below. It spoke directly of Jesus Christ, of whom it affirmed the divine Sonship. To the biblical category of the "only-begotten" (*monogenès*) of the Father it added, by way of explanation (*toutestin*), that of being "from the being" (*ousia*) of the Father, of being born (*gennètos*), not made (*poiètheis*), and—this is the decisive term—of being "of one substance" (*homoousios*) with the Father. The term *homoousios* must, however, be interpreted in the context in which it is being used. In response to Arius's denial of the equal divinity of the Son with the Father, the council affirmed directly the specific identity of nature, not yet—as will be done later—the numerical identity of nature. What was asserted is that the Son of God is as truly divine as the Father, equal in divinity.

In its approach from below, the Symbol of Nicaea continued to affirm in priority the messianic titles of Jesus as the Risen one ("one Lord Jesus Christ"). There followed the affirmation of his divine Sonship in the "ontic" language of John's Gospel (*monogenès*, the "only-begotten"), followed in turn by interpretative explanations coined in hellenistic ontological language (*ousia, homoousios*). The text thus passed through three linguistic registers, showing the continuity between the functional and the ontic language of the New Testament and between the ontic language and the ontological, hellenistic. The third register was added in order to preserve the biblical meaning of Jesus Christ's Sonship of God in its integrity. At the same time, its interpretation in ontological language leads to a discovery of its significance at a deeper level of awareness. Regarding the human condition of Jesus, in order to counteract the Arian reductionism, the Symbol of Nicaea affirmed that in Jesus Christ the Son of God not only "became flesh" (*sarkòtheis*), but added by way of explanation, "was made man" (*enanthròpèsas*).

This "humanization" of the Son of God is seen in a soteriological perspective that prolongs the soteriological motive of the Christology of the Church Fathers. At stake was, as St. Athanasius, the champion of Nicaea, had well understood, the salvation of humankind in Jesus Christ. If Jesus Christ was neither truly God nor truly man, as the *Logos-sarx* Christology of Arius claimed, neither was he capable of saving, nor could humankind have been saved in him. The traditional axiom, "He became man that we might be divinized," was thus being denied from both ends and on both counts, and with it the foundational experience of the apostolic Church, according to which the salvation of humankind consisted in its sonship of God in Jesus Christ, was being threatened. So that humans might be able to share in Jesus Christ's Sonship of God, it was necessary that the Son incarnate be truly God and truly man; that is, the mediator uniting in his person both divinity and humanity—not an intermediary being who is neither one nor the other. Only then could the marvelous exchange of condition and the share in divine Sonship occur between Jesus Christ and us, of which the Fathers had spoken.

Nicaea thus showed the close bond that exists between soteriology and Christology; that is, between *what* Jesus Christ is for us, and *who* he is in himself. It showed, in anticipation of later reductionist tendencies, that all severing of Christ-for-me from Christ-in-himself or Christ-for-God ruins the faith. Involved here was also the necessary bond between the "economic" and the "ontological" or "immanent" Trinity. The economy of salvation realized by God through the mission of the Son and the Spirit leads to the affirmation of the communication between persons within the Godhead; the ontological Trinity is discovered as the source of the divine economy of salvation. Thus the Nicaean profession of christological faith inserts itself in a trinitarian symbol of faith.

The Importance of Nicaea

Arianism represented a hellenization of content of the Church's christological faith. Against it the Nicene dogma affirmed clearly the radical difference between the mystery of Jesus Christ and hellenistic philosophical concepts. It represents a dehellenization of content, even while this is expressed (as had become necessary) in hellenistic language, that is, through linguistic hellenization. No adequate ontological categories existed that could be put to use to express the mystery; these had to be created. Existing terms needed to be used, but in the process of being used to convey the mystery, they received a new, surplus meaning. An authentic inculturation of the faith must account, in the language of the surrounding culture, for the difference in content between the Christian faith and the philosophical concepts supplied by the culture. This is precisely what Nicaea did in regard to hellenistic culture.

The use made by Nicaea of philosophical language has often raised suspicion, especially in recent times. Why not be satisfied with the biblical language? Why use philosophical terms that result in imposing on the object of faith an outward garment of abstract concepts? Why, on the other hand, maintain as normative through the centuries concepts that have been made use of by the christological dogma in a particular cultural historical context, but which are no longer in "symphony" with the surrounding culture of today? A formal answer to these questions will be given later. Meanwhile, attention may be drawn to the historical nature of Christian revelation. This historical nature calls for an ever-new actualization in history and culture of the language through which the abiding content of faith is proposed. Such actualization does not, moreover, consist in a mere translation or transposition; rather, it calls for a reinterpretation of the unchanging content in a new context. In this sense, to answer Arius, a discernment had to be made between two possible ways of understanding the divine Sonship of Jesus Christ. Nicaea interpreted it in keeping with the biblical meaning, but by making use of hellenistic ontological terminology. This choice and the discernment of faith involved in it remains strikingly actual. There is no dearth today of reductionist Christologies that interpret the divine Sonship of Jesus Christ in such a way as to make him somehow divine, yet not truly God and equal with God the Father in divinity.

The Christology of Nicaea also has implications for the Christian concept of God. It underscored its singularity at two distinct levels. God communicates personally in the human existence of the man Jesus; this self-communication of God in God's incarnate Son unveils the self-communication between persons that exists in the mystery of God's inner life. The economic Trinity manifests the ontological Trinity. Arius failed to recognize in Jesus Christ the "human face of God" (J. A. T. Robinson), according to Jesus' word in St. John's Gospel: "He who has seen me has seen the Father" (Jn 14:9). Appealing to God's transcendence, Arius refused to admit that God might be subject to becoming and submit to humiliation and a human death. Christian faith, on the contrary, professes, like the New Testament, the self-emptying (*kenòsis*) of God in Jesus. It boldly affirms that God's absolute transcendence and freedom make God capable of total self-communication to human beings in a man. Such divine self-communication to humankind, in turn, opens up a new perspective on who God is: eternal self-communication between Father and Son. Nicaea's Christology thus leads to new insights into the mystery of God: Jesus Christ is truly God, because he is the true Son of God.[15]

THE COUNCIL OF EPHESUS

The Problematic of Ephesus

At Ephesus, as at Nicaea, the problem posed was how to understand the divinity of Jesus Christ, but the question was asked from the opposite perspective. Nicaea's problematic had been from below: Is Jesus Christ truly Son of God? That of Ephesus was the reverse, from above. It asked, In what sense and in what manner has the Son of God become human in Jesus? The discourse was directly concerned with the Son of God, not with the man Jesus. It follows (as does Jn 1:14), the movement of the incarnation of the Son of God, to inquire about the reality and the modality of God's union with the man Jesus.

This reversal of perspective from ascending to descending reproduces what had previously occurred in the New Testament. The postbiblical christological reflection thus follows the same path as New Testament Christology. In both perspectives the danger of leaving a distance between God and the man Jesus was real; but while at Nicaea this would have meant that Jesus was not truly God, at Ephesus it would make the Son of God stay at a distance from the man Jesus, not being really one with him. In question was the unity of Jesus Christ, true God and true man, and in this, it is the scandal of the incarnation of the Son of God which is at stake. Could it be thought that the eternal Son of God *himself* was subjected to becoming a human, subjected to humiliation and a human death?

Nestorius, a priest in Antioch who had become patriarch of Constantinople, asked the question of the true divine-human unity in Jesus Christ in an ascending, from below perspective. Starting according to the Antiochian tradition from the man Jesus, he asked how he was united with the

Son of God. His was a Christology of the *homo assumptus*. His opponent, Cyril of Alexandria, bishop of that city, held the opposite, from above, perspective. Starting from the Word of God, he asked how God had assumed true humanity in Jesus Christ. His was a *Logos-sarx* Christology.

We may note that at the time of the contest between Nestorius and Cyril, ambiguity and confusion still remained concerning the terminology. When Cyril spoke of "one nature (*phusis*) only in Jesus Christ," he meant the unity of person (*hupostasis*). When Nestorius spoke of two "natures" (*phuseis*), he seemed to intend two persons (*prosòpon*).

The decisive point in the debate between Nestorius and Cyril became Nestorius's refusal to attribute the events of the human life of Jesus personally to the Word of God. In particular, human generation could not be predicated of the Son of God. Consequently, though she could be called mother of Christ (*khristotokos*), Mary could not be said to be the mother of God (*theotokos*). This implied positing two distinct subjects: the Word of God on the one hand and Jesus Christ on the other. The unity between them was conceived by Nestorius as "conjunction" (*sunapheia*), supposing two concrete existing subjects.

Nestorius rejected the realism of the incarnation. While docetism had reduced the humanity of Jesus to an appearance, what Nestorius made apparent and unreal was the humanization of the Word of God. The humanity of Jesus is no doubt real, but it only seems to belong to the Word of God. Or, the other way around, the Word appears in the human subject of the *homo assumptus*, as in another. The man Jesus is not the Word of God become man, one and the same; nor was the Word personally humanized. Rather, the Word was present in the man Jesus as in a temple, and operative in him. With this, the reality of the mediatorship of Jesus Christ vanishes. Once a separating distance is established in Jesus Christ between God and humanity, the death of Jesus on the cross is no longer that of the Son of God.

In response to Nestorius, Cyril of Alexandria noted that the Symbol of Nicaea attributed personally to the Son of God—the only begotten from the Father, personally identified with Jesus Christ—the events affecting Jesus' human life. "For us men and for our salvation he came down and became flesh, was made man, suffered, and rose again on the third day. He ascended to the heavens. . . ."[16] This language follows that of the New Testament, as where John attributes personally to the Son of God the human becoming of the incarnation (Jn 1:14; cf. also Gal 4:4; Rom 1:3). Similarly, in the New Testament, expressions referring to divinity and humanity are attributed to one and the same "I" (*ego*): The same "I" is used in John's Gospel to refer to Jesus' human being and to the Son originated from the Father (cf. Jn 8:58; 8:40; 8:38; 14:9; 10:30; 17:5). Again, according to the apostolic kerygma, only one subsistent subject is acting in Jesus, whether in the humiliation of the human condition or in the divine deeds of power.

The Meaning of Ephesus

As had been the case at Nicaea in the context of the Arian crisis, the problem consisted in interpreting in hellenistic cultural categories the christological faith of the New Testament—here, specifically, the authentic humanization of the Son of God—by way of explanatory phrases added to the biblical language. The key phrase used by Cyril in his Second Letter to Nestorius[17] to explain the true meaning of the incarnation of the Son of God (Jn 1:14) affirms that the Word of God has united to himself the humanity of Jesus "according to the *hypostasis*" (*henòsis kath' hupostasin*). This meant, in opposition to Nestorius's union by conjunction (*sunapheia*), according to which Jesus was made to personify (*prosòpon*) the Word of God, that the relationship between the Word and Jesus is one of real, concrete identity. Not in the sense that the nature of the Word was changed into the flesh of the man Jesus, but that the Word of God personally took human flesh in him. It must, however, be noted that in the historical context of Nestorius's denial, the hypostatic union referred to by Cyril does not convey the fulness of meaning with which later terminological precision will invest it. What it really affirms is that the "mysterious and ineffable coming together" that takes place between the Word and the humanity of Jesus results in true unity (*pros henòtèta sundromè*): The Word of God has personally become human in the man Jesus. Between both there is only one concrete, subsistent subject: not in the sense that the one subject results from the union of both, but rather that in Jesus Christ the eternal Word has united to himself in time a humanity that never existed (or could exist) independently from and prior to that union. What is in question in these affirmations is the recognition of the fact that the Word of God personally became man, was born and suffered; that which constituted the paradox of the Gospel message and a scandal for hellenistic speculation.

The Council of Ephesus (431) produced no dogmatic definition. The dogma of Ephesus is to be found in Cyril's Second Letter to Nestorius, which was officially approved by the council; not in the "Twelve Anathemas" of Cyril against Nestorius,[18] which in some parts represent an extreme Alexandrian perspective and use formulations that remained controversial from the Antiochian perspective.

After Ephesus a compromise was sought between the Antiochian and Alexandrian approaches, in the "Formula of Union" (433). A profession of christological faith written by John of Antioch in Antiochian key was accepted by Cyril of Alexandria, in which the unity of Christ and the attribution of the incarnation to the Word of God are clearly affirmed. The document represents a first successful attempt at a synthesis between the two approaches, in which the differences in perspective are acknowledged while unanimity in the same faith is expressed. Commenting on this document, A. Amato writes as follows:

The formula takes into account the essential elements of both the Alexandrian Christology (unity of subject; usage of the term *henòsis* and not *sunapheia* to indicate the unity of the two natures; the attribution of the incarnation to the Logos; the affirmation that Mary is *theotokos*), and the Antiochian (the affirmation of two natures; their union in one *prosòpon* only). It makes use of the term *homoousios* to indicate the consubstantiality of Christ, not only with God the Father, but also with us human beings. The importance of this formula resides in that the two currents of thought find a common way of expressing consciously the faith of the Church through a language which is not strictly scholastic.[19]

The soteriological argument undergirds the decision of faith of Ephesus, as it did that of Nicaea. But while the reduction of the divinity of Christ or his humanity threatenend the reality of the salvation of humankind in him, here the loosening of the bond of union between them threatened to suppress the truth of the one mediatorship of Jesus between God and humankind (cf. 1 Tim 2:5). This mediatorship required that there be but one subject, in Christ, of divinity and humanity; that, both being united in one person, he might truly belong to and be in solidarity with the divine and the human. The Incarnate Word could save humankind inasmuch as he is at once God-and-man, the God-man. The marvelous exchange of which the Fathers had spoken implied no less: He needed to share in what is ours, that he might make us share in what is his. Thus the hypostatic union of divinity and humanity in Jesus Christ accounted for his true and unique mediation between God and humankind. His humanity was God's very presence among human beings; his human action, God's action on their behalf.

The Importance of Ephesus

One of the questions raised today in christological discussions is whether the mystery of the hypostatic union depersonalizes Jesus. If his human nature is assumed by the person of the Word of God, does this leave Jesus without a singular, concrete, original, human personhood? Is not his humanity thereby reduced to an abstraction, indeed rendered unreal?[20]

An answer to this difficulty must take into account the evolution undergone by the concept of *person* in modern times. In christological dogma, *person* refers to a concrete, individual, existent subject; its meaning is ontological. Modern philosophy, on the contrary, often adopts a psychological concept of person, referring to a subjective centre of consciousness and will. This latter concept could be designated with the term "personality," "personhood" referring rather to the former. In the case of the mystery of the hypostatic union in Jesus Christ, it is clear that there exists but one ontological personhood, that of the Son of God who personally has become human. This, however, keeps intact the human personality of the man Jesus, in the psychological sense of a human centre of consciousness and activity. Jesus' humanity is not therefore depersonalized in the modern sense of the term, even while — in the terminology of the Fathers after Ephesus — his humanity is (ontologically) anhypostatic (*anhupostasia*), having been assumed into the personhood (*enhupostasia*) of the Son of God. The assumption of the humanity of Jesus by the person of the Word (*enhupostasia*) is not a depersonalization but an impersonalization, inasmuch as the personhood of the Son of God is communicated to and extends to the humanity of Jesus, whereby the Son becomes truly human.

More must be said. While in the ontological sense of the term there are not two distinct subsistent subjects in Jesus Christ, the Word of God has truly become a human person in Jesus. The incarnation of the Son of God is a true humanization. The divine person having once become human has henceforth a divine-human personhood, and a divine-human person is one who is also truly human. The Son of God has all the characteristics of the human person, having lived a historical human existence. Jesus, in fact, more than any other human person, has been an altogether original personality. In him, the Son of God has personally made the experience of living a human life in historical becoming.

The mystery of the hypostatic union is therefore that of the humanization of God. In the man Jesus, God has taken a human face (cf. Jn 14:9). Jesus Christ is God humanized, not man divinized. Whereby it becomes clear that Christology from above cannot be dispensed with once the christological faith becomes reflective and is articulated. The incarnation is an event of which God is the source and agent: It is God's becoming human; not a human being made into God. The authentic humanization of God in Jesus Christ is at once the foundation of God's self-communication to humankind and the revelation to it of the mystery of God.

Jesus is the Son of God as man. This does not mean that he is Son of God because of his humanity, which is created, but because of the incarnation, his humanity is that of the Son of God. He is therefore Son, also as man. Given the unity in person of Jesus' humanity with the Son of God, the human story of the man Jesus is that of the Son of God, and Jesus' human death is God's own. Through the incarnation, God has entered history; conversely, human history has become God's own. The realism of the incarnation calls for a reconsideration of the philosophical concept of God's immutability. Since in the event of the incarnation God becomes personally subject to a human becoming, a real change affects personally the divine person who becomes man. However, change does not refer here to a necessity by virtue of which God would acquire infinite perfection. It refers, on the contrary, to the absolute freedom by which, while remaining God, God can personally unite with a human existence. K. Rahner writes: "God can become something, he who is unchangeable in himself can *himself* become subject to change *in* something else."[21] Explaining further how God can become something which God is not in and by Godself, the same author writes:

> We learn through the doctrine of the incarnation that God's immutability, without thereby being eliminated, is by no means simply the only thing that characterizes God, but that in and in spite of his immutability he can truly become something: he himself, he in time. Moreover, this possibility is not to be understood as a sign that he is in need of something, but rather as the height of his perfection. This perfection would be less perfect if he could not become less than he is and always remains.[22]

THE COUNCIL OF CHALCEDON

The Problematic of Chalcedon

Ephesus had explained the meaning of the incarnation in terms of union in the hypostasis. Underlining the unity, it had left the distinction between divinity and humanity unexplained. This is where Chalcedon completes Ephesus. Chalcedon represents progress with regard to the terminology in which the mystery of Jesus Christ is expressed. At Ephesus the ambiguity between *hupostasis* and *phusis* remained. In particular, some of the formulations of Cyril of Alexandria, though given a correct meaning, were in themselves ambiguous and potentially misleading, especially the expressions "one nature of God, incarnate" (*mia phusis tou theou sesarkòmenè*) or "unity of nature" (*henòsis phusikè*). Chalcedon will correct the language of Cyril. More deeply, the schema of Ephesus ran the risk of not accounting adequately for the true consistency and authenticity of the humanity of Jesus. Chalcedon would have to remedy this danger.

In fact, the problematic of Chalcedon is one in which the humanity of Jesus is put in question. The question is raised: If the Word of God has taken on human nature, what happens to that nature in the process of union? Is it maintained in its human reality? Or is it absorbed in the divinity of the Son of God? The Formula of Union between John of Antioch and Cyril of Alexandria affirmed the Son of God to be "consubstantial (*homoousios*) with us as to the humanity."[23] What did this mean?

Eutyches, a monk in Constantinople, though admitting that Christ is *from* (*ek*) two natures, refused to affirm that he remains *in* (*en*) two natures after the process of union. He conceived the union of the two natures as a mixing (*krasis*), by which the human was absorbed into the divine, with the result that Christ is not consubstantial with us in humanity. Making use of the controverted formulas of Cyril in a sense not intended by him, he ended by affirming one nature in Christ after the process of union, the humanity being absorbed into the divinity. With this the reality of the one mediatorship of Jesus Christ between God and humankind was once more placed in jeopardy. If his humanity was absorbed into the divinity of the Word, Jesus did not remain truly man after the union, and with the truth of Christ's mediation, the scandalous reality of the incarnation also vanished once again. Such were the implications of monophysitism.

In this connection, Pope Leo the Great wrote a dogmatic Letter to Flavian, patriarch of Constantinople, known as the "Tomus."[24] The pope concurs with Cyril of Alexandria in affirming the unity in Christ: "The true God, therefore, was born with the complete and perfect nature of a true man; he is complete in his nature and complete in ours. . . ." But Leo's language comes much closer to that of Antioch. As the Formula of Union had done,[25] Leo speaks explicitly and deliberately of "two natures," each of which maintains its own properties: "The character proper to each of the two natures which come together being therefore preserved . . ."; "For each of the two natures performs the functions proper to it in communion with the other. . . ." There remains to be sought an agreement in language between the Antiochian school, represented by the "Tomus" of Leo to Flavian, and that of Alexandria, exemplified in Cyril's Letter to Nestorius.

The Meaning of Chalcedon

The definition of Chalcedon (451) is a new actualization of the revealed mystery of Jesus Christ, in keeping with the Church's tradition, by way of additional explanatory clauses.[26] It consists of two parts, the first of which resumes the previous teaching about Jesus Christ, mostly following the Formula of Union,[27] while the other adds further explanations making use of hellenistic concepts.[28]

The discourse of the first part of the definition takes as its starting point the union in Jesus Christ of divinity and humanity. Within this unity, the distinction of the two natures is affirmed. The "same" is "consubstantial" with the Father as to the divinity and with us as to the humanity. In the context of the monophysite reduction, the consubstantiality with us in humanity needed to be stressed. It answered the question raised by Eutyches: The human nature keeps its integrity and authenticity after the union, the exception of sin (Heb 4:15) notwithstanding. It may be noted, however, that consubstantiality does not carry exactly the same meaning in the case of both natures. Where the divinity is concerned, the numerical consubstantiality of the Son with the Father is now being affirmed—which had not been the case in Nicaea—while the consubstantiality of Jesus' humanity with ours is, of course, specific. The two components of the one Christ having thus been analyzed in Antiochian key, the end of the first part of the definition turns toward his twofold origin: the double generation from the Father before the ages as to the divinity, and in the last days from Mary as to the humanity. With this the definition shifts to the schema of Ephesus, and reference is made to history and to the soteriological motive that governs the becoming man of the Son of God: "in the latter days," "for us and our salvation." The twofold solidarity with the divine and the human involved in the soteriological motive is also brought out, as is Mary's title of Mother of God (*theotokos*). Chalcedon thus truly links with Ephesus.

The second part of the definition, however, contains additional explanations in philosophical language that intend to show how unity and distinction coexist in the mystery of Jesus Christ. The concepts of person (*hupostasis, prosòpon*) and nature (*phusis*) are clearly distinct here. The same Lord and Christ, the only begotten Son, is one in two natures, without confusion or change (against Eutyches), without division or separation (against Nestorius). "In" (*en*) two natures affirms the perdurance of the duality after union: He is not only "from" (*ek*) two natures, as Eutyches admitted, but "in" (*en*) two natures. This means that the hypostatic union of the Word with humanity maintains the otherness of humanity within the one person. The humanity is not absorbed into divinity, as Eutyches claimed. "Without confusion or change" stresses the fact that the distinction of natures endures and that the properties of each are maintained. "Without division or separation" explains that the two natures are not one beside the other, as though they were distinct subsistent subjects. What belongs to each of the two natures is preserved, merging in a unique person (*prosòpon*) and hypostasis (*hupostasis*). One and the same Jesus Christ acts both as God and as man, just as one and the same is at once God and man. Chalcedon thus exposes in Antiochian key the hypostatic union Ephesus had expressed in the Alexandrian schema. The modality of union of divinity and humanity in Jesus Christ appeared altogether singular, but it alone could account for his unique mediatorship between God and humankind.

The Importance of Chalcedon

About the Chalcedonian definition the question has often been raised, and is still being asked today, whether the ontological determinations to which it subjects the mystery of Jesus Christ are necessary and, for that matter, really helpful. The question is whether faith cannot be adequately expressed in functional language, but really needs to be coined in ontological terminology. Must Christology necessarily pass from the functional to the ontological register? M. Luther is quoted as establishing a partition between *what* Jesus Christ is *for us* and *who* he is *in himself*. Without repudiating the Chalcedonian Christology, he questioned strongly its bearing on faith:

> Christ has two natures. In what way does this concern me? . . . That he is by nature man and God, that is for himself. . . . To believe in Christ does not mean that Christ is one person who is man and God — which is of no use to anybody; that means that that person is Christ, that is to say, that for us he went out of God and came into the world: from this function he bears his name.[29]

R. Bultmann echoes and radicalizes Luther's question when he asks, "Does he help me because he is the Son of God, or is he the Son of God because he helps me?"[30]

For Chalcedon and the postconciliar tradition, no separation can be established between the function of Jesus Christ and his being; one does not go without the other. The being of Jesus Christ in himself is the necessary foundation of his salvific function toward us. He can be *what* he is for us because of *who* he is in himself. Function and ontology are mutually interdependent. The Christian tradition was bound, therefore, to develop an ontological Christology. By doing so, it was following the same impulse of faith as had already prompted in the apostolic Church the development from the functional Christology of the early kerygma to the ontological Christology of later writings. This is not to say that the development, as it historically took place, mostly at Chalcedon, was without limitations and shortcomings. These will be looked into hereafter, while a general appraisal of the christological dogma is attempted. Meanwhile, it is the actuality, even today, of Chalcedon's questions and answers that needs to be shown.

This consists in helping to maintain, against the ever actual danger of monophysitism, the truth and reality of Jesus' humanity in its state of union with the Son of God. No matter how closely related he has become to God, Jesus Christ is neither absorbed nor suppressed. The humanization of God does not mean the assimilation of Jesus' humanity into the Godhead. Indeed, K. Rahner shows that the contrary is true; the authenticity and reality of the manhood of Jesus is in direct, not inverse proportion of his union with God. Far from remaining real in spite of the union, Jesus' humanity is enhanced by it, for proper autonomy and nearness to God grow in direct proportion. K. Rahner writes in effect:

> In the incarnation, the Logos creates by taking on, and takes on by emptying himself. Hence we can verify here, in the most radical and specifically unique way the axiom of all relationship between God and creature, namely that the closeness and the distance, the submissiveness and the independence of the creature do not grow in inverse but in like proportion. Thus Christ is most radically man, and his humanity is the freest and most independent, not in spite of, but because of its being taken up, by being constituted as the self-utterance of God.[31]

It becomes clear that the mystery of the hypostatic union affirmed by the Council of Ephesus does not deprive the humanity of Jesus of a human centre of reference for his human awareness and activities. By becoming human, the Son of God personally becomes the subject of human experiences, being Son of God in a human way while living the personal Sonship of the Father in a human life. This is why the dialogue between Jesus and his Father, while revealing his filial identity as a man, opens onto the deeper mystery of the Son's origin from the Father within the inner life of the

Godhead. Jesus' Sonship of God, experienced humanly, prolongs and transposes into human awareness the Son's eternal coming from the Father who begets him. Jesus is at once the Father's human partner in dialogue and eternal Son. Conversely, the Father extends God's fatherly relation to the man Jesus, in whom God recognizes God's own eternal Son. The mystery of the hypostatic union excludes any mutual relationship of subject to subject in Jesus Christ. It postulates, on the contrary, the prolongation on the human plane of the interpersonal relationship between Father and Son in the Godhead. The incarnation is unintelligible without the Trinity.

It has been noted earlier that the terminology of Cyril of Alexandria remained controversial for the Antiochian party and that to a great extent the Council of Chalcedon transposed the doctrine of Ephesus in Antiochian key. After the council there arose a "non-Chalcedonian" current which, meaning to abide by the terminology of Cyril, especially the expression "one nature" (*mia phusis*), refused to speak of "two natures" in Jesus Christ. Non-Chalcedonian Churches exist today in the East, such as the Coptic Church of Egypt, some Armenian Churches, and the Syrian Orthodox Church. However, in the wake of the recent ecumenical dialogue, common professions of christological faith have been made between Pope Paul VI and the heads of those non-Chalcedonian Churches, and more recently still between Pope John Paul II and similar authorities on the other side. The common declarations and professions of faith[32] make it clear that the churches concerned share the same christological faith with the Roman Catholic Church, expressed in such a way as to avoid controverted expressions — especially the Chalcedonian formula of two natures — or strongly partisan terminology. It is being recognized that the schisms of the past were not caused by substantial differences in christological faith but related to differences in terminology, culture and theological formulations. This lesson in practical ecumenism shows that the same christological faith can be expressed differently in diverse historical and cultural contexts; dogmatic plurality is possible in the unity of faith. It also raises questions regarding the binding value that needs to be assigned to the Church's traditional dogmatic definitions, and their relationship to the *norma normans* of the revealed truth of the New Testament. These questions will be raised hereafter.

THE COUNCIL OF CONSTANTINOPLE III

The Problematic of Constantinople III

We have shown earlier that, while the problematic of the Council of Nicaea (and Constantinople I) had been that of the two natures, the divine and the human, it shifted thereafter to the problem of unity in distinction between them. We have further observed that, whereas Ephesus stressed the unity, with Chalcedon the pendulum shifted to the distinction that remains. The same movement of the pendulum was reproduced again after Chalcedon. The Council of Constantinople II (553) turned once more toward the pole of unity (in the direction of Ephesus), while Constantinople III (681) followed the inverse process, turning after Chalcedon toward the pole of distinction.

The context and content of Constantinople II will not be exposed here in any elaborate form. The following will suffice. The context is that of the neo-Chalcedonian current, a sort of "verbal monophysitism" which, abiding by the ambiguous formulas of Cyril of Alexandria, advocated a compromise between the Chalcedonian formulation and monophysitism. In this context, and in order to reconcile the monophysites, an interpretation of Chalcedon was needed that would show its agreement with the doctrine of Cyril. The new council condemned the "three chapters,"[33] the work of three long-dead writers who were now accused of Nestorianism, even though their doctrine had been judged orthodox by Chalcedon. This disowning has the value of a new condemnation of Nestorianism.

More important, however, are the christological canons of Constantinople II.[34] These rejected both the Nestorian (canons 5-7) and the Eutychian (canon 8) interpretations of Chalcedon, explaining that the unity of *hupostasis* refers to the one and only subsistent subject, while the duality of natures (*phusis*) expresses the difference that endures in the incarnation of the Son of God. Between the "one nature" of Cyril and the "two natures" of Chalcedon, there is parity of intention and doctrine in diversity of expression (canon 8). Canon 4 further explains the hypostatic union as "union by way of synthesis" (*katha sunthesin*), by which is meant that the Word of God becomes one concrete existing subject with his humanity, even while the otherness is maintained in him between God and man. In other words, the human nature subsists in the *hupostasis* of the Word; it does not constitute a distinct subject. Or, again, the Word communicates its own personal existence to the humanity of Jesus. In him it is truly humanized. Where Chalcedon had distinguished the two natures against the monophysite tendency to mix them up (*krisis*), without articulating the relation between unity and distinction, Constantinople II explained this relationship by referring to the hypostatic union as "union of synthesis." The divine person of the Son has become authentically human. Jesus Christ, therefore, is a composite divine-human person, as truly human as he is divine. The unity of person presides — and prevails over — the distinction of natures.

After Constantinople II, however, the pendulum shifted once more from the pole of unity to that of distinction, but with a difference. Constantinople III will shift the problem of unity in distinction from the level of the "natures" — the divine and the human — to that of the two actions and wills that proceed from them. How did this new problematic come to the fore?

It has to do with the human existence of Jesus and marks a return to his historical existence to which the Gospels testify. Jesus distinguished the will of the Father, which he had come to do, from his own (Jn 6:38; cf. Mk

15:36). How was this to be understood? The clarifications offered by Constantinople II did not suffice to forestall the possibility of a monophysite interpretation of Jesus' human will and action. Sergius, patriarch of Constantinople, in fact — basing himself on Cyril of Alexandria — spoke of "one theandric operation only" in Jesus Christ. The formula was open to a monophysite understanding, as though to the one acting subject there corresponded only one modality of action in the sense that the human action was absorbed by the divine principle of activity. Such "mono-energism" (*mia energeia*) would extend monophysitism from the level of nature to that of action.

The same problem arose regarding the will or wills. Was it necessary to affirm two wills in Jesus Christ, the divine and the human — corresponding respectively to the two natures — from which there proceeded two distinct modes of action, without separation? But, if so, would there not be contrariness or clash between the divine will and the human will? To avoid the appearance of clash, Sergius of Constantinople refused to speak of a twofold will; there was but one will in Jesus. This theory will be called thereafter monothelitism.

At stake once more in this contest was the authenticity of the humanity of Jesus and the reality of humankind's salvation in him. Deprived of an authentic human will and action, Jesus Christ would not be truly man, as we are. Deprived of a human free will, he would only have been able to passively comply with a course of action predetermined for him by divine will. The salvation of the human race could not have proceeded from a free human act of Jesus' self-offering on the cross; nor could he have assumed in a free human act of will his passion and death in faithfulness to his messianic mission and in voluntary compliance and obedience to the will of the Father.

Hoping to accommodate the monophysite current and end the monophysite crisis, Sergius appealed to Pope Honorius in favour of his own dangerous theory, suggesting that for the sake of maintaining peace among the Churches, the expression "two actions," which divided them, be avoided. The pope, in a Letter to Sergius (634),[35] consented to the use of the expression "one will only," and suggested that all controversial expressions be proscribed. Embolded by the pope's apparent support, Sergius went on to expose the doctrine of monothelitism more firmly. This amounted to reviving the monophysite crisis.

The Meaning of Constantinople III

A council was convened at the Lateran (649) by Pope Martin I to condemn monothelitism.[36] The main formulations of its canons are borrowed from St. Maximus the Confessor, the champion of the doctrine of the "two wills" of Jesus Christ.[37] They reaffirm the Chalcedonian doctrine of the two natures and apply it by way of additional elucidation to the two wills. The

"Symbol" of the council affirms "two natural wills," the divine and the human, in full concordance. Its canons explain that if Christ has two natures, he also has two wills and two modes of action, belonging respectively to each nature, both of which are "intimately united in one and the same Christ God." Thus, "one and the same has willed our salvation by each of his two natures" (canon 10) and worked it (canon 11).[38] The soteriological motive is once more placed at the service of Christology: It was necessary that the salvation of humankind proceed also from a true human will, freely acting. The problem, in effect, was being formulated from the historical standpoint of the human story of Jesus, specifically of the attitude of his human will in the mystery of the agony at Gethsemane.

The Council of Constantinople III taught the same doctrine.[39] It resumed the Chalcedonian affirmation of two natures, adding to it that of the two wills and natural actions. The same qualifications were added as at Chalcedon: The two wills and operations are united in one and the same person Jesus Christ, without division, without change, without separation, without confusion. In answer to the alleged contradiction between the two wills, the council explains that no opposition occurs between them, the human will being in full conformity with the divine. For "it was necessary that the will of the flesh move itself (*kinèthènai*), but also that it be submitted to the divine will." In such a way, as St. Leo had said in his "Tome" to Flavian, "each of the two natures performs the function proper to it in communion with the other"; in such a way too, "the two natural wills and actions concur together for the salvation of the human race."

The Importance of Constantinople III

This last phrase indicates once more the soteriological motive that governs the further elaboration of the christological dogma made by Constantinople III. While this council prolonged Chalcedon by way of further articulation, it was inspired by a return to the Jesus of history witnessed to by the Gospel tradition. It testified to the fact that the Church's dogmatic pronouncements find their ultimate source and point of departure in the foundational text of the New Testament. The revealed word of God is the ultimate norm of the Church's dogmatic interpretation: Dogma must be read in relation to the Scriptures it explains.

The enduring of the human nature of Jesus in its union with the Son of God, affirmed by Chalcedon, could seem abstract. The alleged absorption of his human will and action into the divine, propounded by monophysitism and monothelitism, makes it clear that the reality of Jesus the man and his human story, witnessed to by the Gospel narrative, was at stake here. The authenticity of his human existence was being threatened by the denial of its natural autonomy. The confirmation by Constantinople III of the authenticity of Jesus' humanhood, of his human free will and action, remains of great actuality at a time when much christological thinking is

done to rediscover fully the human authenticity of the man Jesus. K. Rahner, not without reason, has shown that monophysitism always remains a
threatening danger, and is one even today. He asks pointedly: Does the
affirmation of the existence in Christ of a human nature suffice in practice
to safeguard the autonomy required by his function as mediator? And he
asks the further question: Is our current conception of the term "person-
nature" free of all monothelitism?[40]

The risk of a monophysitism and monothelitism based on a modern
understanding of the "person" as centre of reference of consciousness and
activity is not fictitious today. The unity of personhood in Jesus Christ would
then be understood as meaning one centre of activity. This centre being
the divine person, a human centre of consciousness and activity, in Jesus,
or a human personality, would practically be denied. With this, the interpersonal dialogue of Jesus the man with God his Father, in prayer and
obedience, would be nullified and, the human will being absorbed into the
divine, the authenticity of Jesus' freedom and human actions—his being
man in historical becoming—would disappear.

The two wills must, however, be correctly understood. Just as the two
natures are not juxtaposed alongside each other, so neither are the two
wills. Just as the Son of God is also human, so too the Son of God also
wills humanly. In fact, the human will of Jesus Christ is the one will that
is his personally, while the divine will is common in the Godhead to the
Father, Son and Holy Spirit, even as the divine nature is common to them.
The dialogue between two wills initiated by the mystery of the incarnation
took place not between the Son of God and Jesus the man, but between
the Father's will and the human will of God's Son made man. This dialogue
of wills between Father and Son prolongs on the human level, and extends
to the human key in compliance and obedience, the relation of origin by
which in the mystery of God the Son receives himself from the Father.
Jesus lived this relationship humanly through his entire human life and
death; he actualized it progressively through his human choices and deci-
sions. In this sense it is true to say that, as a human, Jesus grew in his
Sonship of the Father by living out his human history and destiny, until in
his agony and death he submitted in a final act of surrender to the Father's
will. "Although he was Son, he learned obedience through what he suffered" (Heb 5:8).

Where the ontological considerations of Chalcedon risked becoming
abstract, Constantinople III partly reintroduced the historical dimension
into the christological dogma. The two dimensions need to complete each
other, as Christologists are better aware today. Furthermore, the personal
insertion of God into history through the incarnation must be given its full
significance. By God's entering into history, history itself has entered into
God, just as by God's Son becoming man, humanity has been integrated
into the mystery of God itself. As through the incarnation God has become
subject to a human becoming, so too has God become subject to history.

To affirm less would be to evacuate the realism of the incarnation, as well as the dynamic of God's revelation in history that takes place through it. The axiom of the Scythian monks that "one of the Trinity suffered," equivalently taken up by the Council of Constantinople II,[41] is rigorously correct, even as it is correct to speak of the "crucified God" (J. Moltmann); and, since the Son incarnate has experienced a true human history and suffering, there exists a human story of God.

Between the ontological and historical aspects of the mystery of Jesus Christ there is an indissoluble bond: The personal identity of Jesus as the Son of God is expressed and realized in history. The mystery of the incarnation consists in the self-expression and communication of God in human history. One of the tasks of today's Christology consists of fully rediscovering the historical dimension of the mystery of Jesus Christ and integrating the ontological dimension with it.

THE CHRISTOLOGICAL DOGMA: APPRAISAL AND PERSPECTIVES

THE ABIDING VALUE OF THE DOGMA

The Christology of the New Testament was an interpretation of the person and event of Jesus Christ made by the apostolic Church in the light of the Easter experience under the inspiration of the Holy Spirit. It belongs to the foundational event of revelation and remains forever the ultimate norm (*norma normans*) for the Church's faith in the mystery. The christological dogma of the Church is a further progressive interpretation of the same mystery made by the postapostolic Church, under the guidance of the Holy Spirit guaranteed by the Church's teaching authority. It consists of a set of documents in which the sense and meaning of the revealed mystery receive further elaborations and explanations rendered necessary by the reductionist tendencies of christological heresies. It has the regulative value that the Church's teaching authority lends to it, but always in relation to the *norma normans* of the Scripture. Scripture is read in the Church and interpreted by it; but the Scriptures, not the Church's dogma, belong to the Church's foundational event.

Being interpretation, the christological formulations of the councils are subject to a hermeneutics. Their regulating value is related to the founding witness of the Scriptures, specifically to the Christology of the New Testament, of which it represents an additional elaboration in an evolving historical context. Every dogmatic formulation, thus, sends us back to the New Testament. It never is an absolute point of departure in the faith reflection of the Church. A reciprocal relationship exists between the foundational act of the Scriptures and the dogmatic formulations of the Church. The Scriptures are read in the Church with the added light of the Church's definitions; these in turn must be read in relation to the Scriptures. In the interpretation of dogma, a mutual interaction is at work between text and context that determines the hermeneutical circle — or the hermeneutical triangle of text, context and interpreter.

If the christological dogmatic formulations are never absolute points of departure, they also never represent final words in the Church's faith reflection on the mystery of Jesus Christ. They are additional interpretations rendered necessary by the concrete circumstances of historical contexts. These are always particular by definition, that is, determined and limited in space and time, and thus depending upon a surrounding culture. We have observed that the christological dogma expressed the mystery of Jesus Christ in terms of hellenistic culture. This contextualized interpretation was perfectly legitimate; it preserved the mystery from philosophical reductionisms while making it intelligible in the surrounding culture. It represents not a hellenization but a dehellenization of content in a linguistic hellenization. R. H. Fuller, a Scripture scholar, has expressed felicitously the necessity, legitimacy and true value of the christological dogma developed by the postapostolic Church on the foundation of New Testament Christology, wherein from the ontic linguistic register of the New Testament a shift takes place toward the ontological language of the Greek philosophical tradition. Referring to the "ontological questions which (were) posed by the ontic Christology of the Gentile mission," he writes:

> If the Church was to preserve and to proclaim the Gospel in the Graeco-Roman world, it had to answer [the ontological questions posed by the ontic Christology of the Gentile mission] in terms of an ontology which was intelligible to that world. Its answer to these questions was the doctrine of the Trinity and the Incarnation. These doctrines took the ontic language of the New Testament, *theos, patèr, monogenès, huios, sarx and anthròpos* (God, Father, only-begotten, Son, flesh, and man), and explained them in ontological language derived from the Greek philosophical tradition (*ousia, homoousios, phusis, hupostasis*), or in Latin dress, *substantia, consubstantialis, natura,* and *persona.* With these tools it defined the pre-existent as "begotten of the Father" and as "of one substance with him," and the Incarnate one as "one person," uniting in himself the "two natures" of God and of man. Perhaps, as is often said, these answers were not really answers at all, but only sign-posts indicating the direction in which the answers were to be found or boundary marks beyond which all answers would distort the ontic affirmations of the New Testament. At least they were valid attempts within a given intellectual framework. And so far as they went they have on the whole prevented serious distortions of the Gospel.

> We must recognize the validity of this achievement of the Church of the first five centuries within the terms in which it operated. It is sheer biblicism to maintain that the Church should merely repeat

"what the Bible says"—about Christology as about everything else. The Church has to proclaim the Gospel *into* the contemporary situation. And that is precisely what the Nicene Creed and the Chalcedonian formula were trying to do. "The definition of Chalcedon was the only way in which the fifth-century Fathers, in their day, and with their conceptual apparatus, could have faithfully credalized the New Testament witness to Christ" (H. W. Montefiore).[42]

"The Church had to proclaim the Gospel *into* the contemporary situation." This indicates both the validity of the process of contextualization and inculturation that is at work in the christological dogma, and its limitations. Contexts and surrounding cultures are by definition limited and particular, being determined by space and time. The dogmatic determinations made by the Church, being dependent on particular, relative concepts, subject to evolution and change, are by necessity fragmentary, incomplete and perfectible, subject to further evolution and precisions—or even to change. We have referred earlier to the possibility of a "dogmatic plurality" in the sense in which it can be derived from recent authoritative Church documents.[43] The "sense" or "meaning," the unchanging content of faith, is what needs to be preserved, not necessarily the language in which it has been coined, even by an authentic tradition. The case may arise when, the meaning of terms changing in an evolving culture, new enunciations may be needed in order that the content of faith may be preserved unaltered or other ways of expressing the mystery may be required as the Christian message meets cultures into which it has not yet taken roots. The dogmatic value of the christological definitions is, therefore, not absolute but relative and relational. Relational, in content, to the New Testament Christology; relative in expression, insofar as it does not represent the only possible way of expressing the mystery, one that would be valid for all times and places. It continues to function in the living tradition of the Church as regulative within the parameters of the cultural context in which it was historically coined and within which it needs to be understood. Moreover, it belongs, and will continue to belong, to the "memory of the Church" to which it bears witness.

A correct appraisal of the christological dogma also needs to take note of its limitations and shortcomings. These have often been pointed out in recent years, especially in relation to the Chalcedonian definition.[44] It is all the more important to indicate the weaknesses of the Chalcedonian definition in view of the central place it occupies in the development of the dogma and of the overwhelming influence it has had on all later christological reflection. P. Smulders sums up the situation aptly when he writes:

The result that the Council of Chalcedon brought with it, after a struggle which had lasted for centuries and through which its confession of faith became common property for nearly all the Churches till our own days, does not allow us to ignore its shortcomings. Tight discussions had drawn the attention ever more closely to the formal constitution of the God-man, God and man. The salvific meaning, which however had been the point of departure of this entire process of reflection, was mentioned only inasmuch as the confession of faith of Nicaea was incorporated in the text. Emphasis is not placed on the fact that it is the Son and the Word that became man, but rather that God became man; nor on the fact that he has lived a truly human life, but rather that he has assumed a complete human nature. Is it possible to speak with such simplicity of the "nature" of God, and to consider it so completely immutable and impassible, as the Antiochians presupposed and the others admitted? Does not the Scripture speak of a God who is personally involved? Is not, moreover, the nature of man also conceived in too Greek a fashion: as a static composite of soul and body? And is it not considered too scarcely in its historical becoming, as conscious and free? If the "natures" of God and of man can be distinguished so easily, as is presupposed by Chalcedon, is the human appearance and the human conduct of Jesus still the self-revelation of God? Is it not rather only concealment? . . . The static vision which prevails in the constitution of the God-man, as it is expressed by the Council of Chalcedon, also brought with it the danger that the genuine character of the human life of Jesus fall into oblivion. On this point the following centuries will add a valid complement; but it is not without significance that they will understand the human will and the human action of Jesus prevalently as a consequence of his genuine human nature, not as his sharing genuinely in our life and our human destiny.[45]

The main shortcomings and dangers inherent in the christological dogma of Chalcedon are the following: the soteriological motive tends to recede in the background as prominence is given to the ontological constitution of the person of Jesus Christ; the personal and trinitarian dimension of the Son incarnate gives way to an impersonal consideration of the God-man; the historical dimension of the Christ-event and of the human life of Jesus is overshadowed by the abstract consideration of the integrity of his human nature; the personal involvement of God in history through the incarnation gives way to philosophical conceptions. In sum: ontology versus function; impersonalism versus personalism; abstraction versus history; philosophy versus ontic language. From it all there ensued in Chalcedon an essentialist language that ran the risk of dualism.

To illustrate the shift of perspective that the christological mystery has undergone from the New Testament to Chalcedon, it may be said that while the New Testament was centred on Christology as event, Chalcedon enunciated Christology as a truth of faith. The New Testament Christology distinguished stages in the historical unfolding of the Christ-event: from preexistence through kenosis to glorification. Chalcedon affirms the union of two natures, the divine and the human, in the one person of Jesus Christ. While in the New Testament *sarx* and *pneuma* referred to Jesus' kenotic human life and his glorification in resurrection, respectively (cf. Rom 1:3-4), as the attention turned later to ontology, the same terms came to refer to the human and the divine natures of Jesus Christ, sometimes conceived — against the dogma's intention — as juxtaposed alongside each other in an apparent dualism. One of the concerns of recent Christologists consists, in fact, in attempting to overcome the covert dualism of much earlier Christology by a return to Christology as event and, in particular, to the functional Christology of the early kerygma. W. Kasper writes in this regard:

> The fundamental christological theme of scripture is the unity of the earthly Jesus and the glorified Christ; *the* fundamental christological motive of tradition is the unity of true divinity and true humanity.

He adds:

> The content of Christology is . . . the earthly Jesus and the glorified Christ of faith. . . . Not the Chalcedonian model of the unity of true divinity and true humanity, but the unity of the earthly Jesus and the glorified Christ form the scope of Christology.[46]

The relational nature of the christological dogma and the need for every christological reflection to be firmly grounded in the foundational event of the New Testament could not be more clearly stated. There remains to indicate what direction a renewed Christology should take, if it wishes to remedy the weaknesses and overcome the shortcomings of the past.

FOR A RENEWAL OF CHRISTOLOGY

That a post-Chalcedonian model of Christology developed in the past that was to a great extent one-sided is to be assigned less to the council itself than to the theology that followed thereafter. The council itself did not claim to offer a complete treatment of the christological mystery, but only to show the direction in which to seek a correct expression of it and to provide signposts indicating the limits not to be crossed on either side in the direction of one of two opposite reductionist readings — Nestorianism and Monophysitism. The fact remains that later Christology has often tended to absolutise Chalcedon, as though it constituted the absolute point of reference, thus overlooking the relational nature of the conciliar Christology in regard to that of the New Testament. There followed a one-sided stress on the formal ontological composition of the person of Jesus Christ, to the neglect of the Christ-event.

Chalcedon's immediate intent had been to preserve the integrity of the human nature of Jesus Christ against the monophysite claim of its absorption into the divine. It expressed in a predominantly Antiochian key the distinction of natures in the unity of personhood. Paradoxically, however, the post-Chalcedonian model of Christology that developed and held the hegemony until recent years was a from-above model that layed heavy stress on the divinity of Jesus Christ, not without danger to the integrity and authenticity of his human existence. The further elaborations on the human will and action of Jesus provided by the Council of Constantinople III, which prolonged the line of interpretation of Chalcedon, did not remedy the situation. It may be said that the traditional christological reflection that followed the period of development of the christological dogma has, until recent years, adopted a from above, descending approach. Only recently did a reaction set in, with a massive return to an ascending, or from below Christology.

Much traditional Christology has thus been marked by a double tendency: toward a one-sided ontology of Christ divorced from soteriology, and toward a unilateral descending approach severed from the necessary complement of an ascending perspective. The previous section has shown the main shortcomings of the christological model of Chalcedon. The present one aims to indicate the corresponding aspects of the mystery that need to be recovered in view of a renewed, integrated Christology.

The Historical Aspect

First to be recovered is the historical aspect, which ought to be combined with the ontological. Central to the Christian message is not a doctrine but an event, that of God's personal entry into, and decisive commitment to, history in Jesus Christ. This event takes place in the concrete history of humankind and is subject to a historical process of becoming. The concrete "story" of Jesus must be rediscovered as the embodiment of the personal commitment and self-communication of God to humankind. This implies rediscovering the revelatory and salvific content of the events of Jesus' human life, of his "historical mysteries." In particular, the New Testament perspective of distinct phases in the Christ-event must remain central. The real transformation that took place in Jesus' human existence as he passed from the state of kenosis to that of glory in his resurrection must govern the treatment of his human psychology, of his awareness and will, of his actions and attitudes. The abstract notion of a complete, integral human nature must not be allowed to obscure the truth of an authentic development to which his human existence is subject. Nor may an a priori principle of absolute perfections be invoked to undermine the concrete reality of Jesus' identification with our own historical human condition.

The Personal or Trinitarian Aspect

Jesus Christ is not a God-man in impersonal terms. He is the Son of God incarnate in history and become a member of the human race. For an impersonal Christology of "God humanized" must be substituted a personalized Christology of the Son with us. This means that the trinitarian dimension of the mystery of Jesus Christ must once more be placed in evidence. His divine identity consists in the personal relationship of Son to Father that he lived in his human existence and expressed in the term Abba. The singularity and unique character of this interpersonal relation of the Son to the Father, experienced by Jesus the man, embodies the concrete reality of the mystery of the hypostatic union. It has its ultimate foundation in the Son's origin from the Father in the life of the Godhead. The intratrinitarian personal relationship of the Son to the Father is humanized in Jesus and experienced by him in humanity. Christology cannot be severed from the mystery of the Trinity.

The Soteriological Aspect

Nor can Christology be severed from soteriology. The soteriological aspect of the mystery also needs to be rediscovered and reintegrated into Christology. In the early tradition, the soteriological motive was the springboard of Christology. Christology came as a second act. It explained the a priori conditions without which the reality of human salvation in Jesus Christ could not be accounted for: In order to be *what* he was for us, he needed to be *who* he was, namely the Son of God. Human salvation consisted not in an impersonal redemption or offer of grace, but in human persons becoming sharers, in Jesus Christ, of the personal Sonship of the Son. The severing of Christology from soteriology is an added reason why Christology has often been impersonal and abstract. The soteriological motive needs to be reintegrated in Christology in its personal form: not as God's humanization for the sake of our divinization, but as the marvelous exchange by which the Son of God shared our concrete human existence in order to make us share in his own Sonship of the Father.

The Dynamism of Faith

The Christology of the New Testament developed, under the impulse of faith, from the paschal functional Christology of the early kerygma to the ontological Christology of later writings. It witnesses to the necessary complementarity and mutual interaction between Christology from below and from above, between an initial ascending approach to the mystery of Jesus Christ and the inverted descending perspective of a reflexive, articulated faith. We have suggested earlier that the same road needs to be traveled by christological reflection today. The unity in tension between Christology from above and from below must be rediscovered and reappropriated for the renewal of Christology. Only their mutual interaction can help balance, in an integral approach, the various aspects of the mystery of Jesus Christ that will forever remain beyond full human comprehension and elaboration.

NOTES

1. *Adv. Haer.*, III,19,1; Sources chrétiennes 34,332.
2. *Contra Ar.*, 1,38; PG 26,92B.
3. *De Incarn.*, 54; PG 25,192.
4. See Piet Smulders, "Dogmengeschichtliche und lehramtliche Entfaltung der Christologie," in Johannes Feiner and Magnus Löhrer (eds), *Mysterium Salutis* III,1: *Das Christusereignis*, Einsiedeln: Benziger Verlag, 1970, pp. 389-476.
5. See Bernard Sesboüé, *Jésus-Christ dans la tradition de l'Eglise*, Paris: Desclée, 1982, pp. 55s.
6. See chapter 3, note 13.
7. See Henricus Denzinger and Adolfus Schönmetzer, *Enchiridion Symbolorum Definitionum et Declarationum de Rebus Fidei et Morum*, Freiburg: Herder, 1965, n.421; cf. Neuner and Dupuis, *The Christian Faith*, n.620/1.
8. See especially Robert Dewart, *The Future of Belief. Theism in a World Come of Age*, New York: Herder, 1966; Id., *The Foundations of Belief*, London: Burns & Oates, 1969.
9. See, for instance, Sebastian Kappen, *Jesus and Freedom*, Maryknoll, New York: Orbis Books, 1977.
10. See Bernard Lonergan, "The De-hellenization of Dogma," *Theological Studies* 28 (1967) 336-351; Aloys Grillmeier, "De Jésus de Nazareth 'dans l'ombre du Fils de Dieu' au Christ, image de Dieu," in *Comment être chrétien? La réponse de H. Küng*, Paris: Desclée de Brouwer, 1979; Aloys Grillmeier, *Christ in Christian Tradition*. Volume I: *From the Apostolic Age to Chalcedon (451)*, London: Mowbray, 1975; volume II: *From the Council of Chalcedon to Gregory the Great (590-604)*, London: Mowbray, 1986.
11. See art. cit., p. 128.
12. Marcello Bordoni, *Gesù di Nazaret. Presenza, memoria, attesa*, Brescia: Queriniana, 1988, p. 324.
13. On the following section the following books can be especially consulted: Angelo Amato, *Gesù il Signore*, Bologna: Dehoniane, 1988, pp. 147-302; Piet Smulders, op. cit., pp. 389-476; Bernard Sesboüé, *Jésus-Christ dans la tradition de l'Eglise*, Paris: Desclée, 1982; Bruno Forte, *Gesù di Nazaret. Storia di Dio, Dio della storia*, Roma: Paoline, 1981.
14. For the text, see Denzinger and Schönmetzer, *Enchiridion*, n.125; Neuner and Dupuis, *The Christian Faith*, nn.7-8; Amato, *Gesù il Signore*, p. 608.
15. The Christology of the Council of Constantinople I (381) only adds further precisions to that of Nicaea; these can be left out of consideration here. For the Symbol of Constantinople I, see Denzinger and Schönmetzer, *Enchiridion*, n.150; Neuner and Dupuis, *The Christian Faith*, n.12; Amato, *Gesù il Signore*, p. 185.
16. Denzinger and Schönmetzer, *Enchiridion*, n. 125; Neuner and Dupuis, *The Christian Faith*, n.7.
17. See text in Denzinger and Schönmetzer, *Enchiridion*, nn.250-251; Neuner and Dupuis, *The Christian Faith*, nn.604-605.
18. See text in Denzinger and Schönmetzer, *Enchiridion*, nn.252-263; Neuner and Dupuis, *The Christian Faith*, nn.606/1-12.
19. Amato, op. cit., p. 206.
20. See Piet Schoonenberg, *The Christ*, London: Sheed and Ward, 1970.

21. Karl Rahner, "Theology of the Incarnation," *Theological Investigations*, vol. 5, London: Darton, Longman and Todd, 1974, p. 113.

22. Karl Rahner, *Foundations of Christian Faith*, London: Darton, Longman and Todd, 1978, pp. 221-222.

23. See Denzinger and Schönmetzer, *Enchiridion*, nn.272-273; Neuner and Dupuis, *The Christian Faith*, nn. 607-608; A. Amato, op. cit., p. 205.

24. See text in Denzinger and Schönmetzer, *Enchiridion*, nn.291-294; Neuner and Dupuis, *The Christian Faith*, nn.609-612.

25. See note 23.

26. See text in Denzinger and Schönmetzer, *Enchiridion*, nn.300-303; Neuner and Dupuis, *The Christian Faith*, nn.213-216; Amato, op. cit., pp. 219-220.

27. See Amato, op. cit., p. 219, nn.1-15.

28. See Amato, op. cit., p. 220, nn.16-24.

29. Yves Congar, *Le Christ, Marie et l'Eglise*, Bruges: Desclée de Brouwer, 1952, p. 33.

30. Rudolf Bultmann, *Glauben und Verstehen*, Band II, Tübingen: Mohr, 1952, p. 252.

31. Karl Rahner, "On the Theology of the Incarnation," *Theological Investigations*, vol. 4, London: Darton, Longman and Todd, 1974, p. 117.

32. The documents are the following: Profession of faith signed by Pope Paul VI and Shenouda III, patriarch of Alexandria of Egypt (10 May 1973)(AAS 65 [1973] 299-301); Common Declaration signed by Paul VI and Ignatius Jacob III, patriarch of Antioch of the Syrians (27 October 1971) (AAS 63 [1971] 814); Common Declaration of John Paul II and Ignatius Zakka I Iwas, Syro-Orthodox patriarch of Antioch (23 June 1984) (*Enchiridion Vaticanum*, IX, 839-841).

33. See canons 12-14, in Denzinger and Schönmetzer, *Enchiridion*, nn.434-437; Neuner and Dupuis, *The Christian Faith*, nn.621-623.

34. Canons 1-10, in Denzinger and Schönmetzer, *Enchiridion*, nn.421-432; Neuner and Dupuis, *The Christian Faith*, nn.620/1-10.

35. Text in Denzinger and Schönmetzer, *Enchiridion*, nn.487-488.

36. Ibid. nn.500-522; Neuner and Dupuis, *The Christian Faith*, nn.627/1-16.

37. On the influence of Maximus the Confessor in defense of the two wills in Jesus Christ and the authenticity of his free human will, see François-Marie Léthel, *Théologie de l'agonie du Christ*, Paris: Beauchesne, 1979.

38. Text in Amato, op. cit., p. 258.

39. See text in Denzinger and Schönmetzer, *Enchiridion*, nn.553-559; Neuner and Dupuis, *The Christian Faith*, nn.635-637; Amato, op. cit., p. 260.

40. See Karl Rahner, "Current Problems in Christology," *Theological Investigations*, vol. 1, London: Darton, Longman and Todd, 1974, pp. 157s, 159s.

41. See canon 10, in Denzinger and Schönmetzer, *Enchiridion*, n.432; Neuner and Dupuis, *The Christian Faith*, n.620/10.

42. Reginald H. Fuller, *The Foundations of New Testament Christology*, London: Collins, 1969, pp. 249-250.

43. See chapter 1 on a "critico-dogmatic approach" to Christology, pp. 20-22.

44. See, for instance, Bernard Sesboüé, "Le procès contemporain de Chalcédoine," in *Recherches de science religieuse* 65 (1977/1) 45s.

45. Piet Smulders, "Dogmengeschichtliche und lehramtliche Entfaltung der Christologie," in Johannes Feiner and Magnus Löhrer (eds.), *Mysterium Salutis*,

III,1: *Das Christusereignis*, Einsiedeln: Benziger Verlag, 1970, pp. 467-468.

46. Walter Kasper, "Christologie von unten? Kritik und Neuansatz gegenwärtiger Christologie," in AA.VV., *Grundfragen der Christologie heute*, Freiburg im Br.: 1975, pp. 142, 166.

5

The Problem of the "Human" Psychology of Jesus

The Third Council of Constantinople partly reintroduced a historical perspective in its doctrine of Christ's human will. In the mystery of his suffering, agony and death, Jesus submitted to the will of the Father by an authentic act of human will. The Council of Constantinople III was thus directly orienting the Church's christological reflection toward problems of the human psychology of Jesus that were already latent in its doctrine of Jesus' human will and action. To do justice to these problems, a return to the Jesus of history and to his human life, witnessed to by the Gospel tradition, was necessary; only then would a priori theories and abstract deductions be avoided. This explains how in recent decades the human psychology of Jesus has been the object of explicit study centred on the concrete, historical human story of Jesus as the memory of the apostolic Church has preserved it in its oral and written tradition. Such a concrete study of the human psychology of Jesus will be the object of the present chapter.

This is not to say that recent christological reflection centres exclusively on such study. The conciliar tradition left unsolved problems concerning the formal ontological constitution of Jesus Christ, to which much christological reflection was dedicated during the following centuries. There is no room here to follow the theories proposed by various classical schools to account rationally for the mystery of the hypostatic union. The same, however, continues to engage the reflection of Christologists even today. It does so predominantly — not exclusively — from an upward, ascending perspective. Among the main questions concerning the ontological constitution of Jesus Christ that retain the attention of Christologists, the following may be mentioned, which have already been alluded to in the course of former developments.

If the ontological personhood of the Son of God is communicated to Jesus' humanity, and consequently Jesus' humanity exists by the "act of being" of the Son, is not his humanity impersonal and, in the last analysis, his human existence unreal? Is the "ecstasy of being" (H. M. Diepen) of Jesus the man in the Son of God conceivable? We have noted earlier that the christological dogma implicitly contained the response to this question, which is in fact a fallacy. The act of being of the Son provides Jesus' humanity with a real, authentic human existence; it makes him personally human. Nevertheless, the question is urged whether Jesus is not being made unreal as long as a human person is denied in him. In what sense then is it possible to speak of Jesus as a human person? In this sense, at least, that a "divine-human" person is one who is also truly human; and in the further sense that the Son of God made man enjoys, actualizes and develops a genuine human personality, W. Kasper writes:

> The assumption of Jesus' humanity, the act of highest possible union, at the same time posits this in its own creaturely reality. Jesus' human-ity is therefore hypostatically united with the *Logos* in a human way, and this means in a way which includes human freedom and human self-consciousness. Precisely because Jesus is no other than the *Logos,* in the *Logos* and through him, he is also a human person. Conversely, the person of the *Logos* is the human person.[1]

Connected with the previous questions is a further one: Has not the traditional christological model of one person in two natures failed to do justice to the authentic, concrete, historical humanity of Jesus? Is it in any way capable of doing justice to it? Piet Schoonenberg, who formulated these questions, sharply suggested that a complete reversal of perspective in the ontological constitution of Jesus Christ is all that is capable of making good the losses and restoring the true balance. Jesus would not be a divine person assuming human nature, but a human person in whom God in God's Word is fully present and operative. The apparent dualism of the Christology of two natures would thereby be overcome, and his divine condition would be placed where the early kerygma discovered it, not beyond and above his human existence, but within it and in the depth of it. Such a reversal of perspective does not seem necessary or theologically practicable; nor is a choice to be made between the Christology of the early kerygma and later New Testament developments. Nevertheless, attention must be drawn to the need of returning to the concrete reality of Jesus and of keeping in touch with the functional, from below, Christology of the kerygma, where Jesus is spoken of as a man in whom God was present and active (cf. Acts 2:22).

Our present chapter attempts to show that both the upward and down-ward perspectives must be combined in a theology of the human psychology of Jesus that would do justice both to the reality of his historical human condition and his personal identity as Son of God.

Such a theology must make good the losses suffered in the past by much christological speculation. It must recover the historical dimension of Jesus' human life in his state of kenosis; the personal aspect of his dealings with God his Father in obedience and free submission; and the soteriological motive that underlies his messianic mission. This return to, and renewed look at, the real Jesus of history submits the theology of his human psychology, of his consciousness and knowledge, of his will and freedom, to a profound revision. What is called for is a theology of the "historical mysteries" of Jesus' human life: the mysteries of his baptism and transfiguration; of the agony in the garden and the cry on the cross; of his awareness of messiahship and sonship; of his knowledge and ignorance; of his prayer and faith in God; of his commitment to his mission and his obedience to the Father's will; of his free gift of self and abandonment into his Father's hands.

The Gospel tradition has kept the memory of those historical mysteries of Jesus' life. It has done so in different ways. Each of the synoptic Gospels has its own connotations and specific interest. After a prolonged period of meditation on the mysteries of Jesus' life, the Gospel of John penetrates most deeply into Jesus' self-understanding and human psychology. But all four accounts contain the memory of the same person and the same event. We have shown earlier how through the witness of the Gospels the Jesus of history can be recovered in such a way that the interpretation of Jesus by the apostolic Church may be said to be truly based on Jesus' own self-understanding and revelation. Remaining within the apostolic Church's faith understanding of the man Jesus contained in the Gospel tradition and other New Testament writings, it is now possible to show what portrait it conveys of the man Jesus and how it perceives his human psychology. To the objection that we have no access to Jesus' psychology and that it is presumptuous to build an account of it on the testimony of the Gospels, the answer is that, inasmuch as the Gospel tradition has preserved, in general traits, a picture of Jesus showing the kind of man he was, it also gives us access to his self-understanding, for people's attitudes and actions naturally reveal and spontaneously unveil their mind and intentions.

JESUS' SELF-AWARENESS AND HUMAN KNOWLEDGE

JESUS' PSYCHOLOGICAL UNITY AND SELF-AWARENESS

The Problematic of Unity-in-distinction

The ontological unity of person in Jesus Christ postulates a psychological unity as well. On the other hand, the human existence of Jesus introduces in the Son of God a distinction that extends from the ontological level to that of self-perception or awareness. How, then, is the psychological unity of Christ to be conceived? Which is the centre of reference of human actions? The divine consciousness? But is not the divine consciousness common to the three divine persons? Is it then the human consciousness? But, if there is in Jesus Christ no human personhood, can the human consciousness serve as centre of reference? Three aspects of the question can be distinguished as follows:

1. Can, or must, a human psychological centre of reference be affirmed in Jesus, that is, a human *ego*?

2. Is Jesus' human nature autonomous or heteronomous?

3. More importantly, How was Jesus the man aware of being the Son of God?

The christological dogma provides some orientations that must be briefly recalled. Constantinople III affirmed in Jesus an authentic human will and action not contrary to, but perfectly submitted to, the divine will. It was necessary, it said, that the human will "move itself" (*kinèthènai*), but, on the other hand (*de*), that it be submitted to the divine will.[2] How is this self-determination of the human will of Jesus, in full conformity with the divine will, to be understood? The two wills and actions cannot be placed alongside each other or seen as parallel in Nestorian fashion. On the other hand, the divine will cannot be thought to act as the hegemonic principle regulating and determining, in a monophysite way, a human will that would be guided by it passively. How to combine, then, the authentic initiative of Jesus' human will and his moral submission to the will of God? There are not two parallel lines of action in Jesus, nor is there one fused theandric action. An organic unity of the two wills in communion and subordination must be affirmed. The human acts keep their authenticity, but they are the human acts of the Son of God. Just as by becoming human, the Word of God has also become "something less than that which he is in himself" (K. Rahner), the Word's human actions are something less than the divine actions. Yet, as Jesus is personally the Word Incarnate, so too his human actions are personally those of the Son Incarnate.

The solution to the question of the psychological unity of Jesus must also be sought in the direction of a correct equilibrium between two opposed, extreme positions. As would be expected, there exist two approaches to the problem, both starting from opposite ends—from below and from above. Both perspectives are equally valid within lawful limits; there is not one absolute Christology of the human psychology of Jesus. Both, however, need to complement each other or, becoming one-sided, they would undermine either the unity or the distinction. The controversies of recent decades bear witness to the reality of such danger.

An extreme Antiochian approach can be exemplified by the Christology of Déodat de Basly and L. Seiller, both Franciscans and Scotists. Starting from the *homo assumptus* Christology of the Antiochian school, Déodat conceived the dialogue between Jesus and God as a "duel of love" between Jesus the man and the Triune God. Though the "man assumed" is no human person, since he is subjoined to the Word, yet Jesus' human ego is fully autonomous. The man assumed meets the triune God in a duel of love. L. Seiller, Déodat's disciple, hardened his master's view. While continuing to profess that there is in Jesus no human person, he held that the hypostatic union does not affect the human psychology of Jesus. The man assumed functions as though he were a human person. He is the human subject, fully autonomous, of those actions, on which the Word of God exercises no influence whatever. Seiller's work[3] was placed on the index of forbidden books in 1951.[4] By conceiving the human ego of Jesus as an autonomous subject, it failed to preserve the unity of the divine ontological person.

Though following the Antiochian approach of the *homo assumptus* Christology, the position of P. Galtier[5] is much more cautious and nuanced. He held that Jesus, the *homo assumptus,* though not being a human person, had a human psychological ego, that is, a human centre of reference of his human actions. The ego of the sayings of Jesus in the Gospel did not refer to the divine person of the Word, but expressed the human personality. Moreover, since Jesus' human nature is complete, it possesses a human consciousness as well, by which — since consciousness belongs to nature — the human nature of Jesus becomes intentionally present to itself in its human acts. Thus the human actions and experiences of Jesus are referred to a human, psychological and empirical centre. The human ego is the centre of Jesus' psychological life. It enjoys full psychological autonomy, for the human nature determines itself, though in moral conformity with the divine will. The Word of God exercises no influence on the human acts of Jesus, of which he is merely the subject of attribution. Furthermore, the human nature is aware of its actions; it refers them to itself as to their immediate subject.

This is where a difficulty arises in Galtier's position. How does Jesus know that he is the Son of God, and not merely a human person? How does he know that his human ego is only a psychological centre of reference, not an ontological person? Galtier seeks the solution to this question in the "beatific vision," that is, the immediate objective knowledge of the Triune God that Jesus is presumed to have had throughout his earthly life. In fact, according to Galtier, the beatific vision is required in Jesus to prevent what otherwise would have been an erroneous subjective perception of being a human ontological person. In the beatific vision of the Triune God, the human intellect of Jesus sees his humanity hypostatically united to the second person of the Trinity. This objective knowledge of his divine person is the key to the mystery of the psychological unity of Jesus. In sum, according to Galtier's theory, there is in Christ a human psychological ego. The human nature enjoys full autonomy. Christ has, through the beatific vision, an objective knowledge of his divine identity.

In the opposite direction, an extreme Alexandrian approach to the psychological unity of Jesus Christ is represented by P. Parente.[6] Parente's thesis consists in a complete reversal of Galtier's positions: there is no

human psychological ego in Jesus; the human nature is entirely "heteronomous"; Christ has a direct, subjective awareness of his divine identity.
While for Galtier the human nature acted as though it constituted a human
person, according to Parente, the Word of God not only acts personally in
and through the human actions of Jesus, but is their "hegemonic," regulating, determining principle. It follows that the only principle of unity,
even psychological, is the divine person of the Word, there being no human
psychological ego to serve as centre of reference of the human actions. The
ego of the Gospel sayings of Jesus is directly the divine person. The human
nature is not only substantially "self-dispossessed" through the hypostatic
union; it is hegemonically governed, guided by the Word in all its actions.
It is therefore entirely heteronomous. Moreover, the human consciousness
of Jesus reaches out to the divine person of the Word. Christ is directly
aware of his divine personhood. The evangelical sayings of Jesus express
such an immediate awareness: "I and the Father are one" (Jn 10:30).

Toward a Solution of the Question

On the occasion of the 1500th anniversary of the Council of Chalcedon,
Pope Pius XII published the Encyclical Letter *Sempiternus Rex* (1951), in
which he enunciated the basic principles for a correct understanding of the
psychological unity of Jesus.[7] The Pope recalls that the unity of person in
Jesus Christ may not be put into danger. "Though it is legitimate to study
the humanity of Christ from the psychological view-point," yet the definition
of Chalcedon must be respected. He goes on to point to new theories that
rashly substitute for it their "novel constructions." "These theologians
describe the state and condition of Christ's human nature in such terms
that it seems to be taken for an independent subject (*subjectum sui iuris*),
as though it did not subsist in the person of the Word."[8] The meaning of
the document is the following: It is legitimate to speak of a human psychological ego in Jesus Christ, provided the ontological unity of person is preserved. Consequently, it is not licit either to suppose two individuals in him,
nor to conceive a *homo assumptus* with full autonomy, placed, as it were,
by the side of the Word (*penes Verbum*).

The one-sidedness of both positions described above is assignable to a
failure to distinguish clearly between person and nature. By making nature
the subject of consciousness, Galtier wrongly conceived nature as the subject of actions. On the opposite side, by making the Word the hegemonic
principle of the human acts, Parente wrongly attributed to the Word the
role of specifying those actions. To find the right equilibrium, it is necessary
to preserve the distinction between person and nature intact. However, the
problem of Jesus' knowledge of his divinity can be approached either in
the Antiochian or the Alexandrian key.

The divine person and the human psychological ego. The ego of the human
consciousness of Jesus is not the human nature in intentional self-posses-

sion (Galtier); it is the divine, ontological person. Awareness is the act of the person in and through nature, hence the ultimate centre of reference of the human acts of Jesus is the divine person of the Word. The ego of the evangelical sayings of Jesus is ultimately the Word of God in human awareness: Jesus is humanly self-aware, as truly as he acts humanly.

This, however, does not mean that there is in Jesus no human personality or human ego acting as human centre of reference of Jesus' human experiences. The ego of the evangelical sayings is the Word, but precisely as humanly conscious in his manhood: It is the expression of the human self-awareness of the Word. The mystery of the hypostatic union extends to the order of human intentionality. Consequently, the human psychological ego of Jesus is, in effect, nothing else but the prolongation, in human self-awareness, of the ego of the person of the Word. It does not compete with it, but is essentially related to it. Without such a human centre of reference, the Word could not be humanly aware of his human experiences as his own. It is in this sense that K. Rahner writes:

> Jesus . . . has a subjective centre of action, which is human and crea-
> turely in kind, such that in his human freedom he is in confrontation
> with God the inconceivable, such that in it Jesus has undergone all
> those experiences which we make of God not in a less radical, but on
> the contrary in a more radical way . . . than in our own case. And this
> properly speaking not in spite of, but rather because of the so-called
> hypostatic union. For the more radically any given individual is related
> to God existentially, and so too in his concrete mode of existence as
> a creature, the more such a creature achieves the state of self-reali-
> zation; again the more radically any given individual is able to expe-
> rience his own creaturely reality, the more united he must be with
> God.[9]

Autonomy and heteronomy of Jesus' human nature. To solve the question of human autonomy or heteronomy in Jesus, autonomy needs to be clearly defined and the distinction between person and nature kept in mind. Jesus' human nature is autonomous, as the specifying, determining principle of the human actions and reactions. The substantial "dispossession" of the human nature hypostatically united to the Word takes away none of its spontaneity. The human psychology of Jesus is similar to our own: Human nature specifies his human actions, ensuring their human authenticity.

On the other hand, being hypostatically united to the Word, the human nature of Jesus is entirely dispossessed, ontologically, in the order of the person. The human actions of Jesus are truly those of the Word of God: It is the Word who is acting in them, exercising his "personal causality." But such total dispossession in the order of person takes nothing away from Jesus' sense of responsibility and human initiative. It ensures that in Jesus, God's Son responds as man to the mission he has received from his Father.

The Word of God fulfills personally the human mission in total dedication and commitment. Here too the axiom posited by K. Rahner concerning every relationship between God and creature is valid:

> The closeness and the distance, the submissiveness and the independence of the creature do not grow in inverse but in like proportion. Thus Christ is most radically man, and his humanity is the freest and most independent, not in spite of, but because of its being taken up, by being constituted as the self-utterance of God.[10]

Jesus' awareness of divine Sonship. This is the most mysterious aspect of the human consciousness of the Word incarnate. To explain Jesus' knowledge of his divinity through the beatific vision does not satisfy on more than one count. First, Jesus' knowledge of his personal identity would be inferior to that of ordinary human persons. A person has a subjective awareness of, not only an objective knowledge of, his identity. Second, the beatific vision leaves unexplained how Jesus knows his humanity is united to the second person of the Trinity, which he is presumed to see through the immediate objective knowledge of the vision. Third, the beatific vision during Jesus' earthly life is gratuitously postulated; it is not affirmed by New Testament evidence.

It is therefore necessary to speak of Jesus having a subjective awareness of his divinity, but how can a human intellect be the instrument whereby a divine person becomes self-aware? Two distinct, opposite approaches are possible here. That from below, represented by K. Rahner and E. Gutwenger among others, asks how the man Jesus is subjectively aware of his divinity. That from above, exemplified by H. U. von Balthasar, inquires how the Word incarnate becomes humanly self-aware in Jesus' human consciousness. Both roads are, within the parameters of the mystery of the hypostatic union, valid and complementary.

The enunciation from below. Jesus the man is subjectively aware of his divinity through a direct awareness of the hypostatic union. That is to say, the hypostatic union falls under the purview of the human consciousness of Jesus. The human self-awareness of divinity is not a new reality added to the hypostatic union; it represents the subjective aspect of the hypostatic union. The hypostatic union could not exist without it, since it is the natural prolongation of the hypostatic union itself in the sphere of the human intellect. Thus it is that the ego of Jesus' evangelical sayings refers to the person of the Word as humanly self-aware.[11]

The enunciation from above. The perspective is reversed. The problem is not how can the man Jesus know that he is God? It is, how does the Son of God know that he is man? Having assumed human nature and a human consciousness, the Word of God becomes humanly self-aware. The ultimate centre of reference of such an act of awareness is the divine person. But how can a human intellect be the instrument by means of which a divine person becomes self-conscious — a task to which it would seem unequal by nature? It needs to be adapted to the task; not, however, by a reality added to the hypostatic union. Rather, the assumption of the human nature by the Word extends its effects to the human consciousness of Jesus. The human awareness of the Son of God is thus the prolongation in human consciousness of the mystery of the hypostatic union. As the communication of the "act of being" of the Word to the human nature adapts it to subsist in him and causes it to exist, in similar fashion it adapts the human consciousness to be the channel for the human self-awareness of the Word. Thus the hypostatic ego of the Logos becomes self-aware in the human nature and consciousness. The ego is the divine person humanly conscious, the human ego of the Word.

In conclusion, the following may be said. The one divine person of the Word is humanly self-aware in Jesus; this postulates a human psychological ego. The human awareness is proper to the Word, while the divine consciousness is common to the three divine persons. In the divine intratrinitarian life there emerges a "We" awareness, with three focusing centres of consciousness. The human self-awareness of Jesus, on the contrary, introduces an "I"-"Thou" relationship of dialogue between the Father and the Word incarnate: "I and the Father are one" (Jn 10:30); "The Father is greater than I" (Jn 14:28). These Gospel data, which express the human awareness of the incarnate Son, transpose in human key and extend to the human level the interpersonal relation of the Son to the Father within the divine life.

The Human Knowledge of Jesus

The Problem of Knowledge and Nescience

What human knowledge did Jesus have? What perfection is to be assigned to his human knowledge, and what limitations affirmed? A study of the human knowledge of Jesus must take account of two facts. It is the human knowledge of the Son of God. The Word, incarnate in kenosis, did not possess during his earthly life the perfection (*teleiòsis*) (cf. Heb 5:9) that became his in his resurrection. Surely, some human perfections must be affirmed in Jesus because of his personal identity as the Son of God. On the other hand, not only does his human nature remain human, but his human existence in kenosis implies voluntarily assumed imperfections.

That the two natures do not mingle together by the hypostatic union — the human nature keeping its integrity — implies that the perfections of the divine nature, in this instance the divine knowledge, is not directly communicated to the human nature. That the two natures are not separated means that the human knowledge of Jesus is that of the Son of God. The perfections of that knowledge must be neither exaggerated nor unduly reduced. Furthermore, the state of kenosis of Jesus' human existence means that the divine glory (*doxa*) is not allowed to shine forth through it during his earthly life until the time of his glorification. The Word has assumed the concrete sinful condition of the human race, sin excepted (cf. Heb 4:15), and shares with human beings their condition—suffering and death included. The Word has freely assumed the consequences of sin that could be assumed and turned into the instrument of salvation.

All this goes to show that the "absolute principle of perfections" that has often been applied to the humanity of Jesus, in particular to his human knowledge, is without foundation. The human perfections of Jesus are proportionate to his kenotic state and related to his mission. As to the first, it needs to be remembered that a real transformation distinguishes Jesus' kenotic from his glorious state. He will be in possession of the fulness of his messianic and saving power only in his resurrection. As for the second, Jesus possessed during his earthly life the human perfections and human knowledge that were needed for the fulfillment of his mission.

Above all, it is necessary to turn to the Gospels to see how the apostolic tradition understood the humanity of Jesus. The Gospel tradition testifies not only to astonishing perfections of Jesus' humanity, but also to obvious imperfections: his nescience, temptation, the agony in the garden, the cry on the cross. Such Gospel indications are all the more trustworthy because they could seem to raise difficulties for the faith in Jesus Christ that the Gospel tradition meant to communicate.

The human psychology of the Word incarnate in kenosis thus appears as a deep mystery. How do we reconcile and combine in it elements that seem to contradict and cancel each other, such as the absence of sin with true temptation? the vision of God with the sense of being abandoned on the cross? the obedience to God's will in death and a free offering of self? In all these, a priori deductions are futile and out of place. What is required is to follow the story of Jesus and his mission. On the one hand, he must reveal the Father (Jn 1:18); on the other, he must suffer for the salvation of humankind (Lk 24:26).

Concerning Jesus' knowledge, the Gospel tradition reports its extraordinary perfection: He speaks of the Father as one who sees (Jn 1:18); he manifests an astonishing knowledge at the age of twelve in the temple (Lk 2:40); the people marvel at his doctrine (Mt 7:28); he teaches with a unique personal authority (Mk 1:22); he possesses a surprising knowledge of the Scriptures without having formally studied them (Jn 7:15); he knows the secrets of the hearts (Lk 6:8); he foretells the future—even though the prediction of his death and resurrection must be dealt with cautiously. John sums it all up by saying that he knew everything (Jn 16:30). Luke affirms that the child Jesus was "filled with wisdom" (Lk 2:40). On the other hand, the Gospel tradition also testifies that Jesus learned through experience and that he "increased in wisdom" (Lk 2:52). He showed surprise, asked questions, and even admitted to not knowing (Mt 24:36; Mk 13:32).

In the failure of a priori deductions, guidance for a theology of the human knowledge of Jesus must be sought in the Gospel tradition. Surely some perfections need to be affirmed in him. He must have known his personal identity as the Son of God. He must have had a special knowledge of the Father, in order to reveal him. But which knowledge? Nor can the limitations of the knowledge of Jesus of which the Gospel speaks — his nescience and doubt, its progress and limitations — be rendered inexistent by a priori deductions that can be qualified as mythical (K. Rahner). Arguing from the "absolute principle of perfections," theology has affirmed in Jesus a threefold kind of human knowledge: the beatific vision of the blessed in heaven, an infused (angelic) knowledge, and an experiential knowledge. All three are sometimes conceived as exhaustive and all-comprehensive. Jesus would have known all things, humanly, in three different ways! To such mythical construction it must be objected that, since during his earthly life Jesus has not reached the "end of his course," but remains on the way, it is preposterous to postulate in him the vision of the blessed; that the Word of God has become man, not an angel (cf. Heb 2:16); and that an exhaustive experiential knowledge is a contradiction in terms. Furthermore, had Jesus enjoyed the beatific vision during his earthly life and throughout it, how could the mystery of his suffering and agony be accounted for? To distinguish different levels in his human soul and to affirm that the apex of the soul enjoyed the beatific vision while the lower part remained subject to suffering, is to lend to Jesus an "artificial psychology with different storeys" which in the end explains nothing, for by nature the beatific vision invades the entire human psychology of the person.

What orientation is found in the christological dogma for a solution to the question of the human psychology of Jesus? While Constantinople III spoke explicitly of "two wills and natural operations" of Christ, no christological council made a similar affirmation concerning two kinds of knowledge, the divine and the human. However, the existence in Jesus of human knowledge is part of the doctrine of faith, being implied in the integrity of the human nature. Here too the principle first affirmed by St. Leo's "Tomus"[12] and repeated by Constantinople III[13] applies: "Each of the two natures performs the function proper to it in communion with the other: the Word does what pertains to the Word and the flesh what pertains to the flesh." In recent times, in the context of modernism, a decree of the Holy Office (1918) declared that it cannot be taught safely (*tuto*) that no evidence shows (*non constat*) that Jesus' soul had during his earthly life the beatific vision of the blessed (*comprehensores*).[14] This disciplinary decree, concerned with public teaching, had no intention of closing the discussion between Christologists. While speaking of the beatific vision of the blessed, it meant to attribute to Jesus an "immediate" vision of the Father. What mattered was the modality of Jesus' knowledge of the Father, not the effects that accompany the vision in the blessed who have reached the end of their human course and, with it, the definitive fruition of God. The same interpretation holds for the Encyclical Letter *Mystici Corporis* (1943), where the beatific vision (*visio beata*) is also attributed to Jesus during his earthly life.[15]

Toward a Solution of the Problem

The immediate vision of the Father. It cannot be proved that during his earthly life Jesus had the beatific vision. His intimate knowledge of the Father, while it implies a direct, immediate contact, does not of necessity postulate the beatific vision. What is true is that Jesus has a personal, human experience of the Father. The Gospel saying "I and the Father are one" (Jn 10:30) refers to this immediate experience of an intimate, personal relationship with the Father, the source of which is in the divine life itself. An infused or prophetic knowledge would hardly account for the immediacy and intimacy of this personal rapport. But, while an immediate vision of the Father is involved here, nothing is presumed as to its beatific character, such as follows in the case of the blessed from the decisive fruition of God they enjoy once they have reached their final goal at the end of their earthly course. As for the Christian tradition, only one text of St. Augustine could seem to affirm the beatific vision of Jesus Christ during his earthly life.[16]

What must be affirmed is that Jesus had the immediate vision of the Father during his earthly life. This was implied in the human subjective awareness of his divine Sonship, which has been mentioned earlier. Jesus was subjectively aware of his personal identity as Son; or, the Word was humanly self-aware. The "absolute *ego eimi* sayings" (Jn 8:24; 8:28; 8:58; 13:19) of Jesus in John's Gospel enunciate such a direct subjective awareness. Involved in this human self-awareness of Jesus as the Son is the immediate, intuitive vision of the Father. But while one is subjective consciousness, the other is objective knowledge.

The Son incarnate lived in his human consciousness the mystery of his personal, essential relationship to the Father within the divine life. The subjective awareness of the Son in humanity involved the objective intuitive knowledge of the Father, from whom within the divine life the Word proceeds as Son. Jesus saw the Father *because* in his human awareness he lived consciously his personal relationship with the Father. His personal awareness as Son implied the immediate vision of the Father.

Such an immediate vision is to be distinguished from the beatific vision of the blessed on more than one count. First, it is the immediate interpersonal rapport between the Son as a human being and his Father, not the vision of the Triune God by a human person. In the "I"-"Thou" relationship between Jesus and the Father, the Father becomes the "Thou" of the Son in humanity. This immediate rapport of the Son in humanity with the Father differs from the objective vision of the Triune God by a human person. The blessed in heaven contemplate the Trinity and say, "Thou art." Jesus on earth, in the "I am" of his self-awareness as Son, sees the Father—

not himself. Second, the immediate vision of the Father on the part of Jesus does not imply the beatific fruition that results in the blessed from the definitive union with God at the end of their earthly pilgrimage. The earthly pre-paschal Jesus remains on his way to the Father. In his state of kenosis, his human soul has not reached the divine glory. Jesus' immediate vision of the Father will become beatific only in his glorified state as the Risen one. Meanwhile, in its kenotic state, it leaves room for human suffering, for the mystery of the agony, and for Jesus' sense of God's dereliction on the cross—without postulating in him a "many storey psychology."

Furthermore, Jesus' self-awareness and immediate vision of the Father are liable to grow and be subject to development, which the beatific vision is not. Jesus' humanity is subject to the laws of human psychology and spiritual activity. As self-awareness grows through the exercise of a person's spiritual activity, so too Jesus' human self-awareness as Son and the accompanying vision of the Father grew from the early years through the mature age of his public mission. Jesus' awareness of his messianic mission and of the way in which he was to fulfil it also grew accordingly, from his baptism in the Jordan, where he became identified with God's suffering Servant, down to Jerusalem, where he faced his impending death on the cross. The Encyclical Letter *Mystici Corporis* notwithstanding,[17] nothing indicates or requires that Jesus was aware of his divinity or had the vision of the Father from the moment of the incarnation. Hebrews 10:5 refers to the kenotic state of the Son's earthly life in general, not to the punctual moment of the incarnation.

Finally, Jesus' immediate vision of God during his earthly life need not have been all-comprehensive. It certainly did extend to the interpersonal relations with the Father and the Spirit, but nothing indicates that it should have extended—as would the beatific vision of the blessed—to God's plan of salvation. Jesus no doubt knew all that he needed to know for the exercise of his saving mission, including the salvific meaning of his death on the cross. But this knowledge did not come to him through the vision of his Father. Another kind of human knowldedge was required for it.

The experiential knowledge. Nothing needs to be said about Jesus' experiential knowledge, except to insist that it was entirely normal and ordinary. As experiential knowledge is by nature limited, that of Jesus too was limited, subject to growth, and neither complete nor comprehensive. Jesus learned from people, from events, from nature, from experience. In his experiential knowledge he shared the ordinary condition of human beings; like them he grew to mature manhood, learning progressively to live out his human life in total proexistence for others.

The infused knowledge. Some theologians, E. Gutwenger for one, have denied Jesus' infused knowledge, which they considered superfluous in view of his immediate vision of God. They thought the vision of God to extend to whatever Jesus needed to have known in view of his mission, or, eventually, that it was all-comprehensive. That Jesus knew whatever he needed to have known for the exercise of his mission is certain, but this is the reason it seems necessary to affirm an "infused" knowledge in him. Such a knowledge is not to be affirmed a priori, but in view of the role it plays in the exercise of Jesus' mission. Nor is it to be understood as "angelic" knowledge, but rather compared to the infused knowledge of the prophets. As through their experience of God the prophets received a message that it was their mission to convey to Israel, in a somewhat similar manner Jesus came to know from God whatever he needed to know to fulfil his mission or was to convey in revelation. In particular, Jesus' vision of the Father, because immediate, was not by itself liable to communication. It needed to be transposed into conceptual, communicable knowledge in order that Jesus might reveal the Father. The infused knowledge had the function of effecting that transposition. Moreover, Jesus' immediate vision of the Father was not all-inclusive. It extended primarily to the intratrinitarian relationships that Jesus lived in his human consciousness. Other knowledge came to him by infusion, such as his deep sense of the meaning of the Scriptures (cf. Jn 7:15); his intuition into God's plan of salvation for humankind; the salvific meaning of his death on the cross. In all these, the infused knowledge was entirely ordained to the fulfilment of Jesus' mission. He knew all that was needed for it; but he need not have known more!

The nescience of Jesus. The knowledge of all that was required for Jesus' mission does not exclude a real nescience. The question of Jesus' nescience has mainly been posed in connection with the day of judgment. The Gospel tradition makes Jesus emphatically affirm that he does not know the day (Mk 13:32; Mt 24:36). Exegetes discuss whether the texts refer to the destruction of Jerusalem or to the last judgment. The eschatological texts are ambiguous. Confronted with the frequent denial on the part of theologians of any nescience in Jesus and the decree of the Holy Office according to which the existence of any ignorance in Jesus cannot safely be taught,[18] K. Adam asked pointedly, "Who is right here? Jesus or the theologians? Jesus or the Holy Office?"[19]

Some Church Fathers (Athanasius, Cyril of Alexandria) admitted that Jesus did not know the day; others said that he knew but professed not to know because revealing it did not pertain to his mission (Jerome, John Chrysostom). Since, for Augustine, ignorance is a consequence of sin and leads to sin, Jesus could not be ignorant of anything. Some later theologians said that Jesus both knew and did not know. He knew in the beatific vision, supposed to be all-inclusive; he did not know in the sense that, since it was not for him to reveal, this knowledge was not transposed into communicable language. Jesus could therefore sincerely profess his ignorance.

Leaving aside such subtle constructions, there is no theological reason for not admitting plainly that Jesus did not know. We have seen that during his earthly life Jesus' vision of God was not all-comprehensive. He knew through infused prophetic knowledge whatever he needed to know for his revealing and salvific mission. If the day of judgment was not part of Jesus' revealing mission, he need not have known it, and simply did not. Nescience was part of Jesus' kenotic state.

Further questions may be asked. If Jesus had no special knowledge of the day of judgment, as the Gospel evidence makes clear (Mk 13:32), is it lawful for theologians to think that he may have been mistaken on that account? In the confusion of various opinions circulated in his time on this subject, can it be thought that Jesus had no clear opinion of his own? Or could Jesus have shared the widespread mistaken opinion that the parousia was to occur soon? This question is formulated by R. E. Brown as follows:

> Is it totally inconceivable that, since Jesus did not know when the parousia would occur, he tended to think and say that it would occur soon? Would not the inability to correct contemporary views on this question be the logical effect of ignorance? . . . Because there is evidence, nay more a statement, that Jesus did not know when the ultimate victory would take place, many Catholic theologians would propose that such knowledge was not an essential of Jesus' mission. Could theologians then also admit that Jesus was not protected from the confused views of his era about the time of the parousia? An exegete cannot solve such a question; he can only point out the undeniable confusion of the statements attributed to Jesus.[20]

This amounts to passing from nescience to doubt and from doubt to mistaken opinion. Could theology admit that Jesus shared mistaken opinions of his time on subjects not pertaining to his revealing mission? Once more it needs to be said that Jesus knew — nor could he be mistaken about — all that pertained to his mission. But, besides this, there could be opinions largely common in his time that he would have shared. Whether the imminence of "the hour" can be thought to be among these is difficult to admit, insofar as it would seem to contradict his will that his mission be continued in the Church. However, if nescience was part of the kenotic state of Jesus' earthly life, the possibility of holding current opinions about things not affecting his mission must be seen as part of his sharing in our human condition.

The Prayer and Faith of Jesus

The prayer of Jesus. Jesus Christ, the Mediator, is a divine-human person who unites in himself the Godhead and humanity. He is at once God turning to us, in his Word, in self-communication and self-gift, and humankind — which he recapitulates and represents — turned to God in grateful response. He is a "mystery of saving worship" (E. Schillebeeckx) made up of a twofold movement: from God to humankind in salvation; from humankind to God in worship. Hence the two directions of Jesus' human actions.

In a descending movement, his human actions can become the human expression of God's saving power. Such is the case with the miracles of Jesus, in which his human will becomes the expression of a divine power. In the ascending movement, Jesus' human actions are perfect divine worship.[21]

To be considered in the second category is the "religion" of Jesus, his prayer, worship and adoration of the Father. Beyond the concrete outward circumstances of Jesus' prayer life, what needs to be delved into is the meaning of his prayer and the depth of his worship of God.[22] In extreme Antiochian key, Galtier pictured Jesus the man as turned in prayer toward the Triune God, the Son included. Jesus as man would then have also prayed to Christ as God. This understanding of Jesus' prayer is based on a mistaken interpretation of the Gospel data. It is alleged that, when Jesus is said to pray to "the Father" (Mk 14:36), God (*theos*) is really meant.[23] In fact, however, the opposite is true: Jesus prays to the Father even when God (*theos*) is mentioned in the Gospel text (v.g. Mk 15:34). K. Rahner has shown convincingly that *theos* in the New Testament refers to the person of the Father (Yahweh of the Old Testament), except where the concept is made to apply to Jesus Christ also. Never does it refer to God in an indeterminate way, or to the Trinity.[24]

To substantiate his view theologically, Galtier notes that Jesus' prayer is the acknowledgment by him of his relationship to the Trinity in creation. Furthermore, Jesus' human nature is the principle of the human acts; and, though hypostatically united with the Son, it is not assumed into the intra-trinitarian relationships. In answer to this argumentation, it must be said that, though created by the Trinity, the human nature of Jesus is assumed into personal union with the Son. Therefore it is also indirectly assumed into the intratrinitarian relationships. The entire religious life of Jesus, his obedience and self-offering in death, his prayer and worship, are directed not by Jesus the man to the Trinity, but by the Son-incarnate, in his humanity, to the Father. All those actions are the human expression, in the humanity assumed by the Son, of his interpersonal relationship toward the Father, to whom he is substantially related in the Godhead.

Jesus prayed to the Father, not to God in general or to the Trinity — neither to the Son nor to the Spirit. Jesus lived his intratrinitarian personal relationships to the Father and to the Spirit on the human level. Lived and experienced consciously in his human psychology, his intratrinitarian eternal origin from the Father through generation became expressed in prayer and in a sense of total dependence upon the Father. This is why Jesus prayed to the Father, and to the Father only, as the Gospel testifies. Where the Spirit is concerned, the Gospel witnesses to Jesus promising to send the Spirit from the Father after his resurrection and glorification (Jn 15:26). This promise expressed on the human plane the relationship by which, within the divine life, the Holy Spirit originates from the Father through the Son. In both cases and on both sides, there took place in Jesus' human psychology a transposition on the human plane of the intratrinitarian relationships within the Godhead.[25]

The eternal origin of the Son from the Father by generation, once transposed to the human plane in Jesus' human psychology, became a sense of total dependence. It is this sense of total dependence upon the Father that is expressed in Jesus' prayer. His prayer to the Father is the expression of a consciousness that is essentially filial.

The faith of Jesus. Many theologians refuse to speak of faith in Jesus. Some have argued the absence of faith in him from the beatific vision: the vision and the decisive fruition of God exclude faith, as Paul himself testifies (1 Cor 13:8-13). Others base their denial of Jesus' faith on his self-awareness as Son and his immediate vision of the Father, which would leave no room for faith. Yet there has been no dearth of theologians in recent years who affirmed that Jesus lived a true life of faith, indeed that he exemplifies the perfect model and the paradigm of faith.[26]

Faith must not be conceived primarily as adherence to revealed truths, but in the biblical sense of a personal commitment and trust in God. Jesus' self-commitment, however, is addressed to the Father. It is part of Jesus' "religious life" and prayer life. Jesus entrusted himself to the Father throughout his earthly life. He sought and did the Father's will and only the Father's will; not in the sense that he followed it passively, but that he freely complied with it and invested all his human energy in fulfilling it. This compliance with the Father's will became, however, "blind faith" when, in the scene of the agony in the garden, the will of the Father became obscure and Jesus sought it in anguish and tears. A mysterious distance intervened then between the Father's will and Jesus' own human will, which he experienced profoundly and overcame in prayer. The words of the Letter to the Hebrews apply to the scene of the agony when they say:

> In the days of his flesh Jesus offered up prayers and supplications, with loud cries and tears, to him who was able to save him from death, and he was heard for his godly fear. Although he was Son, he learned obedience through what he suffered; and being made perfect, he became the source of eternal salvation to all who obey him (Heb 5:7-9).

Here we have the perfect description of what Jesus' life of faith meant in its most tragic and deepest aspect: the struggle involved in the search of, and compliance with, the will of the Father; an unwavering trust in the Father and the decisive commitment of self in obedience; and, through it all, the growth of the man Jesus in his Sonship of the Father and in his saving power toward humankind. Characteristically, the Letter to the Hebrews also describes Jesus as "the pioneer and protector of faith" (Heb 12:2). Whatever interpretation of Hebrews 12:2 may be preferred, the letter stands out — with John's Gospel — as the deepest expression of Jesus' faith in God his Father. That such faith was compatible with Jesus' self-awareness as Son and his immediate vision of the Father will be shown more clearly hereafter, when speaking explicitly of Jesus' human will and suffering. Inasmuch as Jesus' sense of dependence upon the Father was the human expression of his intratrinitarian filial relationship, it presupposed rather than contradicted his identity as Son. The faith of Jesus does not cancel faith in Jesus, but establishes it. It is part of the implicit Christology of the earthly Jesus on which the explicit Christology of the apostolic Church is based.

JESUS' HUMAN WILL AND FREEDOM

JESUS' HUMAN WILL AND ACTIONS

The Problem of Distinction-in-unity

The Council of Constantinople III (680-681) affirmed two wills and natural actions united in Jesus Christ without division, without change, without separation, without confusion. It explained that no opposition occurs between the two, the human will being in full conformity to the divine. For "it was necessary that the will of the flesh move itself (*kinèthènai*),[27] but also that it be submitted to the divine will."[28] The council did not, however, explain how the divine and the human will and action combine in the one person of Jesus Christ, or what kind of autonomy the human will and action have in relation to the divine. How then can the self-determination of the human will of Jesus as the determining principle of authentically human actions and its perfect, unwavering submission to the will of the Father be combined? That the human actions of Jesus are the human actions of the Son of God, who exercises upon them the causality proper to the person, has already been shown. Similarly, it has been affirmed that human nature specifies and determines Jesus' human acts that — their belonging to the person of the Son of God notwithstanding — remain authentically and integrally human. The theological problem under consideration is that of reconciling and integrating the truth and authenticity of Jesus' human will and action with the compelling character of their subjection to the Father's will.

In seeking an answer to this question, it is necessary to remember once again the kenotic state of the pre-Easter Jesus and his real identification with the concrete condition of humankind (cf. Heb 4:15), which forbids applying to Jesus' earthly life the fallacious principle of absolute perfections. True, some perfections can and must be affirmed in Jesus' human will in virtue of his personal identity as the Son of God, such as the absence of sin and absence of the inclination to sin, which is named concupiscence. But Jesus' divine personhood does not prevent the existence of genuine temptation in him, much less of human weakness, despondency, fear, sadness—as the Gospel tradition testifies. The guiding principle for a theological evaluation of perfections and imperfections of Jesus' human will and human knowledge is that the Son of God has assumed all the consequences of sin—suffering and death included—that could be assumed by him and given a positive significance and value for the salvation of humankind. Truly, "in every respect he has been tempted as we are, yet without sin" (Heb 4:15). For the rest, a priori deductions of perfections and imperfections are out of place here. Recourse must be had to the Gospel tradition, taken at its face value. Not naively, as though every scene recorded in the Gospel were to be considered literally historical, but because the memory of the apostolic Church, contained in the Gospel tradition, witnesses to the understanding of Jesus' humanity by eyewitnesses, once their eyes were open to his mystery in their Easter experience. It is in the Gospel tradition, then, that we need primarily to discover how the human perfections owing to Jesus' identity as the Son and the imperfections following upon his state of self-emptying (*kenòsis*) combine together.

Apparent contradictions are not wanting here. How to reconcile Jesus' sinlessness—and, more radically, his theological "impeccability"—with the reality of temptation? And, again, his sinlessness and impeccability with genuine human freedom? Similarly, once the beatific vision has been denied in Jesus during his earthly life, the problem remains of how to combine his immediate vision of the Father with the moral suffering he endures, with the despondency, fear and anguish he experiences in the struggle of the agony, and even more so, in his cry on the cross and his sense of being abandoned by God? These and other apparent contradictions help to fathom the depth of the humanness of the Son of God, like unto us in all things but sin.

Toward a Solution of the Problem

Jesus was immune to sin. The New Testament affirms clearly Jesus' sinlessness (Heb 7:26; 1 Pet 1:18; 2:22; 1 Jn 3:5). The same is affirmed by the Council of Chalcedon as doctrine of faith, with reference to Hebrews 4:15.[29] That Jesus was born without original sin is likewise doctrine of faith affirmed by the Council of Toledo XI (675)[30] and repeated by the Council of Florence (1442).[31] Also doctrine of faith is the absence in Jesus of any inclination to sin, or concupiscence. This is affirmed by the Council of Constantinople II (553).[32] Theologically, this perfect harmony in Jesus' humanity is explained by the absence of original sin in him. As for the intrinsic and absolute impeccability of Jesus, it represents a "theologoumenon," not the doctrine of faith as such. It is deduced theologically from the mystery of the hypostatic union. If Jesus were to commit sin, God would be the author of sinful actions, which is a contradiction.

However, neither Jesus' sinlessness nor his impeccability made him immune to temptation. The Gospel witnesses clearly to the reality of temptation in Jesus (Mk 1:12-13; Mt 4:1-11; Lk 4:1-13; cf. also Heb 2:18). This witness must be taken at its face value. Jesus' temptation cannot be reduced to being merely extrinsic. It was real and experienced inwardly; it provoked in him a genuine struggle. Jesus felt deeply in his humanity the heavy demands that the Father's will and the faithfulness to his own messianic vocation were making on him. His obedience and submission were not painless, even while his will never wavered, but always complied. The genuine character of Jesus' temptation stands out all the more clearly in the Gospel tradition by the fact that it has to do with the way in which he was to fulfil his messianic vocation not as a triumphant Messiah, but as realizing the type of the Servant of Yahweh. Characteristically, in each of the synoptic Gospels the temptation narrative follows immediately after Jesus' baptism in the Jordan, by which his messianic ministry is inaugurated and his vocation as the servant of Yahweh manifested. The three synoptics note, moreover, that Jesus was led into the desert by the Spirit, to be put to the test (cf. Mt 4:1; Mk 1:12; Lk 4:1).

Jesus was not immune to suffering. That Jesus has been subject to bodily suffering is amply testified by the Gospel tradition, especially in the four Passion narratives. It is insisted upon by the Letter to the Hebrews (Heb 4:15; 2:17-18; 5:8). The same is affirmed as doctrine of faith by the Council of Lateran I (649),[33] and repeated by the Council of Lateran IV (1215)[34] and that of Florence (1442).[35] As for moral suffering in Jesus, it is evidenced principally in the Gospel narrative by the scene of the agony or struggle (*agonia*), as it is called by the Gospel of Luke (according to some manuscripts which include Lk 22:43-44 in the Gospel text): "And being in an agony he prayed more earnestly . . ." (Lk 22:44). The agony is undoubtedly one of the most mysterious episodes of Jesus' life, as it is understood by the Gospel tradition. Characteristically, the three synoptic Gospels abound in observations that describe in great detail the human sentiments and reactions experienced by Jesus as he is faced with an imminent violent death and searches in darkness for the will of the Father. Matthew and Mark speak of sorrow unto death (Mt 26:38; Mk 14:34); they add distress (Mt 26:37; Mk 14:33) and trouble (Mk 14:33). Luke, more explicitly, describes Jesus' agony as follows: "and his sweat became like great drops of blood falling down upon the earth" (22:44). All three synoptics speak of Jesus' earnest prayer in seeking the Father's will, which in this supreme trial has become mysteriously obscure. Jesus, it may and must be said, has experienced anguish and sadness, despondency and struggle. Truly, he has shared with humankind the fear that the imminence of death—especially of a violent death—inspires, as nature rebels against its imminent tearing apart. Through this struggle Jesus sought in solitude and darkness the will of God, which had become strangely obscure and incomprehensible.

How to reconcile with such moral suffering and struggle the immediate vision of the Father that has been previously affirmed? Surely the beatific vision would have made all suffering impossible. The blessedness involved in the definitive fruition of God is incompatible with any sense of suffering. Nor can recourse be had, to make them compatible, to artificial devices, such as the momentary interruption of the beatific vision or the division of Jesus' human soul into two parts, of which the higher part would have enjoyed the vision of God, leaving the lower part of the soul liable to suffering. By its nature, the decisive possession and vision of God invades the entire human psyche. The state of glory consists precisely in this.

Jesus is not in the state of glory during his earthly life, but in one of kenosis; not at the end of his human course, but on his way to the Father. In his state of self-emptying, and while in pilgrimage to the Father, he does not enjoy the beatific vision of the blessed in heaven. He has, nevertheless, the human awareness of his identity as Son of God and the accompanying immediate vision of the God he calls Father. This immediate vision of God, unlike its beatific counterpart, was compatible with human suffering. Jesus was conscious of suffering as Son and of having to suffer, even though he was the Son (cf. Heb 5:8). Only beyond the resurrection was Jesus destined to enjoy the decisive possession of God, being then united with him in his glory. Only then was his vision of God to become beatific. Meanwhile, Jesus was conscious of being the-Son-of-God-in-self-emptying; the awareness of the kenotic condition, imposed upon him by his messianic mission, became more vivid than ever as he faced the imminence of a violent death. This explains how in the struggle of the agony the vision of the Father endured, even while Jesus was overcome by human anguish.

Jesus' cry on the cross, "My God, my God, why have you forsaken me?" (Mk 15:34; Mt 27:46) must be understood in the same way. That Jesus experienced a sense of being abandoned by the Father is certain. This does not, however, imply, as has sometimes been supposed, that the Father had in effect abandoned his Son and withdrawn from him, leaving him to suffer in divine forsakenness and dereliction.[36] Jesus did, no doubt, feel on the cross all the distance which lies open between God's infinite goodness and the sinfulness of humankind, that imposed on him the death on the cross, but this in no way involves God's forsakenness of the Son. On the contrary, the Father "sympathised" (suffered with) and empathised with the suffering and dying Son. This is so true that, in the mystery of the cross most of all, the depth of God's infinite love stands revealed in all clarity. The God of Jesus Christ is revealed here as a God who suffers and suffers with, not out of necessity, but out of the superabundant goodness which God has shown toward humankind in the suffering and dying Son. As for Jesus himself, in the sense of being abandoned by the Father, he continues to be united with the Father and commits himself to the Father. He is not abandoned by God. Rather, he abandons himself into the Father's hands. The Gospel itself witnesses to this: "Father, into thy hands I commend my spirit" (Lk 23:46). Jesus' cry on the cross is borrowed from Ps 22:1. As is well known, this psalm, which starts with a sense of forsakenness from God, ends up proclaiming deliverance by God. In keeping with the Hebrew literary device, applying to oneself the first verse of a psalm meant implicitly to identify oneself with it in its integrity. In the darkness of the situation, Jesus on the cross overcomes the sense of being forsaken by the Father to express his total commitment of himself into the Father's hands in trust and confidence.

The sense of forsakenness from God experienced by Jesus on the cross was compatible with his union with and vision of God. To show it, recourse may be had analogically to the experience of the mystics. When they speak of the "dark night of the soul," this does not mean that God has withdrawn from them or become remote. Rather, a sense of remoteness goes together with the abiding close presence, thus allowing for the supreme purification of the soul in view of its perfect union with God. It is such a supreme trial that Jesus — a fortiori — suffered on the cross as he was about to pass from self-abasement to exaltation, from this life and death to the glory of his Father. He experienced forsakenness from the God who was close to him and accompanied him in his suffering. He committed himself in full confidence into the hands of one whom he trusted and who would vindicate him from death.

Jesus' human acts as expression of divine saving power. Jesus Christ, it has been observed earlier, is at once God turning to humankind in self-communication and humankind turned to God in acceptance and response. His mediatorship has been described as a mystery of "saving worship" made up of a twofold movement: from God to humankind, in salvation; from humankind to God, in worship. Hence the two directions of Jesus' human actions: from above and from below. Belonging to the ascending direction are Jesus' "religion," prayer life and worship of God, which have been analysed in the first section of this chapter. In this second section, something remains to be said about Jesus' human acts that follow the opposite, descending movement.

Of all the human actions of Jesus, it is necessary to affirm that they are the human acts of the Son of God, who posits them personally, and that they are specified and determined by the human nature, and hence authentically and exclusively human. The personal causality of the Son of God does not interfere with the natural autonomy of Jesus' human acts, since autonomy and self-determination grow in direct proportion to union with and nearness to God. In Jesus the highest modality of union with God combines with total autonomy of nature; absolute intimacy with complete authenticity.

In the descending line, some human acts of Jesus are the human expression of the divine power to save. Such are the miracles that characterised Jesus' ministry as integral part of the coming of the Kingdom God was establishing on earth through him: cures and exorcisms, resurrections, moral miracles, as well as miracles "of nature." In all of these, Jesus' human act of will becomes the vehicle of the divine power to heal and to free, to restore and to save.

How then did Jesus perform miracles? Not merely by praying to God that God, intervening with infinite power, might produce the healing and saving effect. Not, therefore, in the manner in which the prophets brought about miraculous effects by having recourse to and invoking God's intervention. Jesus, on the contrary, works miracles through the exercise of his own human will: "I will, be healed" (Mk 1:41); "Lazarus, come forth" (Jn 11:43).

To understand this, recourse must be had once more to the mystery of the Son made man, of the Word incarnate. *"Ipsum Verbum personaliter est homo"* (St. Thomas). The Word of God has become personally man in Jesus Christ; he is God in a human way, or God humanized. This means that Jesus' humanness becomes the self-expression of God in the world and history. Therefore Jesus' human actions, which are the human actions of the Word of God, can be the human expression of a divine action, the efficacious sign or the visible channel of the divine power, humanly operative in the world.

Jesus therefore performed miracles through an act of his human will, not by intercession with God in prayer. His human will was efficacious, as the human expression of the divine will, that is, as the efficacious sign of the divine power: "Power came forth from him and healed them all" (Lk 6:19). When prayer is associated with the miracles of Jesus, it is not by way of intercession with God on behalf of people, in order that God may intervene directly to heal them. Rather, Jesus sought the will of the Father in each concrete situation and attuned his own human will with the Father's will. Once in syntony with the Father's will, the human will of Jesus became the channel through which God's healing and saving power flowed and operated.

JESUS' HUMAN FREEDOM

The Problem of Freedom in Dependence

That Jesus during his earthly life enjoyed authentic human freedom must be considered certain, as it is implied in the integrity of his human will and activity, which endures in union with the Son of God. The doctrine of the Third Council of Constantinople (681) supposed it when it affirmed that Jesus' human will remains unaltered after that union.[37] The council did not, however, explain how Jesus is a "free man." The question of Jesus' human freedom is, in fact, fraught with difficulties and apparent contradictions, especially in view of Jesus' sinlessness and impeccability.

We must first make it clear that Jesus exercised genuine freedom of choice as to the course of action through which he would best fulfil his mission. It must be stressed that Jesus invested in such choices an extraordinary sense of initiative, invention, and responsibility. Nor was scope for such choices wanting. The Gospel tradition witnesses, in effect, to a change of strategy on the part of Jesus in the course of his public life after the crisis of the Galilean ministry. Faced with apparent rejection, Jesus decided to concentrate on the training of a core group of disciples. Later he would make up his mind to go down to Jerusalem to meet his fate there. If freedom is the supreme perfection of the person and the highest sign of human dignity, it would do grave injury to Jesus' true and authentic humanity to think him less than a free man. Rather, the contrary needs to be affirmed: As the perfect man, Jesus needed to be endowed with perfect freedom.

The difficulty of Jesus' human freedom arises where Jesus is bound by what appears to be a strict command on the part of the Father, as seems to be the case where his passion and death are concerned. True, these were the natural outcome of the unavoidable clash between the mission to which he would remain faithful and the powers that acted in collusion against him. Nor did God directly will the death of Jesus on the cross. Jesus' faithfulness to his saving mission inexorably led him there. The fact remains, however, that Jesus' death on the cross was in the logic of God's loving and saving design for humankind; it showed in the depth of the Son's self-emptying, the depth of God's own outgoing love for humankind. In that sense it is true to say that according to God's plan, Jesus had to die on the cross.

The New Testament affirms no less, as when the Gospel of Luke explains that it was "necessary" that "the Christ should suffer these things and enter into his glory" (Lk 24:26). The necessity (*edei*) referred to here has the biblical sense of that which is implied in God's plan and design for humankind. That Jesus, especially in his passion and death, was in obedience to the Father is clearly affirmed in the New Testament (cf. Rom 5:19; 4:25; Phil 2:8; Heb 5:8). And, while the concept of *thelèma* (Lk 22:42) could be understood as referring to the Father's wish, that of *entolè* (Jn 14:31) can only be taken to mean a precept or command on the part of God in relation to Jesus' mission that calls for strict obedience. Jesus then had no choice to die or not to die.

It is where Jesus is in obedience to the Father that his human freedom becomes problematic, especially in view of his sinlessness and impeccability. The problem can be formulated in the form of a dilemma. Jesus could disobey, but then what about his impeccability? Or he could not disobey, but in that case what liberty is left to him? In other words, how do we combine Jesus' impeccability and obedience with a true human freedom? Faced with this dilemma, some theologians have thought the problem of Jesus' freedom to be insoluble. Others, unable to hold the three factors, chose to uphold two while somehow undermining the third. Hence opinions fall easily into three categories: those that minimize the divine will about Jesus' death; those that relax his impeccability; and those that reduce the field of his freedom. Can a solution be proposed that is capable of combining the three factors without any prejudice to Jesus' impeccability or the Father's will of his death or Jesus' authentic human freedom?

Toward a Solution of the Problem

A solution can only come from a fresh approach to freedom. The essence of freedom does not consist in the exercise of the faculty of choice. If it were so, necessity and liberty would in all cases be mutually exclusive; that this, however, is not so is clear from the fact that, absolutely determined in the act by which he knows and loves himself, God is at the same time supremely, infinitely, free. Again, the blessed in heaven, though necessitated by the love of God, have reached the perfection of their freedom. Freedom is an ontological perfection of the person, realized in different modes and degrees in God and in the human person.

The essence of freedom must be placed in the self-determination that makes the dignity of the person. A person owes to one's own self-determination one's becoming what one is. The essence of freedom stands in that a person's action comes from him, proceeds from his self, is truly his doing. St. Thomas defined it as "one's mastery over one's action" (*dominium sui actus*).[38] One could say that freedom is the "aseity of the will." Freedom then makes for personal responsibility. The person is responsible for his actions because and insofar as these truly proceed from his self-determination. Freedom is not indetermination; rather, it consists in assuming one's determinism and becoming, through self-determination, what one ought to be. Freedom is not a prerogative we possess, but a perfection we must attain and in which we must grow; it is a gift and a task, a vocation. While the faculty of choice is in this life the concrete modality in which the human person exercises freedom, it is also the sign of a person's present imperfection. The more a person becomes perfect, the more that person's will is necessitated by good. The less scope there remains for moral choice, and the more perfect the person's freedom has become, until such time when, fully self-determined in the vision of God and the possession of his last end, the person will have reached full freedom and will exercise perfect liberty.

It becomes clear that not every necessity is opposed to freedom. Surely violence from without suppresses it; so does all blind intrinsic necessity in the human person, over which the will has no power. If, however, the necessity is intrinsic to the will itself — if a person, in full knowledge of the end proposed to oneself and urged by the irresistible impulse of one's own will toward good, determines oneself for it infallibly — such a determination is the sign of fully mature liberty. The perfection of freedom grows in direct proportion to the self-determination of the will toward good. God, in total self-controlled determinism, is infinitely free. The blessed, adhering willingly to the state of blessedness in which they are determined, have achieved complete liberation. The saints, more and more attracted by a

God whose calling they willingly answer, are gaining their freedom as they lose their indetermination. Men and women in this life are groping toward freedom by progressively developing a responsible necessity of adhering to God.

Such a concept of freedom, no matter how philosophical it may appear, coincides strikingly with the biblical notion. To put it briefly: for St. Paul we are "called to freedom" in Jesus Christ (Gal 5:13). The saint is free, while the sinner is a slave. Conversion to God in Christ is the attainment of freedom, for Christ saves us from the slavery of sin (cf. Gal 5:1; 5:13; 2 Cor 3:17); to belong to him is to be free (1 Cor 3:22-23). Similarly, for St. John the only real slavery is the slavery of sin (Jn 8:34). Freedom, on the contrary, comes from adhering to Christ and being freed from sin by him (Jn 8:32, 36); "he who does what is true comes to the light" (Jn 3:21). The newness brought about in Jesus Christ, it may be said, is the human person's promotion to freedom through him in the Spirit, who becomes the principle of our self-determination.

Coming back to Jesus in the light of this analysis of human freedom, it must be said that his human freedom is perfect. Wherever no express will of the Father is determinent, choice perdures. This was the case, to a great extent, where the means and the modality for the accomplishment of Jesus' mission were concerned; full scope remained here for initiative and invention. Yet this is not what made Jesus' freedom perfect. This was the sign that he remained in this life a pilgrim tending to his last end. Once having reached his glory, his human will would be fully determined, fixed definitively in worship of the Father and the exercise of his saving power. Meanwhile, however, whenever he was under strict obedience from the Father, Jesus had no power to choose. Yet, in clear knowledge of the end proposed to him and to which he adhered with his entire being, he determined himself. His will coincided perfectly with that of his Father. What he resolved in an authentic act of self-determination coincided infallibly with the divine will. Whenever a requirement of the divine will came into play, Jesus was determined by it, yet his human will was prompted to elicit its action, to exercise its determination, not by a divine violence endured from without, but by a personal impulse from within. The vision of the Father did not act as an intruding impulse impeding self-decision, but as an end which drew to it, and the intuition of which made for fully enlightened self-determination. This it would seem is what is implied in K. Rahner's assertion — in a quote that bears repeating — that Jesus' closeness to, and disponibility toward God, far from impeding his authentic freedom, made for its perfection. Rahner wrote:

> The closeness and the distance, the submissiveness and the independence of the creature do not grow in inverse but in like proportion. Thus Christ is most radically man, and his humanity is the freest and

most independent, not in spite of, but because of its being taken up, by being constituted as the self-utterance of God.[39]

This is likewise the kind of human freedom that Jesus claimed for himself, according to the Gospel tradition, specifically in the mystery of his passion and death. Nowhere does he affirm to have freely chosen to die. To the contrary, he attributes his death to the Father's choice and will (cf. Mk 14:36 and par.; cf. also Mt 26:53; Heb 5:7). Yet, on the other hand, Jesus does claim to lay down his life on his own accord, that is, in full self-determination, in perfect freedom: "For this reason the Father loves me, because I lay down my life, that I may take it again. No one takes it from me, but I lay it down on my own accord. I have power to lay it down, and I have power to take it again; this charge I have received from my Father" (Jn 10:17-18; cf. Gal 2:20; Heb 7:27; 9:14).

NOTES

1. Walter Kasper, *Jesus the Christ,* London: Burns and Oates, 1976, p. 248.

2. See Denzinger and Schönmetzer, *Enchiridion,* nn.555-557; Neuner and Dupuis, *The Christian Faith,* nn.635-637.

3. Léon Seiller, "La psychologie humaine du Christ et l'unicité de personne," in *Franziskanische Studien* 31 (1949) 49-76, 246-274.

4. Cf. *Acta Apostolicae Sedis* 43 (1951) 561.

5. Paul Galtier, *L'unité du Christ,* Paris: Beauchesne, 1939.

6. Pietro Parente, *L'io di Cristo,* Brescia: Marcelliana, 1955.

7. See text in Denzinger and Schömetzer, *Enchiridion,* n.3905; Neuner and Dupuis, *The Christian Faith,* nn.662-663.

8. The text first published in *Osservatore Romano* had: "ita provehunt . . . ut eadem *saltem psychologice* reputari videatur. . . ." The words "saltem psychologice" seemed to condemn also the theory of Galtier. However, in the official text published in AAS 43 (1951) 638, those two words have been suppressed. Hence what is condemned in the encyclical is the theory of Seiller. Cf. *Gregorianum* 32 (1951) 562, note 68.

9. Karl Rahner, "The Position of Christology in the Church between Exegesis and Dogmatics," *Theological Investigations,* vol. 11, London: Darton, Longman and Todd, 1974, p. 198.

10. Karl Rahner, "On the Theology of the Incarnation," *Theological Investigations,* vol. 4, London: Darton, Longman and Todd, 1974, p. 117.

11. See Karl Rahner, "Dogmatic Reflections on the Knowledge and Self-consciousness of Christ," *Theological Investigations,* vol. 5, London: Darton, Longman and Todd, 1975, pp. 193-215; Id., "Current Problems in Christology," *Theological Investigations,* vol. 1, London: Darton, Longman and Todd, 1974, pp. 149-200.

12. See Denzinger and Schönmetzer, *Enchiridion,* n.294; Neuner and Dupuis, *The Christian Faith,* n.612.

13. See Denzinger and Schönmetzer, *Enchiridion,* n.557; Neuner and Dupuis, *The Christian Faith,* n.636.

14. See text in Denzinger and Schönmetzer, *Enchiridion,* n.3645; Neuner and Dupuis, *The Christian Faith,* n.651/1.

15. See text in Denzinger and Schönmetzer, *Enchiridion,* n.3812; Neuner and Dupuis, *The Christian Faith,* n.661.

16. *De diversis quaestionibus* I,65, PL 40,60.

17. See Denzinger and Schönmetzer, *Enchiridion,* n.3812; Neuner and Dupuis, *The Christian Faith,* n.661. See also *Mediator Dei,* n.17 where Heb 10:7 is applied to the moment of the incarnation.

18. See Denzinger and Schönmetzer, *Enchiridion,* n.3646; Neuner and Dupuis, *The Christian Faith,* n.651/2.

19. Karl Adam, *The Christ of Faith,* London: Burns and Oates, 1957, p. 271.

20. Raymond E. Brown, *Jesus God and Man,* Milwaukee: Bruce Publishing, 1967, pp. 78-79.

21. See Edward Schillebeeckx, *Christ the Sacrament of Encounter with God,* London: Sheed and Ward, 1966, pp. 18-21.

22. See Ignace de la Potterie, *La prière de Jésus,* Paris: Desclée, 1990; Witold Marchel, *Abba Père. La prière du Christ et des chrétiens,* Roma: PIB, 1971; Joachim Jeremias, *Abba,* Göttingen: Vandenhoeck, 1966.

23. See Paul Glorieux, "Le Christ adorateur du Père," *Revue des sciences religieuses* 23 (1949), pp. 249ff; mostly 266-267.

24. Karl Rahner, "Theos in the New Testament," *Theological Investigations,* vol. 1, London: Darton, Longman and Todd, pp. 79-148. For the disputed texts of Paul, cf. chapter 3, n. 13.

25. It is difficult to agree with Karl Rahner when, speaking of the human centre of activity or human self-consciousness of the Logos, he writes that it "faces the eternal Word in a genuinely human attitude of adoration, obedience. . . ." See "Current Problems in Christology," *Theological Investigations,* vol. 1, London: Darton, Longman and Todd, 1974, p. 158. As we have shown earlier, the human psychological ego cannot be severed from the ontological personhood of the Son. Worship and obedience belong to the Son-in-humanity and are addressed to the Father.

26. See mostly Hans Urs von Balthasar, *La foi du Christ,* Paris: Aubier, 1968; Jacques Guillet, *La foi de Jésus-Christ,* Paris: Desclée, 1980; also Piet Schoonenberg, *The Christ,* London: Sheed and Ward, 1971, pp. 146-152; Jon Sobrino, *Christology at the Cross-roads,* London: SCM Press, 1978, pp. 79-145; Gerald O'Collins, "The Faith of Jesus," *Theological Studies* 53 (1992) 403-423.

27. The passsive voice of *kinèthènai* must be understood in the sense of the mediate voice ("move itself"); otherwise the strong opposition (*de*), marked between the first and the second member of the sentence is not intelligible.

28. See text in Denzinger and Schönmetzer, *Enchiridion,* n.556; Neuner and Dupuis, *The Christian Faith,* nn.635-637.

29. See text in Denzinger and Schönmetzer, *Enchiridion,* n.301; Neuner and Dupuis, *The Christian Faith,* n.614.

30. See text in Denzinger and Schönmetzer, *Enchiridion,* n.539; Neuner and Dupuis, *The Christian Faith,* n.634.

31. See text in Denzinger and Schönmetzer, *Enchiridion,* n.1347; Neuner and Dupuis, *The Christian Faith,* n.646.

32. See text of canon 12 in Denzinger and Schönmetzer, *Enchiridion,* n.434; Neuner and Dupuis, *The Christian Faith,* n.621.

33. See text of canon 4 in Denzinger and Schönmetzer, *Enchiridion,* n.504; Neuner and Dupuis, *The Christian Faith,* n.627/4.

34. See text in Denzinger and Schönmetzer, *Enchiridion,* n.801; Neuner and Dupuis, *The Christian Faith,* n.20.

35. See text in Denzinger and Schönmetzer, *Enchiridion,* n.1337; Neuner and Dupuis, *The Christian Faith,* n.644.

36. See, for instance, Jürgen Moltmann, *The Crucified God,* New York: Harper and Row, 1974. In the same line, Hans Urs von Balthasar, "Mysterium Paschale," in Johannes Feiner and Magnus Löhrer (eds.), *Mysterium Salutis,* vol.III, 2, *Das Christusereignis,* Einsiedeln: Benziger Verlag, 1969, pp. 133-326.

37. See text in Denzinger and Schönmetzer, *Enchiridion,* n.556; Neuner and Dupuis, *The Christian Faith,* n.635.

38. See *Contra Gentiles* II,22; "Cum ... liber sit qui sui causa est, illud libere agimus quod ex nobis ipsis agimus" (As he is free who is cause of himself, our free actions are those which we posit from our very self).

39. Karl Rahner, "On the Theology of the Incarnation," *Theological Investigations* vol. 4, London: Darton, Longman and Todd, 1974, p. 117.

6

Jesus Christ the Universal Saviour

Between Christology and soteriology there exists a dialectic, or mutual interaction. We have shown that the soteriological motive has been the springboard and point of departure of the Church's reflection on the mystery of Jesus Christ, both in the apostolic and the later tradition. The question that needed to be answered was: *Who* is Jesus Christ in himself and in relation to God if, as the Church experienced and believed, we have been saved in him and through him? Christology needs to keep in touch with its soteriological foundation at every step of its elaboration. On the other hand, a reflective Christology becomes in turn the starting point for a deeper perception and an explicit treatment of the soteriological mystery. A more profound understanding of *who* Jesus Christ is allows for new insights into the mystery of our salvation in him. In this sense we have spoken of the need to travel the road twice, from one end to the other and vice versa, and of making a full circle.

The present study must be limited to the first way of traveling the road, that is, to Christology proper; it remains open to an explicit treatment of soteriology. Christology proper cannot, however, dispense with asking questions about the inner significance of the mystery of Jesus Christ. What is the ultimate meaning, in God's own mind, of the christological mystery? Why is Jesus Christ central to Christian faith, and what does this centrality imply? In one question: Jesus Christ—why and what for?

This question has different aspects, all equally important. One consists in asking what God's intention is in devising an order of things in which God's self-communication to human beings is made dependent on the historical incarnation and death on the cross of God's Son. Why has God placed Jesus Christ at the centre of the plan of salvation for humankind? Another is to seek how the divine plan unfolds itself through the history of humankind and the world. Assuming that God has placed Jesus Christ at the centre of the plan, what place does the historical event of Jesus Christ occupy in the history of salvation through which God's plan unfolds in history? Connected with these questions is that of the uniqueness and universality of Jesus Christ, Saviour of all humankind—the decisive problem that Christology must answer.

But, again, this problem has different dimensions. One consists in asking the meaning of Jesus Christ for and in the context of the created world and human history. It seeks to situate the Christ-event, according to God's plan, in the history of the cosmos as we know it today, with its immensely increased proportions in space and time. Another, which is attracting the attention of theologians today, consists in seeking the meaning of Christ and the place of the Christ-event in the vast context of the plurality of human cultures and religious traditions. The first way of seeking the place of Jesus Christ in God's plan will naturally lead to a cosmic Christology; the other will call for a Christology of religious plurality. The two parts of this chapter will be dedicated to these two problematics.

Before entering into our material in more explicit detail, let us briefly state the question in its essentials. Very broadly, we wish to know whether the traditional christocentric perspective of Christian faith is still defensible in the new context created by the discoveries of modern science and religious pluralism as we know and live it today. At stake is the traditional Christocentrism of Christian theology, whose profound, seemingly irreducible demands are now judged by some to be passé and no longer defensible. Let us briefly recall these demands.

The uniqueness of Jesus Christ and the universal meaning of the Christ-event represent more than a central belief for Christian tradition. These truths are seen as the very foundation of faith. They have always been, and still are, a stumbling block for those who do not share our faith. To be sure, uniqueness and universality are understood here in the strict sense. We traditionally affirm that Jesus is unique, not only as any person whom God chose as the vehicle of divine self-revelation and self-manifestation would necessarily be unique—so that consequently any divine revelation resulting from this would also be unique—but in the sense that, by and in Jesus Christ, God effected a self-manifestation in a manner that is decisive and can be neither surpassed nor repeated.

It is the same with the universality of the meaning of Christ. Traditionally for the Christian that meaning includes not only the irresistible call represented by the human Jesus for all those who draw near to him, but also the scope and influence of Jesus and his work for the salvation of women and men in every time and place. Jesus is at the centre of God's design for the world and of the process by which this design is deployed in history. In Jesus, God undertook an irrevocable commitment to humanity, in an irrevocable acceptance of that humanity. The human condition of the human Jesus—his words, his deeds, his life, his death, and his resurrection—constitutes God's decisive, and in this sense, final, revelation. However we may formulate this primacy of his, Christ is "the centre." This is the traditional heart of the Christian faith.

However, this uniqueness and universality are not exclusive, but inclu-

sive; not closed, but open; not sectarian, but cosmic. Thus, as regards religious pluralism, the theologies of a Christ present but "hidden" and
"unknown" in the world's religious traditions, or of an "anonymous Christianity," along with still other theologies, strive to reconcile the traditional
Christian position regarding Jesus with the reality of various manifestations.
Christ as mystery is God turning toward men and women in self-manifestation and self-revelation. The Christic mystery, therefore, is present wherever God enters into the life of human beings in an experience of the divine
presence. Nevertheless, this mystery remains anonymous in a certain sense
for whoever has not been enabled, thanks to the Christian revelation, to
recognize it in the human condition of Jesus of Nazareth. All have the
experience of the Christic mystery, but Christians alone are in a position
to give it its name. The Christ of faith is inseparable from the Jesus of
history; but his presence and activity are not limited to the confines of the
Christian fold.

Notwithstanding its favourable approach to other religious traditions,
the theology of the cosmic Christ — or better, of the cosmic meaning of
Jesus Christ — is in danger today of appearing tragically esoteric for some,
who scarcely appreciate being called and regarded as "anonymous Christians," as well as for others — Christians in this case — who regard it as no
longer possible to maintain. True, the uniqueness and universal meaning
of Jesus the Christ create inescapable theological problems. Inasmuch as,
and to the extent that, the Christic mystery is bound up with the Jesus of
history, faith in Christ as the centre involves a claim that may appear incon-
gruous: the attribution of universal meaning to a particular historical event!
The empirical fact of Jesus of Nazareth is essentially conditioned by time
and space. How then can it acquire a universal scope in the realm of
relations between God and human beings?

The difficulty is as old as Christology itself, but it has acquired renewed
importance in recent times. The altogether new dimensions, temporal and
spatial, that the world has gained under the impulse of contemporary science, call, it is said, for a "Copernican revolution" to lay to rest for good
all the "provincial" theology of the prescientific human being. To this must
be added the numerous questions raised among Christians, including theologians, on the basis of their new awareness of religious pluralism in the
world.

All of these considerations conspire to pose the urgent question formulated above: Is traditional Christocentrism still viable? The question
deserves an answer.

JESUS CHRIST IN WORLD AND HISTORY

Jesus Christ at the Centre of Faith

"Christianity is Christ," we have said at the beginning of this work. The
formulation is right, but it is important to understand it correctly. We must

make a distinction. The Christianity lived by Christians or by the Church is not Christ. But Jesus Christ, his person and his work, are at the centre of Christian faith. Indeed, we must say that Jesus Christ occupies in Christian faith a central, unique place such as no other religion attributes to its founder. For Islam, Muhammad is the prophet through whom God speaks, the depository of the divine message, as it were. For Buddhism, Gautama is the Enlightened One showing the way, and in this sense the great teacher. For the Christian, however, it is the mystery of Jesus Christ himself, and not just his message, that is at the very centre of faith. The message and the Messenger blend into one. Christianity is not a "religion of the book," then, in the sense that Islam is. Christianity is the religion of a person, the Christ.[1]

The New Testament forthrightly attests that Jesus Christ is personally at the centre of the Christian faith. Pauline theology puts this in a most striking way when, after having considered as mystery (*mustèrion*), or divine plan, the common inheritance bestowed on the Jews and the nations (see Eph 3:5-7), it comes to identify the mystery with the very person of Jesus Christ (cf. Col 1:26-27; 2:2; see also 1 Tim 3:6). For the Pauline school, Jesus Christ is the sole mediator between God and humankind (see 1 Tim 2:5), precisely at the point at which Paul is stressing the divine will that all men be saved (see 1 Tim 2:4). Such is the clarity with which Jesus Christ appears to him to be the very realization of that will.[2]

Peter thought no differently in his discourse to the Sanhedrin reported in Acts: "There is no other name under heaven given to men by which we must be saved" (see Acts 4:12). We know that the name stands for the person. We could cite the great hymns of Paul and his school, the trinitarian hymn of Ephesians 1:1-13 and the christological hymn of Colossians 1:15-20. Everywhere Christ appears at the centre of the divine work. We could likewise note the New Testament texts, in and out of the Gospels, in which Jesus so clearly emerges as universal Saviour (Jn 3:17; Acts 10:44-48; 17:24-31; etc.). Perhaps such a listing would be superfluous. After all, it is abundantly clear that this is the message of the New Testament in its entirety, the assertion underlying every part of it, the deep faith without which none of the books that comprise it — Gospels, letters, history, treatise — would have been written or be comprehensible.

Let us touch very briefly on the postapostolic tradition. It is arresting to observe that in the analytic table of his magisterial work on the Christology of the Fathers and the councils, A. Grillmeier thought it unnecessary to list an entry on the uniqueness of Jesus Christ.[3] I believe that this absence — surprising at first sight — can be explained by the fact that, for the patristic era, the uniqueness of Jesus Christ, the universal Saviour, was outside the purview of theological discussion, being precisely at the centre of faith. The problem to be attended to was not the fact, but the why and the how. That is, what is it about the personal identity of Jesus Christ that renders the Jesus Christ event unique and unrepeatable? I have written:

One point should be clear as regards the patristic attitude to the uniqueness of Jesus Christ: it is the corner stone of the whole edifice of Christian faith, everywhere implied in the elaboration of doctrine. ... [The Fathers] found the reason for the uniqueness of Jesus Christ in the very nature and exigencies of the incarnational economy of salvation manifested in him. If, as they believed, the Word had become man in Jesus Christ, it was clear that this event could not but be one and have universal, cosmic implications and repercussions.[4]

But is recent Christian tradition stamped with the same Christocentrism as the ancient tradition was? The question has been broached of the Christocentrism of Vatican II. Was the council not too strongly focused on the Church, whether in itself or in its relations *ad extra* (the world, other religions, ecumenism) so that Christ does not appear as its authentic centre?[5] This would not be an altogether fair statement of the case. Over the course of its sessions, the council surely moved toward a more explicit Christocentrism (and pneumatology). Its great christological texts are to be found in the Pastoral Constitution *Gaudium et Spes* (nos. 22, 32, 45, etc.). Indeed, as Paul VI insisted on more than one occasion, in seeking to grasp its own mystery in greater depth, the Church of Vatican II found itself compelled, as it were, to return to the mystery of Jesus Christ that is its source and raison d'être.[6]

This is the viewpoint that we must adopt if we would acquire an adequate perspective on the definition of the Church selected and promulgated by the council from among so many different images: that of the Church as universal sacrament of salvation (cf. *Lumen Gentium,* nos. 1, 48; *Ad Gentes,* no. 1; *Gaudium et Spes,* nos. 42, 45). The Church is "in some way in Christ the sacrament, both the sign and means of intimate union with God and the unity of the whole human race" (*Lumen Gentium,* no. 1). In other words, since Christ is salvation itself, the Church is defined as the sacrament of Christ. Just as Christ himself is the primordial sacrament of the encounter with God, so the Church in turn is the sacrament of Jesus Christ.[7]

But this definition implies a radical decentering of the Church, which now finds itself altogether centred on the mystery of Jesus Christ. He, we might say, is the absolute mystery; the Church, by contrast, is the derived, relative mystery. (Who can fail to see how powerfully such a theological definition of the mystery of the Church militates against concepts of the Church as readily conducive to ecclesiological inflation as is, for example, J. Moeller's "continuous incarnation"?) Proceeding logically from the conciliar definition of the mystery of the Church, we should arrive at a comprehensive christocentric perspective that goes beyond the ecclesiocentric approach.

THE MEANING OF CHRIST IN THE DIVINE PLAN

We have just quoted one of the most explicit texts of the New Testament on the role of Jesus Christ as the universal mediator between God and humanity. God has chosen to save all human beings in him. For Christian faith, this is a fact — a fact, for that matter, whose internal reason has always been a theological problem. The whole of Christian tradition, biblical and postbiblical alike, has inquired about the meaning of Jesus Christ in the divine plan — or, as it has been put, on the motive of the Incarnation. If, as must be understood, not only the creation of the human being called by God to share the divine life, but also the salvation of sinful humanity in Jesus Christ are, and can only be, free and gratuitous deeds of God, the question must be asked: What intrinsic motive or reason can have fixed the choice made by God of a universal salvation effected by the death on the cross, in a determinate time and place, of a human being, Jesus of Nazareth, who claimed to be, and who was, the Son of God?

The particularity of the salvific event and the universal value attributed to it have always been a scandal — a scandal that becomes all the greater if one takes into account the seeming triviality of the event in its historical context and the pluralism of human cultures and religious traditions. The question of the meaning of Christ in the divine plan appears thus in all its amplitude.

The question that has been more or less explicitly posed throughout the whole of Christian tradition was put more clearly in Saint Anselm's *Cur Deus Homo* and later became one of the great theological debates between the Thomists and the Scotists.[8] Here it will suffice to offer a rapid sketch of the basic positions, discuss them summarily to bring out their respective lacunae, and seek a more satisfactory response.

Saint Anselm has often been understood to say that the redemption of sinful humanity requires that God receive justice — the theory of "adequate satisfaction." The offense to God is in one way infinite (by reason of its Object). Adequate satisfaction can be offered only by Jesus Christ, the human being who was God. Thus the Incarnation seemed necessary for the redemption of humanity. This statement of the case presupposed a vengeful, vindictive image of God and a juridical conception of the mystery of salvation, as if it were a matter of appeasing an angry God, which runs counter to the message of the New Testament, where the redemption appears essentially as a mystery of love.[9]

Saint Thomas was not deceived here, and to avoid the negative consequences of a similar conception, he reduced the apparent divine intent in Jesus Christ to "reasons of suitability." Surely the Incarnation was not necessary for the salvation of humanity; still, it was appropriate that the incarnate Son satisfy, as he alone was capable of doing, the demands of justice and earn the salvation of humanity. In the divine plan, then, Jesus Christ was essentially ordered to the redemption, to the point that it was correct to say that if humanity had not had to be saved from sin, the Incarnation would not have occurred. Thus Jesus Christ was reduced to his redemptive function, and a Christic world was purely incidental. Furthermore, Jesus Christ was an afterthought in the divine plan, which now consisted rather in two successive, superimposed plans.

The Scotist reaction ensued. Jesus could not be reduced to an after-thought in God's plan for humanity and the cosmos. Jesus Christ had been willed by God from the beginning of the mystery of creation. He was, as Saint Paul so clearly indicated, the crown and centre, indeed the very prin-ciple of intelligibility, of the created world. He was not willed by God essentially as Saviour. He had become Saviour only incidentally, in view of humanity's sin and need for redemption. Even if humans had not sinned, the Son would have become incarnate in Jesus Christ to crown creation as the divine plan had decreed. Thus, with Jesus Christ the redeemer only incidentally, the world was essentially Christian, being thought and willed by God in Jesus Christ from the beginning.

The Scotist thesis—which is surely closer to the New Testament mes-sage—has the merit of expanding Christ's function vis-à-vis humanity and the world. Its Christocentrism is more accentuated and more radical. Its flaw is the same as that of the Thomist thesis: It supposes two successive plans in the mind of God. While for Saint Thomas, Jesus Christ is absent from the divine plan in a first stage and enters it as Saviour only in a second stage, for Duns Scotus and his successors, Jesus Christ is central to the divine plan from the beginning but becomes Saviour only in a second stage in function of humanity's sin.

It would little serve our purpose to go further into the discussion that continues to divide the two camps or even to dwell on certain "conciliatory perspectives" that seek—perhaps in vain—to combine them. What we need is a more adequate response to the question, "Why Jesus Christ?"—a response at once deeply scriptural and theologically satisfying. It is actually a matter of overcoming or transcending the problematic of the two opposed camps, which seems too narrow. It is too narrow, particularly, in its undue distinction between two successive stages in the divine plan, as if the divine thinking could be fragmented by time. It is also too narrow in its undue reduction of the gratuity of Jesus Christ as a divine gift of salvation. We must ask ourselves what, in the divine plan for humanity (which is only one), is the meaning of the Jesus Christ event—whose entire gratuity on God's part we acknowledge a priori—both in the order of creation, in which God already called the human being to share in the divine life itself, and then in the plan of the redemption, by which God reestablishes the human being in that life. In other words, what is the meaning of Jesus Christ in the gift of being, the gift of the divine self, and the forgiveness of sins?

It seems that we must say that God's formal intent in Jesus Christ is to inject the divine gift of self into humanity as deeply as can be, into the very stuff of the humanity that is called to share the divine life. In other words, to make the divine self-bestowal as immanent as possible. The plenary insertion of God's self-communication into the human race—the total immanence of the divine self-bestowal upon humanity—consists precisely in God's personal self-insertion into the human family and its history, that is, in the mystery of the Incarnation of the Son of God in Jesus Christ. This can be called the principle of God's creative and restorative "immanent self-communication."

If Jesus Christ is Head of created humanity, which is called and restored in him by God—without any need to distinguish successive moments in the divine plan—the explanation is this: In this personal insertion of himself as Son of God into our human condition and history, Jesus Christ has actually placed God within our reach, along with the gift to us of the divine life itself, given on our own level. As Edward Schillebeeckx puts it, while in the Old Testament itself God is already a God-of-humanity, in Jesus Christ, God becomes a God-of-human-beings-in-human-fashion. Indeed, "Christ is God in a human way, and a human in a divine way."[10] This is the key to Christ's actualization in himself of the total—and totally immanent—gift of God to humanity. G. Martelet takes the same direction when, in an article on the motive of the Incarnation, he writes:

> The immediate premise of the Incarnation is not . . . *sin*, but *adoption;* in adoption itself, the essential is not *redemption* as such, but *deification*. . . . Adoption corresponds in us to what Incarnation is in [Christ]: "Being Son of God, he came to make himself son of man, and to grant us, who were children of human beings, to become children of God." In us, then, adoption is the counterpart of what Incarnation is in Christ. . . . Incarnation is our adoption *qua* founded in Christ, and our adoption, in turn, from this viewpoint, the Incarnation of Christ *qua* operative in us.[11]

But is this response to the question, "Why Jesus Christ?" anything more than a theologoumenon among others? Or does it actually present itself as being in profound harmony with the message of the New Testament? Surely the latter is the case. Suffice it to allude here to certain more characteristic passages, such as John 3:16-17, in which the coming of the Son into the world is presented as the paroxysm of the Father's love for humanity, and 1 John 1:1-2, where Jesus Christ, Son of the Father, figures as principle of life, deeply inserted into the very stuff of the human. The most eloquent text, however, is the passage in the Letter to the Romans in which St. Paul establishes a parallel between the two Adams that strikes us all the more by dint of its repetition. In the space of a few verses (Rom 5:12-21), the parallel between Adam and Jesus Christ is either amplified or sketched out no less than six times. The key word throughout the passage is *anthròpos*. It is by the grace of a single *human being,* Jesus Christ, that God has communicated the divine gift, just as it was by a single *human being* that sin had entered the world. Saint Paul is not asserting merely that redemption has been wrought in Jesus Christ, but that it has been wrought by a *human being,* therefore in a manner immanent to humanity itself. The parallel between Jesus and Adam is invoked with a view to a more effective emphasis on the human causality in the free gift of God in Jesus Christ.

We cannot show here that patristic tradition has often understood the mystery of Christ in the same fashion. It was to bring out the immanence of the divine gift made to humanity in Jesus Christ that the Fathers insisted not only on the integrity of Jesus' human nature but on his real identification with the concrete condition of sinful humanity. He sought us out on the level on which we found ourselves. This is the purport of the familiar axioms often repeated by the patristic tradition. "God has become a human being that we may be divinized." But to this end, God must have assumed all that is human, for "what has not been assumed has not been saved." The marvelous exchange between God and the human being in Jesus Christ, of which the Fathers have spoken, required that God first descend to us in Jesus, that in him God might exalt us to divinity.

We must, however, face the problems that are surely posed by the divine plan in Jesus Christ, or the economy of the Incarnation, as we have felt constrained to represent it here. These problems are not new, although they become more urgent and acute in the context of modern science and religious pluralism. As we have seen, in Jesus Christ, God seeks to be a God-of-human-beings-in-human-fashion. But is not this intrusion upon humanity on God's part terribly inhuman? Doubtless the economy of the Incarnation represents on God's part the fullest possible gift of the divine self to humanity. One may also think that it implies on God's part the most profound respect for human dignity without injury to human freedom. Still it seems scandalous, inequitable, and unjust to make the gift of salvation dependent on a necessarily particular, allegedly unique historical event. St. Thomas appears to have admitted the possibility of multiple incarnations. Would they not have seemed desirable to avoid in part the particularity of the single event? This solution however, appears precluded in the New Testament. We need only think of the Pauline "once and for all" (*ephapax*) and of the Letter to the Hebrews. From the Christian viewpoint, it would actually have been superfluous, since "by his Incarnation the Son of God in some sort united himself to every man" (*Gaudium et Spes,* no. 22) and the whole of humanity to God's self. By the Jesus Christ event, a knot that can never more be undone has bound God to humanity. Nor can that event be repeated.

However, the scandal of the temporal and spatial particularity of the event abides. It is discernible in the thinking of the Fathers themselves. In terms of the biblical chronology, according to which 4000 years separated Christ from Adam, the Fathers wondered why Christ had come so late. They replied that humanity had to be prepared for his coming. In the gigantic perspectives that modern science has opened on the history of the world and humanity, that answer may well seem ridiculous. The question only becomes all the more urgent — and the particularity of the event the more scandalous — even if the opposite question too might have to be asked: Why so soon?

However this may be, in the context of the plurality of cultures and religious traditions that we experience today, the spatial particularity of the Jesus Christ event may be even more scandalous. That one particular culture could have received, nearly exclusively, the legacy of a solitary salvation event, an event occurring in a particular religious tradition, seems to constitute a belittling of humanity's other religious traditions and cultures — those of Asia, for example, which are actually older, and certainly no less rich. It is practically impossible to exaggerate the sense of sectarism and parochialism, indeed of arrogance and intolerance, experienced by so many Asians, thoughtful Hindus or Buddhists, when they are confronted with what Christianity claims for such a historically obscure (even though we have better access to it today) event as that of Jesus of Nazareth.

In Eastern eyes, an economy of incarnation as Christianity understands it could never lay claim to universality. Is not the Hindu teaching of the *avataras* more human — and ultimately more divine — in virtue of the very multiplicity of the divine manifestations it posits? The question stands out in all its sharpness: Is the claim of universality that Christianity makes for the Jesus Christ event still possible to sustain? Is it enough, in order to defend it today, to call it "not exclusive, but inclusive"? And what is the actual purpose of such distinctions? In the last analysis, does the traditional Christocentrism of Christian theology stand up to the shock of the current encounter of cultures and religious traditions? These questions will have to be answered. Meanwhile, let us observe, with Karl Rahner, that the most urgent christological task today surely consists in demonstrating the universal significance and cosmic dimension of the Jesus Christ event,[12] with Christ as the pinnacle of salvation history and Christology as that history's sharpest formulation.[13]

A cosmic Christology would, in the first place, have to show the cosmic dimension of the Incarnation, that is, the significance of Jesus Christ not only for the salvation of human beings and their history, but for the whole universe. It would also have to illustrate the relationship between the theology of the Incarnation and the scientific understanding of the universe, and integrate into a holistic vision of reality creation, incarnation, salvation and consummation.[14] A foundation for such a cosmic Christology is not wanting in the New Testament, least of all in Pauline theology (cf. Col 1:15-20; Eph 1:15-23; 2:10) and in John (cf. Jn 1:1-18).

The underlying unity between creation and "re-creation" in Jesus Christ is placed in striking relief when seen in the context of an evolutionary view of the world.[15] Showing this was the intention of P. Teilhard de Chardin when he conceived the world evolutionary process as "Christogenesis."[16] In that view, Jesus Christ is seen at once as the springboard, the driving force and the goal that draws to itself, of cosmic evolution; the beginning, the middle and the end; the first and the last, the Alpha and the Omega. The cosmic Christ, or Omega point, acts as the final cause that directs the entire cosmos to its last end, until God be "everything in everything" (1 Cor 15:28).

This cosmic Christ is the historical Jesus, dead and risen. Nor could he be the Omega point if he had not first been inserted into the "phylum" of the human race and the heart of matter. Again, the Jesus of history who has become the Christ of faith—or, in Teilhard's own terms—Jesus and the "universal Christ"—were intended in God's design for both humankind and the cosmos. In this way, Teilhard hoped to combine together and show the "convergence" that obtained between his scientific "faith" in the evolutionary process of the world and his Christian faith in the cosmic Christ, which he read especially in St. Paul. Teilhard wrote:

> Christ is the Alpha and the Omega, the principle and the end, the foundation stone and the corner stone, the fulfilment and the fulfiller. He brings all things to completion and gives to all things their consistence. . . . He is the unique centre, precious and coherent, which shines forth at the apex of the world still forthcoming.[17]

A "Christified universe" or, to put it the other way round, a "universal Christ," is what Teilhard had in view. We must "frankly Christify evolution."[18] "The universe and Christ, each on his side, find their fulfilment in mutual conjunction."[19] "To discern this marvellous coincidence . . . between Christ directly perceived as the spring of evolution (*comme évoluteur*) and as the cosmic focus which evolution positively requires" is the privilege of the Christian. To the Christian is given to perceive "the astonishing and liberating harmony which exists between a Christic type of religion and a convergent type of evolution."[20] Nor should we fear that the cosmos may take precedence over Christ. On the contrary, "far from obscuring Christ, the universe points to him as the guarantee of its consistence." The evolutionary view of the world does not draw Christ to the universe in such a way as to dissolve him in it. Rather, it is put to use so that the primacy of the risen Christ, already towering over the cosmos that he must one day bring to fulfillment, may be further enhanced. "O Christ ever greater."[21]

The Christ-event, Centre of Salvation History

Jesus Christ is at the centre of God's plan for the creation and "re-creation" of humankind and the cosmos. There remains to show that he is likewise at the centre of the "history of salvation" through which God accomplishes the saving design.

For Christianity, history has a direction, a goal set for it by God. This goal is the definitive fulfillment of the Reign of God. History is a process that—through contingent events and often despite their fortuitous character—is directed toward a transcendent goal: the fulness of the Reign of God. The Christian concept of history is essentially positive and optimistic. It has been called linear, which does not mean that all the elements constituting human history have a positive sense and contribute positively to the achievement of the end assigned by God to the historical process. However, throughout the vicissitudes of time and the interplay of freedoms, the certitude abides that the end decreed by God will one day be accomplished in plenitude. The Reign of God, gradually inaugurated in the world, will reach its term. We know where we are going.[22]

This so-called linear Christian concept of history is readily distinguished from other concepts. We may cite two of these: the so-called circular or cyclical concept characteristic of Greek philosophy and culture, and that of the Oriental philosophies, notably Hindu philosophy, which has been called spiral. Suffice it to recall that the Greek circular model of history is fundamentally pessimistic: Nothing is new under the sun.[23] As for the Hindu concept, even though using a different model, it shares the pessimism of Greek philosophy.[24]

The vast distance separating the Hebrew and Christian conception from the Greek and the Hindu is not without theological consequences for the meaning with which a historical salvific event may be invested. The Christian message, in particular the Christian signification of the Jesus Christ event, is, like it or not, inextricably bound up with a concept of history capable of bestowing all of its density on God's personal involvement in the history of human beings. We must draw one conclusion forthwith. True, the Christian message is in theory open to all cultures and called to express itself in each of them. This does not imply, however, the a priori capacity of that message to accommodate all it encounters in the religious traditions of humanity. Cultures can harbour elements not assimilable by the Christian message because there is no room in these elements themselves for that message. It is scarcely evident how a cyclical or spiral concept of history might leave room for the decisive value that Christianity attributes to the historical, particular Jesus Christ event as representing God's final commitment to humanity. The linear model is inescapable here. Apart from it, history cannot take on the authentic sense of a dialogue between God and humanity through God's historical interventions or have a final destiny actually assigned to it by God. Open as the Christian message would like to be to all cultures, it cannot renounce a view of the world and reality apart from which the Jesus Christ event would find itself bereft of its true sense and genuine meaning.

The history of this dialogue between God and humanity is a history of salvation. This does not mean that it is part of universal history as a part of the whole. True, salvation history is not formally identical with "profane" history; but it is materially coextensive with it. It, too, is universal. Salvation history is universal history itself *qua* salvation dialogue between God and humanity.[25] While distinct from profane history, it is inseparable from it.

This is tantamount to saying that salvation history extends from creation to the parousia of the risen Lord at the end of time. Creation is part of salvation history from the outset; it, too, is mystery of salvation. As we know, Israel's religious experience is totally founded on the covenant struck by Yahweh with the people through Moses, not on some philosophical consideration of creation. It is from a point of departure in the experience of the covenant, and by retrojection, that the mystery of divine creation enters Israel's awareness. Creation is first and foremost a salvation mystery, the starting point of the salvific dialogue between Yahweh and the people of Yahweh. This progressive reflection, leading from the covenant back to creation by retrojection, is part of Israel's long journey to the discovery of the one God, culminating in absolute monotheism, as concretely expressed in the *Shema Yisra'el* — "Hear, O Israel: Yahweh our God is one Yahweh! You shall love Yahweh your God with all your heart, with all your soul, and with all your strength" (Deut 6:4-5) — and as theologically established by the prophets, especially in Second Isaiah.

Thus salvation history extends from the beginning of history to its end, from creation to the end of the world. Christian faith places the Jesus Christ event at its centre. This is to be understood not chronologically, but theologically. The Jesus Christ event is the decisive event of salvation history — the pivot, we might say, upon which the entire history of the dialogue between God and humanity turns, the principle of intelligibility of the divine plan as made concrete in the history of the world. Well does Vatican II's Pastoral Constitution *Gaudium et Spes,* number 10, say that the key, the centre, and the end of all human history is found in Jesus Christ.

This text rightly speaks of a centre and an end. The apostolic faith distinguishes between the event of the coming of Jesus Christ into history and the Lord's eschatological return in the parousia. The Reign of God already inaugurated in the world through the historical Jesus — in his life, his death, and his resurrection — nevertheless is still only *in via* toward its eschatological perfection. As exegesis has shown, a tension prevails between the "already" and the "not yet" of the Reign of God. This tension is constitutive of the time called the "time of the Church," the time in which we live. In virtue of this tension, we can place the accent now on what has already occurred once and for all, not on what remains to be accomplished. As we have already recalled, a "realized" echatology has often been associated with the name of Charles H. Dodd, while a "consequent" eschatology bears that of Albert Schweitzer.

If we realize, however, that in the apostolic Church there was a widespread belief at first that the Lord's return was near and imminent, we shall more readily understand why the emphasis was more on what had already occurred — the historical Jesus Christ event that culminated in his death and resurrection. As Joachim Gnilka, in his contribution to the session of the Pontifical Biblical Commission on "Bible and Christology," said:

A "consequent" eschatology neglects a decisive factor in Jesus' proclamation of the Reign of God, namely: that not only is the *basileia* a *future* event, to which we look forward, but its healing, helping, saving forces are *already present and active* through Jesus' actions and preaching, and that they can be experienced by human beings. The relationship of tension thus established between a salvation already present and a salvation still to come is new, and has no parallel in Judaism. Jesus not only proclaims the *basileia;* he also conveys it. This is why he alone could make such a proclamation.[26]

For the apostolic faith, as for Christian faith thereafter, while our whole present history is steeped in a tension between the already and the not yet — a tension that we must not seek to dissolve — the accent is nonetheless on what has already been accomplished once and for all by God in Jesus Christ.

Oscar Cullmann has excellently shown the contrast prevailing between Israel's religious psychology and that of the first Christians.[27] Israel was totally turned to the future — to the fulfillment of Yahweh's promise and the messianic expectations to be accomplished in a decisive, eschatological salvation event — without knowing when that event was to take place. The apostolic Church discovered, to its astonishment and wonder, that this eschatological event had actually taken place in the immediate past, in Jesus' resurrection from the dead. Thus Jesus' resurrection, the starting point of a christological faith, wrought a 180-degree turn among the first Christians. The faith of their forebears had been oriented to an indefinite future, while the paschal experience riveted their attention on a definite event they had experienced in the immediate past. Not that the first Christians' orientation to the future simply vanished, but their eschatological expectancy was now divided into two times: the already and the not yet — the event accomplished, and its final plenitude. Meanwhile, the role of the axis connecting these twin poles, the pivot of salvation history, fell unambiguously to the already. Christ raised, not the parousia, was at the centre of their faith. The rest — the not yet — would follow as the sure outcome, as a totally reliable development of the potential of the past event. To be sure, the air is electric with the expectancy of the fulness of the Reign of God, the parousia, but it is the Jesus Christ event that is at the centre of salvation history.

That the pivot of salvation history is the already accomplished by the Christ-event does not dispense us from our responsibilities in history. On the contrary. Because Jesus Christ died and is risen, we live in a world that is already saved in principle. Its actual liberation, however, depends on our free cooperation with God's offer of grace. The salvation of the world in Jesus Christ is both a gift and a task. Speaking in terms of the Kingdom inaugurated by God in history, this means that women and men are called to cooperate with God to its advancement and growth. They respond to this calling by the practice and promotion of the values of the Reign of God propounded by Jesus: justice, sisterhood/brotherhood, peace, freedom. Jesus' own praxis teaches us that the Reign of God is being prospered where and when the promotion of justice, healing, forgiveness and reconciliation happen. Liberation Christology, for its part, has shown that the presence and development of the Reign of God is disclosed primarily through the praxis of human liberation; that is, by bringing about justice where injustice prevails and overcoming the ensuing suffering of the poor and the oppressed, whereby Good News is announced to them.

Far from dispensing women and men from a concrete involvement in a liberating praxis — as though, all having been accomplished, there remained no historical task to fulfill — the pivotal role in salvation history of the historical event of Jesus Christ is at once the foundation and the necessary condition for such an involvement. No liberation praxis could contribute to the growth of the Reign of God in history if the Reign had not first been inaugurated by God in the historical event of Jesus Christ. It is this event that opens the way to liberation for us. Moreover, the liberation praxis of Jesus himself throughout his human life and the mystery of his death and resurrection constitute the one paradigm for the growth of the Kingdom in history. Discipleship in relation to Jesus — in whichever way, conscious or unconscious — is the gate through which one enters the Kingdom and cooperates in its growth. The Reign of God cannot merely be viewed as an eschatological reality drawing us toward it by way of a final cause. It needs to be seen primarily as a reality already present and operative, empowering us to contribute our share to its expansion and increment. The interim period of salvation history between the Christ-event and the parousia of the Lord is that of the growth through history of the Kingdom of God as it looks toward its eschatological fulness. Women and men of every generation are called by God to be co-creators and co-builders of this Reign of God.

JESUS CHRIST AND WORLD RELIGIONS

CENTRALITY OF JESUS CHRIST IN THE THEOLOGY OF RELIGIONS

In its Decree on Ecumenism, *Unitatis Redintegratio,* number 11, Vatican Council II introduced the important consideration of an order, or hierarchy, of truths of Catholic teaching. It explains the principle according to which this hierarchy of truths is established in terms of a different relation to the foundation of faith. What the council does not explicitly say is that the foundation of faith governing the hierarchy of truths is the mystery of Jesus Christ, but this emerges from what has been said above on the Christocentrism of Vatican II in general and the relativity of the mystery of the Church in particular.

If we pursue this line of thought opened by Vatican II and apply it explicitly to the theology of religions, we can draw important conclusions. After all, the real question is that of the relationship of the religious traditions of humankind to the primordial mystery of Jesus Christ, the foundation of faith — not of their relation to the mystery of the Church, which is itself a derived truth. It is, therefore, a question of an ecclesiological decentring and a christological recentring of the theology of religions. A correct outlook enjoins an investigation of the vertical relation of the other religious traditions to the mystery of Christ present and at work in the world, not of their horizontal relationship to the Church. Let us see if we are able to extract the immediate implications of this change of perspective.

A certain Church tradition has posed the problem in terms of the horizontal relationship of the other religions to Christianity or to the mystery of the Church. The adage, "Outside the Church there is no salvation" has been the vehicle of this limited perspective. But it is important to observe that the adage in question, *Extra ecclesiam nulla salus,* originated in a different context from that to which it has been more recently applied.[28] It is borrowed from Fulgentius of Ruspe, who applies it not only to pagans but to Jews, and even to Christians who have separated themselves from the Church, whether by schism or heresy.[29] To culpably separate oneself from the Church is tantamount to separating oneself from Christ, the source of salvation.

When the adage is cited in official texts of the magisterium, as in the thirteenth century by the creed of the Fourth Council of the Lateran (1215)[30] and in the fourteenth century by the Bull *Unam Sanctam* (1302) of Boniface VIII,[31] it seems to be intended to refer to those who find themselves outside the Church voluntarily and culpably. The first text of the Church magisterium explicitly to extend its usage beyond heretics and schismatics to pagans and Jews is the Decree for the Jacobites (1442) of the Council of Florence.[32] In the historical context, however, the primary intention of the council continues to be to apply the adage to those who have separated themselves from the Church and who have not been united (*aggregati*) to it before the end of their lives.[33]

These circumstances permit a reduction of the scope of the adage on which an overly narrow ecclesiocentric view of salvation has traditionally been based, even apart from the doubts that prevail as to the properly dogmatic value of the decree of the Council of Florence. However this may be, the adage implied a faulty statement of the question. The requirements for access to salvation were envisaged in a negative way and in virtue of an ecclesiocentric outlook. They should have been enunciated positively, in a christocentric perspective. Thus corrected, the adage would have read, "All salvation is through Christ," and thus would have been in perfect conformity with the New Testament proposition mentioned above.

Has Vatican Council II adopted this positive and christocentric perspective where it addresses the mystery of the salvation of the members of other religious traditions? Or has it prolonged the narrow ecclesiocentric perspective, perhaps in spite of the acknowledgment it makes of certain positive values within these same traditions? An absolute answer to this question cannot be given. On the one side, regarding the salvation of individual persons living beyond the pale of Christianity, the council adopts a decidedly christocentric perspective in the Pastoral Constitution *Gaudium et Spes,* where, having expanded the manner in which the Christian receives salvation in function of his or her association to the paschal mystery of Jesus Christ, the document continues:

> All this holds true not only for Christians, but for all men of good will in whose hearts grace works in an unseen way. For, since Christ died for all men, and since the ultimate vocation of man is in fact one, and divine, we ought to believe that the Holy Spirit in a manner known to God offers to every man the possibility of being associated with the paschal mystery.[34]

The christological perspective is not consistently maintained, however, in the conciliar documents, particularly when it is not a matter of the individual mystery of the salvation of persons, but of the religious traditions themselves, taken in their objective, historical reality. The very title of the Declaration *Nostra Aetate* — "On the Relations of the Church with the Non-Christian Religions" — demonstrates this. The question posed here is not directly that of the vertical relationship of humanity's religious traditions with the mystery of Jesus Christ. It is the question of the horizontal relationship of these same traditions with Christianity or the Church. The first question could have borne on the acknowledgment of a hidden presence of the mystery of Christ in these same traditions, and of a certain mediation of this same mystery through them. The second question, of course, did not naturally lead in this direction. Is not this the reason why, despite the council's assertion of the presence of values and positive elements in these religious traditions, it does not explicitly venture in the direction of an acknowledgment of these same traditions as legitimate paths of salvation for their members, although necessarily in relation to the mystery of Christ?

Without unduly anticipating our coming discussion, we may provisionally conclude that, in the area of the theology of religions, the only outlook that promises appreciable positive results is the christocentric perspective, which overcomes, by transcending it, a stunted ecclesiocentric approach. The real question — the only one open to meaningful answers — is that of the vertical relation of the other religious traditions to the mystery of Christ. The theology of religions must substitute this question for that of the horizontal relation between the other religions and Christianity. The question of the horizontal relationship can find a valid solution only from a point of departure in the more fundamental problem of the vertical relation. Thus we arrive, from another direction, at the conclusion already formulated: A narrow ecclesiocentric outlook must be replaced by a christocentric perspective both more basic and broader. This is what Hans Küng observed, equivalently, when he wrote:

Such, then, is how this problem appears when the starting point is not the Church but God's will and plan of salvation, as it is made known to us, and in so far as it is made known to us, in Scripture. The question of what lies outside the Church is one which can be asked but . . . can only be answered with difficulty. All men can be saved! As to what lies outside *God* and his plan of salvation, this is not a real question at all. If we look at God's plan of salvation, then there is no *extra*, only an *intra*; no outside, only an inside, for "God desires *all* men to be saved and to come to the knowledge of the truth. For there is *one* God, and there is *one* mediator between God and men, the man Jesus Christ, who gave himself as a ransom for *all*" (1 Tim 2:4-6).[35]

JESUS CHRIST IN THE DEBATE ON RELIGIOUS PLURALISM

The foregoing has afforded us a glimpse of the dangers and weaknesses of a rigidly ecclesiocentric perspective on the theology of religions. For that matter, we have cited the challenge posed by the context of religious pluralism to the traditional christocentric perspective of theology. The present section will be devoted to the debate among the various perspectives, as we find it in the abundant literature of recent years on the theology of religions. We shall begin with a presentation and critical examination of the various outlooks proposed. Then we shall attempt to answer the question: Is a christocentric perspective of universal and cosmic dimensions, such as we have sketched it above, adequate to the challenge of the context of theological reflection today, with its new historical and geographical proportions, its pluralism of cultures and religious traditions, and its inter-religious encounter and dialogue?

In an article entitled "Christ and the Church: A Spectrum of Views," J. Peter Schineller has arranged current theological opinions on the relationship of other religious traditions to Christ and the Church in four categories:[36]

1. Ecclesiocentric universe, exclusive christology;
2. Christocentric universe, inclusive christology;
3. Theocentric universe, normative christology;
4. Theocentric universe, non-normative christology.

Despite the admitted merits of this fourfold grouping,[37] many recent authors prefer a tripartite division of opinions. They distinguish three perspectives: ecclesiocentric, christocentric, and theocentric, and in parallel with these, three basic positions respectively designated exclusivism, inclusivism, and pluralism.[38]

These models are readily recognizable from their names, although each may call for various distinctions. The exclusivism governing the ecclesiocentric perspective, in the mind of the authors in question, refers to the exclusivity of salvation through Jesus Christ professed in the Church. If we must give it a name, we might call it the thesis of Hendrik Kraemer.[39] In order to solve the problem of the various religions, it applies the dialectical theology of Karl Barth, according to which the one valid knowledge of God is the Christian knowledge received by human beings in Jesus Christ. The god of others is an idol. It will not be superfluous to observe that the exclusivist thesis, which postulates membership in the Church as a condition of salvation, and in that Church, the explicit profession of Jesus Christ, has been officially rejected by the ecclesial magisterium.[40]

We must note, however, that an ecclesiocentric perspective does not necessarily presuppose exclusivism in Kraemer's sense (and in the footsteps of Barth), which is dependent on a strict interpretation of the axiom "Outside the Church there is no salvation." All Catholic theologians actually admit the possibility of salvation outside the Church, however they may conceive this possibility.

For the moment, let us note that the role of the Church in the mystery of salvation outside the Church can be, and actually is, conceived in various ways. Some theologians posit a constitutive mediation on the part of the Church, in addition to the obligatory mediation — on a different level, of course — of Jesus Christ. Others are closer to the language of the New Testament, according to which Christ is the sole mediator, and conceive the role of the Church not so much in terms of mediation, but rather as a presence, a sign, sacrament and testimony.[41]

It seems difficult to conceive how the salvific mediation of the Church beyond its own frontiers might be understood. As essentially sacramental, the salvific mediation of the Church is exercised by the proclamation of the word and the sacraments. While reaching the Church's members, and to some extent its future members, it does not reach the members of other religious traditions. Thus, although we have come by a different route, we are back at the viewpoint we have considered above. The ecclesiocentric outlook, even in its attenuated form, must be transcended. It is important to avoid, in the theology of religions, an ecclesiological inflation that would falsify perspectives. The Church, as derived mystery, cannot be the yardstick by which the salvation of others is measured.

Once we have admitted this premise, however, the above-cited tripartite division poses a serious challenge to the traditional christocentric outlook. To inclusive Christocentrism is opposed a theocentric view, represented in a model called (rather ambiguously) pluralism. A number of recent authors support this "paradigm change" — this shift from Christocentrism to theocentrism, from inclusivism to pluralism. Their reasoning, broadly speaking, is as follows.

If Christianity sincerely seeks a dialogue with the other religious traditions — which it can only seek on a footing of equality — it must first of all renounce any claim to uniqueness for the person and work of Jesus Christ as a universal constitutive element of salvation. To be sure, this position is open to various understandings in terms of radicality. Following the categories of J. P. Schineller, two divergent interpretations must be distinguished according to which the person of Jesus Christ, understood as nonconstitutive of salvation, is nonetheless normative for some, while for others it is neither constitutive nor normative. If we must give examples, we might cite, for the normative Jesus, Ernst Troeltsch and Paul Tillich;[42] and for the nonnormative Jesus, John Hick, whose representative position deserves some attention here.

The authors who advocate a theocentric pluralism, however, differ from one another in various respects, which we need not detail here. Let us simply note that, while for some of these authors, such as Alan Race, Christianity's renunciation of its christological claims must be irrevocable,[43] others propound it as a working hypothesis, along the lines of a method-ological doubt or as an at least temporary "bracketing" necessary in order for the dialogue with others to be established honestly and authentically. The very practice of dialogue may well reestablish the validity of Christian claims regarding the mystery of Christ. These claims would rest ultimately on the sole foundation that can establish them with solidity: the test of encounter.[44]

John Hick's position is so representative of a theological pluralism understood in the radical sense that it may well be worthwhile to pause a moment to consider it.[45] Hick advocates a "Copernican revolution" in Christology, a revolution that must specifically consist of a shift in paradigm, a movement from the traditional christocentric perspective to a new the-ocentric perspective. "Copernican revolution," an expression we frequently meet in other areas of theological discussion today, is indeed an appropriate term for what is underway here. Originally it designated the passage from one system for explaining the cosmos, now passé and overthrown, to another system that actually corresponds to reality. The Ptolemaic system was replaced by the Copernican. Having believed for centuries that the sun revolves around the earth, we finally discovered, with Copernicus and Gali-leo, that the earth actually revolves around the sun. Just so, having believed for centuries that the other religious traditions revolved around Christianity as their centre,[46] today we must acknowledge that the centre around which all religious traditions revolve (including Christianity) is actually God. Such a paradigm switch necessarily entails the abandonment of any claim to a unique meaning not only for Christianity, but for Jesus Christ himself.

The basic dilemma, as Hick conceives it, is between an ecclesiocentric exclusivism and a theocentric pluralism. That is, between a fundamentalist interpretation of the axiom "Outside the Church there is no salvation" and a radical liberalism that regards all the various divine manifestations in various cultures, including that which takes place in Jesus Christ, as enjoy-ing the same basic equality in their differences.

This is not to say that Hick simply ignores theological writings repre-senting the middle position—that of inclusivism or, in Schineller's termi-nology, an inclusive Christology in a christocentric universe, such as that of

Karl Rahner, for example.[47] Still, for Hick, all of the efforts of an impressive number of recent theologians — especially Catholic theologians — to endow the theology of religions with an inclusive, open Christocentrism that would combine the "constitutive" sense of the Jesus Christ event for the salvation of humanity and the value of other religious traditions as representing interventions of God in the history of human cultures, and comprising "elements of grace" and salvation for their members — all of these efforts may be left out of account as unworthy of serious consideration. Indeed, they are comparable to the "epicycles" concocted by ancient science in its vain attempt to force certain recalcitrant phenomena into the Ptolemaic system, until the latter finally blew up in our faces, taking its epicycles with it and making room for the Copernican revolution. In analogous fashion, the Copernican revolution in theology, which Hick not only enthusiastically approves but is determined to initiate, rejects all inclusive Christologies as if they were useless, abandoned epicycles. The only remaining valid theology of religions will now be that of a theocentric pluralism, which accounts for all the phenomena, transcends any Christian claim to a prioritarian, universal role for Jesus Christ, and at last establishes the interreligious dialogue on a genuinely equal footing.[48]

Let us further observe that Hick's thinking has evolved into a veritable school of thought that vaunts a somewhat militant attitude, as its slogans attest. Besides the "paradigm change," we have heard more recently of "crossing the Rubicon." "Crossing the Rubicon," of course, will designate an irrevocable acknowledgment of the equal meaning and value of the various religions and the renunciation of any claim of exclusivity or even normativity for Christianity.[49] If there is any universalism in Jesus Christ, it can only be that of the appeal his message might have in terms of the aspirations of all men and women. Of course, other salvific figures might have the same appeal.

The price to be paid by the traditional Christian faith in terms of the mystery of the person and work of Jesus Christ is, as we see, considerable. In such a context it is urgent to show that an inclusive, open Christocentrism remains possible and indeed represents the only way available to a Christian theology of religions truly worthy of the name.

Let us be content to observe that some recent authors not only reject Hick's dilemma but show his position to be untenable.[50] A recent book by Gavin D'Costa entitled *Theology of Religious Pluralism* deserves special attention in this respect.[51] The author recalls two basic axioms of the Christian faith: the universal salvific will of God and the necessary mediation of Jesus Christ (and the role of the Church) in every salvation mystery. He then shows that contrasting attitudes toward these two axioms account for the three basic positions that he calls, using current terminology, exclusivism (represented by H. Kraemer), inclusivism (of which Karl Rahner serves as protagonist), and pluralism (illustrated by John Hick).

While exclusivism relies on the second axiom, neglecting the first, and pluralism on the first, to the detriment of the second, inclusivism alone succeeds in accounting for and holding both at once. Expanding first the pluralistic theory, the author shows that despite its seeming liberalism, Hick's either/or dilemma actually represents a rigid, self-contradictory position. Its theocentric view imposes on the encounter of religions a divine model that corresponds exclusively to the God of the so-called monotheistic religions. It is not universal.

Kraemer's exclusivism stands in the diametrically opposite corner but is equally rigid, it, too, being based on a dialectic of either/or. It, too, is untenable from a biblical and theological point of view, and actually involves internal contradictions. An exclusive emphasis on merely one of the pair of crucial axioms that ought to govern a Christian theology of religions leads to insoluble theological problems.

There remains the inclusive paradigm, of which Karl Rahner is the foremost representative. Does this paradigm solve the problems left unsolved by the other two while preserving whatever measure of validity may reside in the two extreme positions? The author shows that this is indeed the case and that the inclusivistic position alone is capable of holding together and harmonizing the two axioms of Christian faith that are obligatory for any Christian theology of religions. On the one side, Jesus Christ is clearly asserted to be God's definitive revelation and the absolute Saviour. On the other side, the door is open to a sincere acknowledgment of divine manifestations in the history of humanity in various cultures and of efficacious "elements of grace" to be found in other religious traditions; elements that are salvific for their members. Revealed definitively in Jesus Christ, God (and the mystery of Christ) is nonetheless present and at work in other religious traditions. How? This is what a Christian theology of religions ought to clarify. Here let us merely cite the author's conclusion. Referring to the stimulating, open theological and phenomenological tasks confronting the Christian in religious pluralism, he writes:

> The form of inclusivism I have argued for tries to do full justice to [the] two most important Christian axioms: that salvation comes through God in Christ alone, and that God's salvific will is truly universal. By maintaining these two axioms in fruitful tension, the inclusivist paradigm can be characterized by an openness and commitment; an openness that seeks to explore the many and various ways in which God has spoken to all his children in the non-Christian religions and an openness that will lead to the positive fruits of the exploration transforming and fulfilling Christianity, so much so that its future shape may be very different from the Church we know today.[52]

Thus, in broad strokes, we have surveyed the current debate on a Christian theology of religions. If there is one important conclusion that is certain, it is that the christological problem constitutes the nub of this debate.

The decisive question that governs everything else is whether a theology of religions that means to be Christian has any real choice between a christocentric perspective, which acknowledges the Jesus Christ event as constitutive of universal salvation, and a theocentric perspective, which, in one fashion or another, places in doubt or explicitly rejects this central datum of traditional faith. In other words, can a theocentrism that is not at the same time christocentric be a Christian theocentrism?

Indeed, we must make no mistake on the meaning with which the christocentric outlook is invested here. To say that Christ is at the centre of the divine plan for humanity is not to consider him as the goal and end toward which the religious life of human beings and the religious traditions of humanity tend. God (the Father) remains the goal and end. Jesus never replaces God. Jesus Christ is at the centre of the mystery as obligatory Mediator, constituted by God and no one else, as the way leading to God. Jesus Christ is at the centre because God, not human beings or Christianity, has placed him there. It follows that, in Christian theology, Christocentrism and theocentrism cannot be mutually opposed as different perspectives between which a choice must be made. Christian theology is *theocentric qua christocentric, and vice versa.* Far from being passé, the christocentric and theocentric perspective (both adjectives at once) seems surely to be the only way open. What is at issue is not, in the last analysis, a choice between two interchangeable theologies, but the free, responsible adoption of the perspective that reveals to our gaze the very heart of faith, the mystery of Jesus Christ in its integrity and universality.

Adherence to the Christian faith is doubtless a free choice. But this choice governs all authentic Christian theology. With this choice as point of departure, it would have to be shown that faith in Jesus Christ is not closed, but open, not stingy or mean, but cosmic in its dimensions, and that the theology of the religions of humanity based on that faith establishes, on a cosmic scale, a wonderful convergence in the mystery of Christ of all that God in the divine Spirit has realized or continues to accomplish in the history of humanity.[53]

NOTES

1. These distinctions have often been noted. See, for example, Hans Küng, *On Being a Christian,* New York: Doubleday, 1976, pp. 150, 212, 278, 283, 334, 346-347; Id., *Christianity and World Religions,* New York: Doubleday, 1986; Gerald O'Collins, "The Founder of Christianity," in Mariasusai Dhavamony (ed.), *Founders of Religions,* Studia Missionalia, no. 33, Rome: Gregorian University Press, 1984, pp. 385-402; Clifford G. Hospital, *Breakthrough: Insights of the Great Religious Discoverers,* Maryknoll, New York: Orbis Books, 1985.

2. See Jerome D. Quinn, "Jesus as Saviour and Only Mediator," in *Foi et culture à la lumière de la Bible: Actes de la session plénière 1979 de la Commission Biblique Pontificale,* Turin: Elle Di CI, 1981, pp. 249-260; Jean Galot, "Le Christ, Médiateur

unique et universel," in Mariasusai Dhavamony (ed.), *Mediation in Christianity and Other Religions,* Studia Missionalia, no. 21, Rome: Gregorian University Press, pp. 303-320.

3. See Aloys Grillmeier, *Christ in the Christian Tradition,* vol. 1: *From the Apostolic Age to Chalcedon (451),* 2nd ed., London: Mowbrays, 1975.

4. Jacques Dupuis, "The Uniqueness of Jesus Christ in the Early Christian Tradition," in "Religious Pluralism," *Jeevadhara* 47 (September-October 1978), pp. 393-408; here, pp. 406-407.

5. See Jacques Dupuis, *Jesus Christ and His Spirit: Theological Approaches,* Bangalore: Theological Publications in India, 1977, pp. 33-58.

6. See the Inaugural Discourse of Pope Paul VI at the Second Session of the Council (29 September 1963), *Documentation Catholique* 60 (1963) 1345-1361; see also the public audience of November 23, 1966, ibid., 63 (1966) 2121-2122.

7. See Edward Schillebeeckx, *Christ the Sacrament of Encounter with God,* London: Sheed & Ward, 1963; Otto Semmelroth, *Die Kirche als Ursakrament,* Frankfurt am Main: Josef Knecht, 1953; International Theological Commission, "Select Themes of Ecclesiology," in Michael Sharkey (ed.), *Texts and Documents 1969-1985,* San Francisco: Ignatius Press, 1989, pp. 266-304; see 294-297.

8. For an extended treatment of the question see, for example, the recent book by J. B. Carol, *Why Jesus Christ? Thomistic, Scotistic and Conciliatory Perspectives,* Manassas: Trinity Communications, 1986.

9. Saint Anselm's position is actually more nuanced. See Michel Corbin's Introduction, "La nouveauté de l'incarnation," in *L'oeuvre de S. Anselme de Cantorbéry,* vol. 3, Paris: Cerf, 1988, pp. 11-163; see also Paul Gilbert, "Justice et miséricorde dans le 'Proslogion' de Saint Anselme," *Nouvelle Revue Théologique* 108 (1986) 218-238. See also John McIntyre, *The Shape of Christology,* London: SCM Press, 1966; Walter Kasper, *Jesus the Christ,* London: Burns and Oates, 1976, pp. 219-221; Gerald O'Collins, *Interpreting Jesus,* London: G. Chapman, 1983, pp. 148-150.

10. See Edward Schillebeeckx, *Christ the Sacrament,* pp. 32-38; also his *Jesus: An Experiment in Christology,* New York: Crossroad, 1979, pp. 626-669.

11. Gustave Martelet, "Sur le problème du motif de l'Incarnation," in H. Bouëssé and J. J. Latour (eds.), *Problèmes actuels de Christologie,* Paris: Desclée de Brouwer, 1965, pp. 35-80; here, p. 51.

12. Karl Rahner, "Jesus Christus," in Josef Höfer and Karl Rahner (eds.), *Lexikon für Theologie und Kirche,* vol. 5, Freiburg: Herder Verlag, 1966, p. 955: on "Kosmische Christozentrik."

13. Karl Rahner, "Current Problems in Christology," *Theological Investigations* vol. 1, London: Darton, Longman and Todd, 1974, p. 167.

14. See Dermot A. Lane, *Christ at the Centre: Selected Essays in Christology,* Dublin: Veritas, 1990, pp. 142-158.

15. See, for instance, Karl Rahner, "Christology within an Evolutionary View of the World," *Theological Investigations,* vol. 5, London: Darton, Longman and Todd, 1966, pp. 157-192.

16. See, for instance: J. A. Lyons, *The Cosmic Christ in Origen and Teilhard de Chardin: A Comparative Study,* Oxford: Oxford University Press, 1982; I. Bergeron and A. Ernst, *Le Christ universel et l'évolution selon Teilhard de Chardin,* Paris: 1986; Chrystopher F. Mooney, *Teilhard de Chardin and the Mystery of Christ,* London: Collins, 1966; Henri de Lubac, *The Religion of Teilhard de Chardin,* New York: Desclée, 1967; Ursula King, *A New Mysticism: Teilhard de Chardin and Eastern*

Religions, New York: The Seabury Press, 1980; George Maloney, *The Cosmic Christ: From Paul to Teilhard,* New York: Sheed and Ward, 1968.

17. See Pierre Teilhard de Chardin, *Science and Christ,* New York: Harper and Row, 1965.

18. Quoted by Henri de Lubac, *The Religion of Teilhard de Chardin,* p. 61.

19. "Le christique."

20. "Le christique."

21. Quoted by Henri de Lubac, *The Faith of Teilhard de Chardin,* New York: Desclée, 1965, p. 39.

22. For the theology of history, the reader may refer, for example, to Jean Daniélou, *Lord of History,* London: Longmans, 1958; Hans Urs von Balthasar, *A Theology of History,* London: Sheed and Ward, 1964; Oscar Cullmann, *Salvation in History,* London: SCM Press, 1967; Wolfhart Pannenberg, *Revelation as History,* London: Macmillan, 1969; Bruno Forte, *Teologia della storia,* Cinisello Balsamo: Paoline, 1991.

23. On the contrast between the biblical concept of history and the Greek concept, see Claude Tresmontant, *Etudes de métaphysique biblique,* Paris: Gabalda, 1955; Id., *Essai sur la pensée hébraïque,* Paris: Cerf, 1953; also Oscar Cullmann, *Christ and Time,* London: SCM Press, 1965; Id., *Immortalité de l'âme ou résurrection des morts?,* Neuchâtel and Paris: Delachaux et Niestlé, 1956; Arthur H. Armstrong and Robert A. Markus, *Christian Faith and Greek Philosophy,* London: Darton, Longman and Todd, 1960; Th. Boman, *Hebrew Thought Compared to Greek,* Philadelphia: Westminster, 1960.

24. See S. J. Samartha, *The Hindu View of History,* Bangalore: CISRS, 1959; also Duraisamy S. Amalorpavadass, *Foundations of Mission Theology,* Bangalore: NBCLC, 1970, pp. 68-69; Robert Smet, *Essai sur la pensée de Raimundo Panikkar,* Louvain-la-neuve: Centre d'histoire des religions, 1986, pp. 84-86.

25. See Karl Rahner, "History of the World and Salvation History," *Theological Investigations,* vol. 5, London: Darton Longman and Todd, 1966, pp. 115-134.

26. Joachim Gnilka, "Réflexions d'un chrétien sur l'image de Jésus tracée par un contemporain juif," in *Bible et christologie,* by Commission Biblique Pontificale, Paris: Cerf, 1984, pp. 212-213.

27. Oscar Cullmann, *Christ and Time.*

28. The reader may consult, for example, Walter Kern, *Ausserhalb der Kirche kein Heil,* Freiburg: Herder, 1979; Hans Küng, "The World Religions in God's Plan of Salvation," in Josef Neuner (ed.), *Christian Revelation and World Religions,* London: Burns and Oates, 1967, pp. 25-66. Also: Jerome P. Theisen, *The Ultimate Church and the Promise of Salvation,* Collegeville, Minnesota: St. John's University Press, 1976, pp. 1-36; and mostly: Francis A. Sullivan, *Salvation outside the Church,* Mahwah, N.J.: Paulist Press, 1992.

29. Fulgentius of Ruspe, *De fide liber ad Petrum* 38:79, 39:80 – PL 65:704 A-B. Likewise, Cyprian of Carthage, Epist. (73) ad Iubaianum, chap. 21 (PL 3:1123 A-B), where "Salus extra ecclesiam non est" is applied to the heretics.

30. Denzinger and Schönmetzer, *Enchiridion,* n.802; Neuner and Dupuis, *The Christian Faith,* n.21.

31. Denzinger and Schönmetzer, *Enchiridion,* n.870; Neuner and Dupuis, *The Christian Faith,* n.804.

32. Denzinger and Schönmetzer, *Enchiridion,* n.1351; Neuner and Dupuis, *The Christian Faith,* n.810.

33. See Josef Ratzinger, *Das neue Volk Gottes,* Düsseldorf: Patmos, 1970, pp. 339-361; Paul F. Knitter, *No Other Name? A Critical Survey of Christian Attitudes toward the World Religions,* Maryknoll, New York: Orbis Books, 1985, pp. 121-123. Also the works mentioned in note 28.

34. *Gaudium et Spes,* no. 22. Please note that the official Latin text does not contain the word "only," to make the key phrase "known only to God," which one often finds as a mistranslation of GS 22.

35. Hans Küng, "The World Religions in God's Plan of Salvation," loc. cit., pp. 25-66; here, p. 46.

36. J. Peter Schineller, "Christ and the Church: A Spectrum of Views," *Theological Studies* 37 (1976) 545-566; reprinted in Walter J. Burghardt and William G. Thompson (eds.), *Why the Church?,* New York: Paulist Press, 1977, pp. 1-22.

37. Paul F. Knitter, *No Other Name?,* also adopts a fourfold division: the conservative evangelical model (one true religion); the most widespread Protestant model today (all salvation comes from Christ); the open Catholic model (various paths, Christ the sole norm); and the theocentric model (various paths, with God as centre). In an article entitled "Catholic Theology of Religion at the Crossroads," in "Christianity among World Religions," *Concilium* 183 (1986/1), pp. 99-107, Knitter partly adopts the categories proposed by H. Richard Niebuhr (*Christ and Culture,* New York: Harper and Row, 1951) for the relationship between Christ and "Culture," and distinguishes a Christ, against religions, in the religions, above the religions, and together with the religions. These categories partly coincide with Schineller's four members.

38. Among authors who take account of the various positions, the following adopt this nomenclature: Alan Race, *Christians and Religious Pluralism: Patterns in the Christian Theology of Religions,* London: SCM Press, 1983; Harold Coward, *Pluralism: Challenge to World Religions,* Maryknoll, New York: Orbis Books, 1985; Gavin D'Costa, *Theology and Religious Pluralism: The Challenge of Other Religions,* Oxford: Basil Blackwell, 1986.

39. Hendrik Kraemer, *The Christian Message in a Non-Christian World,* London: Edinburgh House Press, 1947; Id., *Religion and the Christian Faith,* London: Lutterworth, 1956; Id., *Why Christianity of All Religions?,* London: Lutterworth, 1962.

40. See the letter of the Holy Office to the Archbishop of Boston (August 8, 1949) condemning the rigid interpretation of the axiom *Extra ecclesiam nulla salus* proposed by Leonard Feeney, according to which explicit membership in the Church or the explicit desire to enter it are absolutely required for individual salvation. A relationship with the Church *in desiderio,* even merely implicit, can suffice for the salvation of the person (Denzinger and Schönmetzer, *Enchiridion,* n.3866-3873; Neuner and Dupuis, *The Christian Faith,* nos. 854-857).

41. See, for example, Richard P. McBrien, *Catholicism,* vol. 2, Minneapolis: Winston, 1980, pp. 691-729. In order to account for these two different views of the role of the Church, Schineller introduces a subdistinction under the heading, "christocentric universe, inclusive christology": (a) Jesus Christ and the Church as constitutive, but not exclusive, means of salvation; (b) Jesus Christ as constitutive means of salvation, the Church as a nonconstitutive means. See the schema in *Why the Church?* p. 6.

42. See Ernst Troeltsch, *The Absoluteness of Christianity and the History of Religions,* Richmond: John Knox Press, 1971; Paul Tillich, *Systematic Theology,* vol. 2,

Chicago: University of Chicago Press, 1957; Id., *Christianity and the Encounter of World Religions,* New York: Columbia, 1963.

43. Alan Race, *Christians and Religious Pluralism,* pp. 106-148.

44. Paul F. Knitter, *No Other Name?,* pp. 169-231. More recently, Knitter has proposed to substitute for the paradigm of theocentrism that of "soteriocentrism," and again that of "Regnocentrism." All the religions offer salvation or human liberation. As such, though differing among themselves, they all are equal ways of salvation for their members. The criterion according to which they must be evaluated is the measure in which they contribute to the full liberation of human beings. Similarly, all religions must be signs of the presence of the Reign of God in the world; all can and must contribute together on an equal footing to the growth of the Reign of God. See Paul F. Knitter, "Catholic Theology of Religions at the Crossroads," in Hans Küng and Jürgen Moltmann (eds.), "Christianity among the World Religions," *Concilium* 183 (1986/1), pp. 99-107; Id., "Towards a Liberation Theology of Religions," in John Hick and Paul F. Knitter (eds.), *The Myth of Christian Uniqueness. Toward a Pluralistic Theology of Religions,* Maryknoll, New York: Orbis Books, 1987, pp. 178-200; Id., "Missionary Activity Revised and Reaffirmed," in Paul Mojzes and Leonard Swidler (eds.), *Christian Mission and Interreligious Dialogue,* Lewiston: The Edwin Mellen Press, 1990, pp. 77-92.

45. See especially John Hick, *God and the Universe of Faiths: Essays in the Philosophy of Religion,* London: Macmillan, 1973; Id., *The Centre of Christianity,* London: SCM Press, 1977; Id., *The Second Christianity,* London: SCM Press, 1983; Id., *God Has Many Names: Britain's New Religious Pluralism,* London: Macmillan, 1980; Id., *Problems of Religious Pluralism,* London: Macmillan, 1985; Id., *An Interpretation of Religion. Human Responses to the Transcendent,* New Haven: Yale University Press, 1989.

46. Hick published a book entitled *Christianity at the Centre,* London: Macmillan, 1968, before he himself underwent the Copernican christological revolution. This was transformed into a second edition, *The Centre of Christianity,* to become, in turn, in a third edition, *The Second Christianity.*

47. See Karl Rahner's various essays in *Theological Investigations,* 23 vols., London: Darton, Longman and Todd, 1961-1992 (especially vols. 5ff); also *Foundations of Christian Faith,* New York: Crossroad, 1978.

48. To the theocentric perspective an objection has been made to the effect that, in spite of its apparent universalism, its new model ends up imposing a priori as the necessary interpretative category the concept of God of the monotheistic religions, to which the nontheistic traditions are forced to adapt themselves. To such objection John Hick has responded with a new change of paradigm. In his most recent book, *An Interpretation of Religion. Human Responses to the Transcendent,* he moves from theocentrism to what he calls now "Reality-centredness." Hick holds that all the religions are saving ways, equally valid, leading to "the Real." For an elaborated critique of this latest version of the pluralistic model of Hick, see Gavin D'Costa (ed.), *Christian Uniqueness Reconsidered: The Myth of a Pluralistic Theology of Religions,* Maryknoll, New York: Orbis Books, 1990.

49. See Leonard Swidler (ed.), *Toward a Universal Theology of Religion,* Maryknoll, New York: Orbis Books, 1987, esp. pp. 227-230. See also John Hick and Paul F. Knitter (eds.), *The Myth of Christian Uniqueness: Toward a Pluralistic Theology of Religions,* Maryknoll, New York: Orbis Books, 1987.

50. See, for example, Julius J. Lipner, "Does Copernicus Help?," in Richard W.

Rousseau (ed.), *Inter-Religious Dialogue: Facing the Next Frontier,* Scranton, Penn.: Ridge Row Press, 1981, pp. 154-174, who accuses John Hick of a naive relativism and ahistorical idealism. Also Gavin D'Costa (ed.), *Christian Uniqueness Reconsidered: The Myth of a Pluralistic Theology of Religions,* Maryknoll, New York: Orbis Books, 1990.

51. Gavin D'Costa, *Theology of Religious Pluralism: The Challenge of Other Religions,* Oxford: Basil Blackwell, 1986.

52. Ibid., p. 136.

53. For such development, see Jacques Dupuis, *Jesus Christ at the Encounter of World Religions,* Maryknoll, New York: Orbis Books, 1991, pp. 113-206.

Conclusion

This "Introduction to Christology" has from the outset advocated an integral approach or a comprehensive perspective. What such an approach to Christology would imply has been summed up under various principles: the principle of dialectic tension; the principle of totality; the principle of plurality; the principle of historical continuity; and the principle of integration. Having come to the end of the road, it may be well to stress once more some implications of these principles that in the past have not always been adequately attended to or effectively pursued.

To be credible and convincing, Christology today will have to present itself as a process of reflection on the mystery of Jesus Christ in which continuity-in-discontinuity is made manifest at every step and on every level: between Jesus and the Christ; between the Christ of the kerygma and that of later biblical elaboration; between the Christology of the New Testament and that of the Church tradition; between the christological dogma and today's theological reflection on the mystery of Jesus Christ. It will, moreover, have to give full recognition to the existence and validity of a plurality-in-unity. We have seen that the New Testament testifies to a variety of Christologies among which there obtains a substantial unity, and that opposite approaches to the mystery of Jesus Christ, far from being mutually exclusive, can complement and eventually correct each other. The same interaction between apparently contradictory approaches must be allowed to take place today, lest a fragmentary and one-sided view of the mystery of Jesus Christ be allowed to prevail, falling short of the integral reality. To this must be added the fact that the contextualisation and inculturation of Christology also call today for plurality-in-unity. No Christology can henceforth be considered valid for all times and all places. Inasmuch as reflection on the mystery of Jesus Christ needs to be done in each local church within a definite context and be expressed in the framework of a particular culture, it is bound to be local and historical — safeguarding, however, the communion, both diachronic and synchronic, with the Christology of the apostolic Church and with those of the other local churches of today.

We have drawn attention to some aspects of the mystery of Jesus Christ, inadequately stressed in the past, which a renewed Christology should place in full relief: the historical aspect; the personal or trinitarian aspect; and the soteriological aspect. There is no need to elaborate on each again.

As regards the trinitarian aspect, emphasis has been laid on the fact that

Jesus Christ is not a God-man in a neutral, impersonal way, but the Word or the Son incarnate who in his humanhood relates personally to his Abba-Father and to the Spirit. The implications of Jesus' Sonship of the Father, for him and for us, have been brought out. Those of his relation to the Spirit ought to be equally developed. Attention has rightly been given in recent years to the need of building a "Spirit Christology."[1] Such a Christology would show the influence of the Holy Spirit throughout the earthly life of Jesus, from his conception by the power of the Spirit (cf. Lk 1:35) to his resurrection by God in the same Spirit (cf. Rom 8:11). It would not, however, limit itself to substantiating the influence of the Spirit on Jesus' humanhood during his earthly life, but would extend beyond the resurrection to illustrate the relationship between the action of the risen Lord and the economy of the Holy Spirit. The one cannot be disjoined from the other, for the risen Lord himself confers the Holy Spirit who, in view of this action, is called by St. Paul the "Spirit of Christ" (Phil 1:19; cf. 1 Pet 1:11). Between Jesus Christ and the Holy Spirit there are not two economies of salvation, but one "Christo-pneumatic" economy. The functions are distinct, but rather than being separated or simply parallel, they are interdependent and complementary. Jesus Christ is the event of salvation and, as such, is at the centre of God's design for humankind and of its realization in history; but the Jesus Christ-event remains contemporary at every period of time and becomes present and operative for every generation through the power of the Holy Spirit. If Christology cannot but be "Spirit Christology," pneumatology in turn needs to be christological. This amounts to stating, with regard to the relation between Christology and pneumatology, what has been observed previously concerning Christology and the doctrine of God: Christian theocentrism is of necessity christocentric.

But the reverse is also true: Christocentrism is theocentric by nature. This implies, among other things, that the mystery of Jesus Christ unveils to us the mystery of God in a unique, unprecedented manner. Christology thus ends up by opening up on the mystery of the Triune God. In Jesus Christ, the Word of God has entered human history personally; the Son has stooped to us to share with us his Sonship of the Father. The Jesus Christ-event is in all truth the human story of God. In this human story that the Son assumed for our sake, the secret of God's intimate life stands revealed to us: the Father who is the source, the Son who eternally comes from the Father and through whom eternally the Father breathes the Spirit. By unveiling for us these interpersonal relationships that constitute the inner life and communion of the Godhead, the Christ-event teaches us that "God is Love" (1 Jn 4:8) and that love overflows to humankind.

Thus in Jesus Christ a "different God" stands revealed.[2] Not in the sense of another God, but that the one and only God who spoke and communicated "in many and various ways" (Heb 1:1) throughout salvation history and made with Israel a lasting covenant, "when the time had fully come" (Gal 4:4) spoke a decisive word to humankind in the Word made flesh (cf.

Jn 1:14) and called all human beings to share in the Sonship of the Son (cf. Gal 4:6; Rom 8:15). The "God of Abraham, of Isaac and of Jacob" has become for us the "God and Father of our Lord Jesus Christ" (Eph 1:3; cf. 2 Cor 11:31).[3] In Jesus, and in him alone do we discover truly *what* and *who* God has willed to be for us, *what* and *who* God is. Jesus, it may be said, is "the human face of God"; his human face is in turn the symbol and the image of God's personal dealings with humankind. The image of God inscribed in the face of Jesus is that of a God who has freely chosen to empty God's self in self-giving. In Jesus, God has become "God-of-human-beings-in-a-human-way." Jesus, the "man for others" (Bonhoeffer), unveils God's proexistence for human beings. Free in giving, the God of Jesus is also a God who frees and liberates: "Jesus the Liberator" conveys humanly to us the freedom with which God frees us to be God's children (Rom 8:21; 2 Cor 3:17; Gal 4:31; 5:13). The trinitarian image of God unveiled in Jesus is the symbol of God's outpouring love toward humankind in free, liberating self-gift. No philosophical discourse on God's transcendence and divine attributes — immutability and impassibility — suffices henceforth to account for what God is, for the reality of God's commitment to humankind is only available to us in Jesus Christ. In him our human history has become God's own history. God has once for all bound God's self personally with humankind by an indissoluble bond; to it God remains irrevocably committed today in a dialogue of salvation and self-giving.

NOTES

1. See, among others, James D. G. Dunn, *Jesus and the Spirit*, Philadelphia: Westminster, 1975; Walter Kasper, *Jesus the Christ*, London: Burns and Oates, 1976, pp. 249-274; Philip Rosato, "Spirit Christology: Ambiguity and Promise," *Theological Studies* 38 (1977), pp. 423-449; Alfons Nossol, "Der Geist als Gegenwart Jesu Christi," in Walter Kasper (ed.), *Gegenwart des Geistes,* Freiburg: Herder, 1979, pp. 132-154; Luis Ladaria, "Cristología del Logos y Cristología del Espíritu," *Gregorianum* 61 (1980), pp. 353-360; Raniero Cantalamessa, *Lo Spirito Santo nella vita di Gesù. Il mistero di unzione,* Milano: Ancora, 1982; Yves Congar, "Pour une christologie pneumatique," *Revue des sciences philosophiques et théologiques* 63 (1979) 435-442; Id., *I Believe in the Holy Spirit,* 3 vols., London: G. Chapman, 1983; Id., *The Word and the Spirit,* London: G. Chapman, 1986; H. Mühlen, "Das Christuser- eignis als Tat des Heiligen Geistes," in Johannes Feiner and Magnus Löhrer (eds.), *Mysterium Salutis* III,3: *Das Christusereignis,* Zürich/Koln: Benziger, 1969, pp. 513- 545; Francesco Lambiasi, *Lo Spirito Santo: Mistero e persona,* Bologna: Dehoniane, 1987, pp. 202-217; Angelo Amato, *Gesù il Signore. Saggio di cristologia,* Bologna: Dehoniane, 1988, pp. 320-339; Bruno Forte, *Gesù di Nazareth, Storia di Dio, Dio della storia,* Roma: Paoline, 1981, pp. 287-314; Marcello Bordoni, "Cristologia e pneumatologia: L'evento pasquale come atto del Cristo e dello Spirito Santo," *Lateranum* 47 (1981) 432-492; M. Simonetti, "Note di cristologia pneumatica," *Augustinianum* 12 (1972) 201-232; John O'Donnell, "In Him and Over Him: The Holy Spirit in the Life of Jesus," *Gregorianum* 70 (1989), pp. 25-45; Jürgen Molt-

mann, *The Way of Jesus Christ: Christology in Messianic Dimensions,* London: SCM Press, 1990; Jacques Dupuis, *Jesus Christ and His Spirit,* Bangalore: Theological Publications in India, 1977, pp. 21-31; Joseph H. P. Wong, "The Holy Spirit in the Life of Jesus and of the Christian," *Gregorianum* 73 (1992), pp. 57-95; Piet Schoonenberg, *De Geest, het Woord en de Zoon*, Altoria-Averbode: Verlag, 1991.

2. See Christian Duquoc, *Dieu différent,* Paris: Cerf, 1977.

3. See Jacques Schlosser, *Le Dieu de Jésus,* Paris: Cerf, 1987; D. G. A. Calvet, *From Christ to God,* London: Epworth Press, 1983; Walter Kasper, *Jesus the Christ,* London: Burns and Oates, 1976.

Bibliography

Some Recent Christologies

Amato, Angelo. *Gesù il Signore*. Bologna: Dehoniane, 1988.

Balthasar, Hans Urs von. *Herrlichkeit. Eine theologische Aestetik*. Vol. III/2: "Theologie," Teil 2: "Neuer Bund." Einsiedeln: Johannes Verlag, 1969.

Balthasar, Hans Urs von. "Mysterium Paschale," in Feiner, Johannes, and Löhrer, Magnus. *Mysterium Salutis*. Vol. III/2: "Das Christusereignis." Zürich/Koln: Benziger, 1969, pp. 133-326.

Balthasar, Hans Urs von. *Theodramatik*. Vol. 2: "Die Personen des Spiels," Teil 1: "Die Personen in Christus." Einsiedeln: Johannes Verlag, 1978.

Balthasar, Hans Urs von. *Life Out of Death. Meditations on the Easter Mystery*. Philadelphia: Fortress Press, 1985.

Balthasar, Hans Urs von. *Theologik*. Vol. 2: "Wahrheit Gottes." Einsiedeln: Johannes Verlag, 1985.

Balthasar, Hans Urs von. *Theologie der drei Tage*. Freiburg: Johannes Verlag, 1990.

Boff, Leonardo. *Jesus Christ Liberator*. Maryknoll, N.Y.: Orbis Books, 1979.

Boff, Leonardo. *Passion of Christ, Passion of the World*. Maryknoll, N.Y.: Orbis Books, 1987.

Bordini, Marcello. *Gesù di Nazaret, Signore e Cristo. Saggio di cristologia sistematica*. 3 vol. Roma: Lateranense, 1982-86.

Bordini, Marcello. *Gesù di Nazaret: Presenza, memoria, attesa*. Brescia: Queriniana, 1988.

Bouyer, Louis. *Le fils éternel*. Paris: Cerf, 1974.

Doré, Joseph, et al. *Jésus, le Christ et les chrétiens*. Paris: Desclée, 1981.

Dunn, James D. G. *Christology in the Making*. London: SCM Press, 1980.

Dupuis, Jacques. *Jesus Christ and His Spirit*. Bangalore: Theological Publications in India, 1977.

Duquoc, Christian. *Christologie. Essai dogmatique*. 2 vol. Paris: Cerf, 1968-1972.

Duquoc, Christian. *Jésus homme libre*. Paris: Cerf, 1973.

Feiner, Johannes, and Löhrer, Magnus (eds.). *Mysterium Salutis*. Vol. III/1-2: "Das Christusereignis," Zürich/Köln: Benziger, 1969-1970.

Forte, Bruno. *Gesù di Nazaret, storia di Dio, Dio della storia*. Roma: Paoline, 1981.

Galot, Jean. *Who Is Christ?* Rome: Gregorian University Press, 1980.

Galot, Jean. *Jesus our Liberator*. Rome: Gregorian University Press, 1982.

Galot, Jean. *Abba, Father*. New York: Alba House, 1992.

Gonzalez, Carlos I. *El es nuestra salvación*. Bogota: CELAM, 1986.

Gonzalez Faus, José I. *Acceso a Jesús*. Salamanca: Sigueme, 1979.

Gonzalez Faus, José I. *La humanidad nueva. Ensayo de cristología*. Saltander: Sal Terrae, 1984.

174   Bibliography

Gonzalez Gil, Manuel M. *Cristo, el Misterio di Dios. Cristología y soteriología*. 2 vol. Madrid: Ed. Católica, 1976.

Grillmeier, Aloys. *Christ in Christian Tradition*. Vol. 1: "From the Apostolic Age to Chalcedon." 2nd revised edition. London: Mowbrays, 1975.

Grillmeier, Aloys. *Mit ihm und in ihm. Christologische Forschungen und Prospektiven*. Freiburg: Herder, 1975.

Grillmeier, Aloys. *Christ in Christian Tradition*. Vol. 2: "From the Council of Chalcedon to Gregory the Great (590-604)." London: Mowbrays, 1986.

Guillet, Jacques. *The Consciousness of Jesus*. Paramus, N.J.: Newman Press, 1972.

Hellwig, Monika. *Jesus, the Compassion of God*. Wilmington: Glazier, 1985.

Johnson, Elisabeth A. *She Who Is. The Mystery of God in Feminist Theological Discourse*. New York: Crossroad, 1992.

Kasper, Walter. *Jesus the Christ*. London: Burns and Oates, 1976.

Kereszty, Roch A. *Jesus Christ. Fundamentals of Christology*. New York: Alba House, 1991.

Küng, Hans. *On Being a Christian*. New York: Doubleday, 1976; London: Collins, 1977.

Küng, Hans. *The Incarnation of God: An Introduction to Hegel's Theological Thought as Prolegomena to a Future Christology*. New York: Crossroad, 1987; Edinburgh: T. & T. Clark, 1987.

Lane, Dermot A. *The Reality of Jesus*. Mahwah, N.J.: Paulist Press, 1975.

Lane, Dermot A. *Christ at the Centre*. Dublin: Veritas, 1990.

Lauret, Bernard, and Refoulé, François (eds.), *Initiation à la pratique de la théologie*. Tome II: "Dogmatique 1." Paris: Cerf, 1982.

Mackey, James P. *Jesus the Man and the Myth*. Mahwah, N.J.: Paulist Press, 1979.

Macquarrie, John. *Jesus Christ in Modern Thought*. London: SCM, 1990.

Mascall, Eric L. *Theology and the Gospel of Christ*. London: SPCK, 1977.

Mascall, Eric L. *Whatever Happened to the Human Mind?* London: SPCK, 1980.

Moingt, Joseph. *L'homme qui venait de Dieu*. Paris: Cerf, 1993.

Moiolo, G. *Cristologia. Proposta sistematica*. (ed. F. G. Brambilla). Milano: Glossa, 1989.

Moltmann, Jürgen. *The Crucified God*. New York: Harper and Row, 1974.

Moltmann, Jürgen. *The Way of Jesus Christ. Christology in Messianic Dimensions*. London: SCM Press, 1990.

O'Collins, Gerald. *The Easter Christ*. London: Darton, Longman and Todd, 1974.

O'Collins, Gerald. *Interpreting Jesus*. Mahwah, N.J.: Paulist, 1983; London: G. Chapman, 1983.

O'Collins, Gerald. *Jesus Risen*. Mahwah, N.J.: Paulist Press, 1987.

Pannenberg, Wolfhart. *Jesus—God and Man*. 2nd ed. Philadelphia: Westminster, 1977.

Pannenberg, Wolfhart. *An Introduction to Systematic Theology*. London: T. & T. Clark, 1991.

Pannenberg, Wolfhart. *Systematische Theologie*. Vol. 2. Göttingen: Vanderhoeck & Ruprecht, 1991.

Porro, Carlo. *Gesù il Salvatore. Iniziazione alla cristologia*. Bologna: Dehoniane, 1992.

Rahner, Karl. *Foundations of Christian Faith: An Introduction to the Idea of Christianity*. New York: Crossroad, 1978; London: Darton, Longman and Todd, 1978.

Rahner, Karl. *Theological Investigations*. 23 vol. London: Darton, Longman and Todd, 1992.

Rahner, Karl, and Thüsing, Wilhelm. *A New Christology*. London: Burns and Oates, 1980.

Robinson, John A. T. *The Human Face of God*. London: SCM Press, 1972.

Schillebeeckx, Edward. *Jesus: An Experiment in Christology*. New York: Crossroad, 1979; London: Collins, 1979.

Schillebeeckx, Edward. *Christ: The Experience of Jesus as Lord*. New York: Seabury Press, 1980.

Schillebeeckx, Edward. *Interim Report on the Books Jesus and Christ*. London: SCM Press, 1980.

Schillebeeckx, Edward. *God among Men: The Gospel Proclaimed*. New York: Crossroad, 1983.

Schillebeeckx, Edward. *Church: The Human Story of God*. New York: Crossroad, 1990; London: SCM Press, 1990.

Schoonenberg, Piet. *The Christ*. London: Sheed and Ward, 1971.

Schüssler Fiorenza, Elisabeth. *In Memory of Her: A Feminist Theological Reconstruction of Christian Origins*. New York: Crossroad, 1983.

Schüssler Fiorenza, Elisabeth. *Bread Not Stone: The Challenge of Feminist Biblical Interpretation*. Boston: Beacon Press, 1984.

Segundo, Juan L. *Jesus of Nazareth Yesterday and Today*. 5 vols. Maryknoll, N.Y.: Orbis Books, 1984-88.

Segundo, Juan L. *La historia perdida y recuperada de Jesus de Nazaret: De los Sinópticos a Pablo*. Santander: Sal Terrae, 1991.

Serenthà, Mario. *Gesù Cristo, ieri oggi e sempre. Saggio di cristologia*. Leumann (Torino): Elle Di Ci, 1986.

Sloyan, Gerard S. *Jesus Redeemer and Divine Word*. Wilmington: Glazier, 1989.

Sobrino, Jon. *Christology at the Crossroads: A Latin American Approach*. Maryknoll, N.Y.: Orbis Books, 1976; London: SCM Press, 1978.

Sobrino, Jon. *Jesus in Latin America*. Maryknoll, N.Y.: Orbis Books, 1987.

Sobrino, Jon. *Jesucristo liberador*. Madrid: Trotta, 1991.

Thompson, William. *Jesus Lord and Saviour: A Theopathic Christology and Soteriology*. Mahwah, N.J.: Paulist Press, 1980.

Thompson, William M. *The Jesus Debate: A Survey and Synthesis*. Mahwah, N.J.: Paulist Press, 1985.

Thompson, William M. *Christology and Spirituality*. New York: Crossroad, 1991.

1. CHRIST AND CHRISTOLOGIES

Amato, Angelo (ed.). *Problemi attuali di cristologia*. Roma: LAS, 1975.

Auén, G. *Jesus in Contemporary Historical Research*. Philadelphia: Fortress Press, 1976.

Bouëssé, Humbert, and Latour, Jean-Jacques. *Problèmes actuels de christologie*. Bruges: Desclée de Brouwer, 1965.

Bourgeois, Henri. *Libérer Jésus: Christologies actuelles*. Paris: Centurion, 1977.

Ciola, Nicola. *Introduzione alla cristologia*. Brescia: Queriniana, 1986.

Commission Biblique Pontificale. *Bible et Christologie*. Paris: Cerf, 1984.

Dantine, Wilhelm. *Jesus von Nazareth in der gegenwärtigen Diskussion*. Gütterloh, 1974.

Fitzmyer, J. A. *Scripture and Christology: A Statement of the Biblical Commission with a Commentary*. Mahwah, N.J.: Paulist Press, 1986.

Galot, Jean. *Le Christ. Foi et contestation*. Chambray: CLD, 1981.

Gunton, Colin E. *Yesterday and Today: A Study of Continuities in Christology*. London: Darton, Longman and Todd, 1988.

Iammarrone, Giovanni (ed.). *La cristologia contemporanea*. (Associazione Teologica Italiana). Padova: Messaggero, 1992.

Iammarrone, Giovanni, et al. *Gesù Cristo volto di Dio e volto dell'uomo*. Roma: Herder, 1992.

International Theological Commission, *Texts and Documents (1969-1985)*. Sharkey, Michael (ed.). San Francisco: Ignatius Press, 1989.

Johnson, Elisabeth A. *Consider Jesus. Waves of Renewal in Christology*. New York: Crossroad, 1990.

McFague, Sallie. *Metaphorical Theology. Models of God in Religious Language*. Philadelphia: Fortress Press, 1982.

McFague, Sallie. *Models of God: Theology for an Ecological, Nuclear Age*. Minneapolis: Augsburg-Fortress, 1987.

Miguez-Bonino, José. *Faces of Jesus: Latin American Christologies*. Maryknoll, N.Y.: Orbis Books, 1984.

Mondin, Battista. *Le cristologie moderne*. Roma: Apes, 1973.

Norris, Richard A. *The Christological Controversy*. Philadelphia: Fortress Press, 1980.

O'Collins, Gerald. *What Are They Saying about Jesus?* Mahwah, N.J.: Paulist Press, 1983.

O'Grady, John Francis. *Models of Jesus*. New York: Doubleday, 1981.

Pelikan, Jaroslav. *Jesus Through the Centuries: His Place in the History of Culture*. New Haven and London: Yale University Press, 1985.

Porro, Carlo. *Cristologia in crisi? Prospettive attuali*. Roma: Paoline, 1975.

Rahner, Karl. "Current Problems in Christology" in *Theological Investigations*, vol. 1. New York: Crossroad, 1974; London: Darton, Longman and Todd, 1974, pp. 149-200.

Ruether, Rosemary Radford. *To Change the World: Christology and Cultural Criticism*. New York: Crossroad, 1981.

Ruether, Rosemary Radford. *Sexism and God-talk. Toward a Feminist Theology*. Boston: Beacon, 1983.

Ruether, Rosemary Radford. *Disputed Questions. On Being a Christian*. Maryknoll, N.Y.: Orbis Books, 1989.

Scheffczyk, Leo (ed.). *Problemi fondamentali della cristologia oggi*. Brescia: Morcelliana, 1983.

Schilson, Arno and Kasper, Walter. *Christologie im Präsens: Kritische Sichtung neuer Entwürfe*. Freiburg: Herder, 1974.

Schreiter, Robert J. (ed.). *Faces of Jesus in Africa*. Maryknoll, New York: Orbis Books, 1991.

Segalla, Giuseppe et al. *Il problema cristologico oggi*. Assisi: Cittadella, 1973.

Sesboüé, Bernard. "Esquisse d'un panorama de la recherche christologique actuelle," in Laflamme, Raymond, and Gervais, Michel (eds.). *Le Christ, hier, aujourd'hui et demain*. Quebec, Presses de l'Université, 1976.

Sesboüé, Bernard. *Jésus-Christ à l'image des hommes*. Paris: Desclée de Brouwer, 1978.

Sugirtharajah, R. S. (ed.). *Asian Faces of Jesus*. Maryknoll, N.Y.: Orbis Books, 1993. "Visages du Christ. Les tâches présents de la christologie." *Recherches de science religieuse* 65 (1977/1).

2. JESUS AT THE SOURCE OF CHRISTOLOGY

Beasly-Murray, G. R. *Jesus and the Kingdom of God*. Grand Rapids: Eerdmans, 1986.

Bornkamm, Günther. *Jesus of Nazareth*. London: Hodder and Stoughton, 1960.

Brown, Raymond. *The Virginal Conception and the Bodily Resurrection of Jesus*. New York: Paulist Press, 1978.

Bultmann, Rudolf. *Glauben und Verstehen*. 2 vol. Tübingen: Mohr, 1933-1952.

Bultmann, Rudolf. *Jesus*. Tübingen: Mohr, 1958.

Bultmann, Rudolf. *Jesus Christ and Mythology*. London: SCM Press, 1958.

Bultmann, Rudolf. *Theology of the New Testament*. 2 vols. New York: Scribners, 1951-55; London: SCM Press, 1965.

Caba, José. *El Jesus de los Evangelios*. Madrid: Ed. Católica, 1977.

Caba, José. *Da los Evangelios al Jesús histórico. Introducción a la cristologia*. Madrid: Ed. Católica, 1980.

Caba, José. *Resucitò Cristo, mi esperanza. Estudio exegetico*. Madrid: Ed. Católica, 1986.

Charlesworth, James H. *Jesus' Jewishness: Exploring the Place of Jesus within Early Judaism*. New York: Crossroad, 1991.

Charlesworth, James H. (ed.). *The Messiah: Developments in Early Judaism and Christianity*. Minneapolis: Fortress Press, 1992.

Conzelmann, Hans. *Jesus*. Philadelphia: Fortress Press, 1973.

Crossan, John Dominic. *The Historical Jesus: The Life of a Mediterranean Jewish Peasant*. San Francisco: Harper, 1991; Edinburgh: T. & T. Clark, 1991.

de la Potterie, Ignace (ed.). *De Jésus aux évangiles*. Gembloux: Ducoulot, 1967.

Descamps, Albert. *Jésus et l'Eglise. Etudes d'exégèse et de théologie*. Louvain: Presses Universitaires, 1987.

Dodd. Charles H. *The Founder of Christianity*. New York: Macmillan, 1970; London: Collins, 1971.

Dreyfus, François. *Jésus savait-il qu'il était Dieu?* Paris: Cerf, 1984.

Dupont, Jacques (ed.). *Jésus aux origines de la christologie*. Louvain: University Press, 1975 (rev. ed. 1989).

Fabris, Rinaldo. *Gesù di Nazareth. Storia e interpretazione*. Assisi: Cittadella, 1983.

Flusser, David. *Jesus*. New York: Herder and Herder, 1969.

Gnilka, Joachim. *Jesus von Nazaret. Botschaft und Geschiette*. Freiburg: Herder, 1993.

Guillet, Jacques. *The Consciousness of Jesus*. Paramus, N.J.: Newman Press, 1972.

Hooker, Morna D. *Continuity and Discontinuity: Early Christianity and Its Jewish Setting*. London: Collins, 1971.

Jeremias, Joachim. *New Testament Theology*. Vol. 1, "The Proclamation of Jesus." London: SCM Press, 1971.

Käsemann, Ernst. *Essays on New Testament Themes*. London: SCM Press, 1964.

Latourelle, René. *Finding Jesus through the Gospels*. New York: Alba House, 1979.

Lee, Bernard J. *The Galilean Jewishness of Jesus*. Mahwah, N.J.: Paulist Press, 1988.

Leivestad, Ragnar. *Jesus and His Own Perspective.* Minneapolis: Ausburg Publishing House, 1987.

Léon-Dufour, Xavier. *Les évangiles et l'histoire de Jésus.* Paris: Seuil, 1963.

Léon-Dufour, Xavier. *Face à la mort: Jésus et Paul.* Paris: Seuil, 1979.

Léon-Dufour, Xavier. *Résurrection de Jésus et message pascal.* Paris: Seuil, 1971.

Manicardi, Ermenegildo (ed.). *Il cammino di Gesù nel vangelo di Marco.* Roma: PIB, 1963.

Neusner, J. *Judaism in the Beginning of Christianity.* Philadelphia: Fortress Press, 1984.

Nolan, Albert. *Jesus Before Christianity.* Maryknoll, N.Y.: Orbis Books, 1978.

Perrin, Norman. *The Kingdom of God and the Teaching of Jesus.* London: SCM Press, 1963.

Perrin, Norman. *Rediscovering the Teaching of Jesus.* London: SCM Press, 1967.

Perrin, Norman. *Jesus and the Language of the Kingdom.* Philadelphia: Fortress Press, 1976.

Perrot, Charles. *Jésus et l'histoire.* Paris: Desclée, 1979.

Riches, John. *Jesus and the Transformation of Judaism.* London: Darton, Longman and Todd, 1980.

Sanders, E. P. *Jesus and Judaism.* London: SCM Press, 1985.

Schillebeeckx, Edward. *Jesus: An Experiment in Christology.* New York: Crossroad, 1979; London: Collins, 1979.

Schürmann, Heinz. *Jesu ureigener Tod: exegetische Besinnungen und Ausblick.* Freiburg: Herder, 1975.

Schweizer, Eduard. *Jesus.* London: SCM Press, 1978.

Schweizer, Eduard. *Jesus Christ: The Man from Nazareth and the Exalted Lord.* London: SCM Press, 1989.

Senior, Donald. *Jesus, a Gospel Portrait.* Dayton: Pflaum Press, 1975.

Song, C. S. *Jesus, the Crucified People.* New York: Crossroad, 1989.

Song, C. S. *Jesus and the Reign of God.* Minneapolis: Augsburg Fortress, 1993.

Stanton, Graham N. *The Gospels and Jesus.* Oxford: Oxford University Press, 1989.

Vermes, Geza. *Jesus the Jew.* London: Collins, 1973.

Vermes, Geza. *Jesus and the World of Judaism.* London: SCM Press, 1983.

Vermes, Geza. *The Religion of Jesus the Jew.* London: SCM Press, 1993.

Witherington, Ben. *The Christology of Jesus.* Minneapolis: Fortress Press, 1990.

Zeitlin, Irwin M. *Jesus and the Judaism of His Time.* Cambridge: Polity Press, 1989.

3. THE DEVELOPMENT OF NEW TESTAMENT CHRISTOLOGY

Boismard, Marie-Emile. *Moïse ou Jésus: Essai de christologie johannique.* Louvain: University Press, 1988.

Brown, Raymond E. *Jesus God and Man.* Milwaukee: Bruce Publishing, 1967.

Cerfaux, Louis. *Le Christ dans la théologie de Saint Paul.* Paris: Cerf, 1954.

Cullmann, Oscar. *Les premières confessions de foi chrétienne.* Paris: Presses Universitaires, 1948.

Cullmann, Oscar. *The Christology of the New Testament.* Philadelphia: Westminster, rev. ed., 1980; London: SCM Press, 1963.

Dahl, Nils Alstrup. *Jesus the Christ. The Historical Origins of Christological Doctrine.* Minneapolis: Fortress Press, 1991.

de la Potterie, Ignace. *La prière de Jésus*. Paris: Desclée, 1990.

Dodd, Charles H. *The Apostolic Preaching and Its Development*. New York: Harper and Row, 1964.

Dondeyne, Albert, et al. *Jésus-Christ Fils de Dieu*. Bruxelles: Facultés Universitaires Saint-Louis, 1981.

Dunn, James D. G. *Jesus and the Spirit*. Philadelphia: Westminster, 1975.

Dunn, James D. G. *Unity and Diversity in the New Testament*. London: SCM Press, 1977 (2nd ed. 1990).

Dunn, James D. G. *Christology in the Making*. Philadelphia: Westminster, 1980; London: SCM Press, 1980.

Dunn, James D. G. *The Evidence for Jesus*. Philadelphia: Westminster, 1985.

Dunn, James D. G. *The Parting of the Ways. Christianity and Judaism and their Significance for the Character of Christianity*. London: SCM Press, 1991.

Dunn, James. *Jesus' Call to Discipleship*. Cambridge: Cambridge University Press, 1992.

Dupont, Jacques. *Essais sur la christologie de Saint Jean*. Bruges: Saint André, 1951.

Durrwell, François-Xavier. *The Resurrection: A Biblical Study*. New York: Sheed and Ward, 1961.

Feuillet, André. *Le Christ sagesse de Dieu d'après les épîtres pauliniennes*. Paris: Gabalda, 1966.

Feuillet, André. *Christologie paulinienne et tradition biblique*. Paris: Desclée de Brouwer, 1973.

Fredikson, Paula. *From Jesus to Christ. The Origins of the New Testament Images of Jesus*. New Haven: Yale University Press, 1988.

Fuller, Reginald H. *The Foundations of New Testament Christology*. London: Collins, 1969.

Fuller, Reginald H., and Perkins, Pheme. *Who Is This Christ? Gospel Christology and Contemporary Faith*. Philadelphia: Fortress Press, 1983.

Hahn, Ferdinand. *The Titles of Jesus in Christology: Their History in Early Christianity*. London: Luttherworth Press, 1969.

Hellwig, Monika. *Jesus, the Compassion of God*. Wilmington: Glazier, 1983.

Hengel, Martin. *The Son of God*. Philadelphia: Fortress Press, 1976.

Howard, Marshall I. *The Origins of the New Testament Christology*. Downers Grove, Ill.: Inter-Varsity Press, 1976.

Iersel, Bastiaan M. F. Van. *"Der Sohn" in den synoptischen Jesusworten*. Leiden: Brill, 1964.

Jeremias, Joachim. *The Central Message of the New Testament*. London: SCM Press, 1965.

Jeremias, Joachim. *Abba: Studien zur neutestamentlichen Theologie und Zeitgechichte*. Göttingen: Vandenhoeck, 1966.

Jeremias, Joachim. *New Testament Theology*. London: SCM Press, 1971.

Knox, John. *The Humanity and Divinity of Christ: A Study of Patterns of Christology*. Cambridge: Cambridge University Press, 1967.

Kuschel, Karl-Josef. *Born Before All Time?* Minneapolis: Fortress, 1993; London: SCM Press, 1993.

Lamarche, Paul. *Christ vivant*. Paris: Cerf, 1966.

Longenecker, Richard N. *The Christology of Early Jewish Christianity*. London: SCM Press, 1970.

Marchel, Witold. *Abba, Père. La prière du Christ et des chrétiens*. Rome: PIB, 1971.

Moule, Charles F. D. *The Origin of Christology*. Cambridge: Cambridge University Press, 1977.

Neufeld, Vernon H. *The Earliest Christian Confessions*. Leiden: Brill, 1963.

Neyrey, Jerome H. *Christ Is Community: The Christologies of the New Testament*. Wilmington: Glazier, 1985.

Pollard, T. E. *Johannine Christology and the Early Church*. Cambridge: Cambridge University Press, 1970.

Reid, Jennings B. *Jesus: God's Emptiness, God's Fullness: The Christology of St. Paul*. Mahwah, N.J.: Paulist Press, 1990.

Richards, Earl. *Jesus: One and Many: The Christological Concept of the New Testament Authors*. Wilmington: Glazier, 1988.

Riesenfeld, Harold. *Unité et diversité dans le Nouveau Testament*. Paris: Cerf, 1979.

Sabourin, Léopold. *The Names and Titles of Jesus: Themes of Biblical Theology*. New York: Macmillan, 1967.

Sabourin, Léopold. *Christology: Basic Texts in Focus*. New York: Alba House, 1984.

Sanders, Jack T. *The New Testament Christological Hymns*. Cambridge: Cambridge University Press, 1971.

Schillebeeckx, Edward. *Christ: The Experience of Jesus as Lord*. New York: Seabury Press, 1980.

Schmitt, Joseph. *Jésus ressuscité dans la prédication apostolique*. Paris: Gabalda, 1949.

Schnackenburg, Rudolf. *God's Rule and Kingdom*. London: Burns and Oates, 1968.

Schnackenburg, Rudolf. "Christologie des Neuen Testamentes," in Feiner, Johannes, and Löhrer, Magnus. *Mysterium Salutis*. Vol. III/1: *Das Christusereignis*, Zürich/Köln: Benziger, 1970, pp. 227-388.

Schnackenburg, Rudolf. *Die Person Jesu Christi im Spiegel der vier Evangelien*. Freiburg: Herder, 1993.

Segalla, Giuseppe. *La cristologia del Nuovo Testamento*. Brescia: Paideia, 1985.

Taylor, Vincent. *The Names of Jesus*. London: Macmillan, 1954.

Thompson, William M. *The Jesus Debate: A Survey and Synthesis*. Mahwah, N.J.: Paulist Press, 1985.

Vanhoye, Albert. *Situation du Christ*. Paris: Cerf, 1969.

Vawter, Bruce. *This Man Jesus*. London: G. Chapman, 1975.

4. HISTORICAL DEVELOPMENT AND PRESENT RELEVANCE

Amato, Angelo. *Gesù il Signore*. Bologna: Dehoniane, 1988, pp. 147-287.

Camelot, Pierre-Thomas. *Ephèse et Chalcédoine*. Paris: Orante, 1962.

Cantalamessa, Raniero. "Dal Cristo del Nuovo Testamento al Cristo della Chiesa: Tentativo di interpretazione della cristologia patristica," in *Il problema cristologico oggi*. Assisi: Cittadella, 1973, pp. 147-197.

Daniélou, Jean. *The Theology of Jewish Christianity*. London: Darton, Longman and Todd, 1964.

Daniélou, Jean. *Gospel Message and Hellenistic Culture*. London: Darton, Longman and Todd, 1973.

Doré, Joseph. "Les christologies partistiques et conciliaires," in Lauret, Bernard, and Refoulé, François (eds.). *Initiation à la pratique de la théologie*. Tome II: "Dogmatique" 1. Paris: Cerf, 1982, pp. 185-262.

Grillmeier, Aloys. "Die altkirchliche Christologie und die moderne Hermeneutik," *Theologische Berichte* I, 1972, pp. 69-169.

Grillmeier, Aloys. *Christ in Christian Tradition*. Vol. 1: "From the Apostolic Age to Chalcedon." 2nd revised edition. London: Mowbrays, 1975.

Grillmeier, Aloys. *Christ in Christian Tradition*. Vol. 2: "From the Council of Chalcedon to Gregory the Great (590-604)." London: Mowbrays, 1986.

Grillmeier, Aloys, and Bacht, Heinrich (eds.). *Das Konzil von Chalkedon*. Vols. 1-3. Würzburg: Echter Verlag, 1951-1954.

Hanson, Richard P. C. *The Search for the Christian Doctrine of God: The Arian Controversy 318-381*. Edinburgh: T. & T. Clark, 1988.

Kelly, John N. D. *Early Christian Doctrines*. New York: Harper, 1960.

Kelly, John N. D. *Early Christian Creeds*. London: Longman, 1976.

Liébaert, Jacques. *Christologie: von der Apostolischen Zeit bis zum Konzil von Chalkedon (451)*. Freiburg: Herder, 1965.

Lonergan, Bernard. *The Way to Nicea*. Philadelphia: Westminster, 1976; London: Darton, Longman and Todd, 1976.

Meyendorf, Jean. *Le Christ dans la théologie byzantine*. Paris: Cerf, 1969.

Neuner, Joseph, and Dupuis, Jacques (eds.). *The Christian Faith in the Doctrinal Documents of the Catholic Church*. New York: Alba House, rev. ed., 1983; London: Harper Collins Religious, 1992.

Ortiz de Urbina, Ignatius. *Nicée et Constantinople*. Paris: Orante, 1963.

Prestige, George L. *Fathers and Heretics*, London: SPCK, 1948.

Prestige, George L. *God in Patristic Thought*. London: SPCK, 1964.

Sellers, Robert V. *The Council of Chalcedon*. London: SPCK, 1961.

Serenthà, Mario. *Gesù Cristo ieri, oggi e sempre. Saggio di cristologia*. Torino: Elle Di Ci, 1986, pp. 159-252.

Sesboüé, Bernard. *Jésus-Christ dans la tradition de l'Eglise*. Paris: Desclée, 1982.

Simonetti, Manlio. *Cristianesimo antico e cultura greca*. Roma: Borla, 1983.

Smulders, Piet. "Dogmengechichtliche und lehramtliche Entfaltung der Christologie," in Feiner, Johannes, and Löhrer, Magnus (eds.). *Mysterium Salutis*. Vol. III/1: *Das Christusereignis*. Zürich/Köln: Benziger, 1970, pp. 389-476.

Young, Frances. *From Nicea to Chalcedon. A Guide to the Literature and Its Background*. Philadelphia: Fortress Press, 1984.

5. "HUMAN" PSYCHOLOGY OF JESUS

Balthasar, Hans Urs von. *La foi du Christ*. Paris: Aubier, 1968.

Bouëssé, Humbert, and Latour, Jean-Jacques (eds.). *Problèmes actuels de Christologie*. Bruges: Desclée de Brouwer, 1965.

Brown, Robert E. *Jesus God and Man*. Milwaukee: Bruce Publishing Company, 1967.

de la Potterie, Ignace. *La prière de Jésus*. Paris: Desclée, 1990.

Diepen, Herman M. *La théologie de l'Emmanuel*. Paris: Desclée de Brouwer, 1960.

Dreyfus, François. *Jésus savait-il qu'il était Dieu?* Paris: Cerf, 1984.

Dupont, Jacques. *Les tentations de Jésus au désert*. Bruges: Desclée de Brouwer, 1968.

Duquoc, Christian. *Christologie: Essai dogmatique*. 2 vol. Paris: Cerf, 1968-72.

Duquoc, Christian. *Jésus homme libre*. Paris: Cerf, 1973.

Galot, Jean. *La conscience de Jésus*. Paris: Letthielleux, 1971.

Galtier, Paul. *L'unité du Christ*. Paris: Beauchesne, 1939.

Guardini, Romano. *The Humanity of Jesus: Contributions to a Psychology of Jesus.* New York: Pantheon Books, 1964.

Guillet, Jacques. *The Consciousness of Jesus.* Paramus, N.J.: Newman Press, 1972.

Guillet, Jacques. *La foi de Jésus-Christ.* Paris: Desclée, 1980.

Gutwenger, Engelbert. *Bewusstsein und Wissen Christi.* Innsbruck: Rauch, 1960.

Lafont, Ghislain. *Peut-on connaître Dieu en Jésus-Christ?* Paris: Cerf, 1969.

Lonergan, Bernard. *De constitutione Christi ontologica et psychologica.* Roma: Pontificia Universitas Gregoriana, 1956.

Malmberg, Felix. *Ueber den Gottmenschen.* Freiburg i. Br.: Herder, 1960.

Marchel, Witold. *Abba, Père. La prière du Christ et des chrétiens.* Rome: PIB, 1971.

Mouroux, Jean. *Le mystère du temps.* Paris: Aubier, 1962.

Nigro, Carmelo. *Il mistero della conoscenza umana di Cristo nella teologia contemporanea.* Rovigo: 1971.

Parente, Pietro. *L'io di Cristo.* Brescia: Morcelliana, 1955.

Rahner, Karl. "Dogmatic Reflections on the Knowledge and Self-Consciousness of Christ," in *Theological Investigations,* vol. 5. London: Darton, Longman and Todd, 1975, pp. 193-215.

Riedlinger, Helmuth. *Geschichlichkeit und Vollendung des Wissen Christi.* Freiburg i. Br.: Herder, 1966.

Rizzi, Armido. *Cristo, verità dell'uomo.* Roma: AVE, 1972.

Ternus, Josef. "Das Seelen-und Bewusstseinsleben Jesu. Problem-geschichtlich-systematische Untersuchung," in Grillmeier, Aloys, and Bacht, Heinrich (eds.). *Das Konzil von Chalkedon,* Vol. 3, Würzburg: Echter Verlag, 1954, pp. 81-238.

Vögtle, Anton. "Exegetische Erwägungen über das Wissen und Selbstbewusstsein Jesu," in Vorgrimler, Herbert (ed.). *Gott im Welt.* Festgabe für Karl Rahner. Vol. 1. Freiburg i.Br.: Herder, 1964, pp. 608-67.

Weber, Edouard-Henri. *Le Christ selon Saint Thomas d'Aquin.* Paris: Desclée.

Wiederkehr, Dietrich. "Entwurf einer systematischen Christologie," in Feiner, Johannes, and Löhrer, Magnus (eds.). *Mysterium Salutis.* Vol. III/1: "Das Christusereignis," Zürich/Köln: Benziger, 1970, pp. 477-648.

Xiberta, Bartolomé M. *El Yo de Jesus-Cristo.* Barcelona: Herder, 1954.

6. Jesus Christ the Universal Savior

Anderson, Gerald H., and Stransky, Thomas F. (eds.). *Christ's Lordship and Religious Pluralism.* Maryknoll, N.Y.: Orbis Books, 1981.

Ariarajah, Wesley. *The Bible and People of Other Faiths.* Geneva: WCC, 1985.

Balthasar, Hans Urs von. *A Theology of History.* London/New York: Sheed and Ward, 1964.

Balthasar, Hans Urs von. *The Moment of Christian Witness.* New York: Newman Press, 1969.

Balthasar, Hans Urs von. *Das Christentum und die Weltreligionen.* Freiburg: Informationscentrum Berufe der Kirche, 1979.

Barnes, Michael. *Christian Identity and Religious Pluralism.* Nashville: Abingdon Press, 1989.

Bergeron, I., and Ernst, A. *Le Christ universel et l'évolution selon Teilhard de Chardin.* Paris: 1986.

Boublik, Vladimir. *Teologia delle religioni.* Roma: Studium, 1973.

Burghardt, Walter J., and Thompson, William G. (eds.). *Why the Church?* New York: Paulist Press, 1977.

Cantone, Carlo (ed.). *Le scienze della religione oggi.* Roma: LAS, 1981.

Carol, J. B. *Why Jesus Christ? Thomistic, Scotistic and Conciliatory Perspectives.* Manassas: Trinity Communications, 1986.

Coward, Harold. *Pluralism: Challenge to World Religions.* Maryknoll, N.Y.: Orbis Books, 1985.

Cragg, Kenneth. *The Christ and the Faiths.* London: SPCK, 1986.

Cullmann, Oscar. *Christ and Time.* London: SCM Press, 1965.

Cullmann, Oscar. *Salvation in History.* London: SCM Press, 1967.

Cuttat, Jacques-Albert. *The Encounter of Religions.* New York: Desclée, 1960.

Cuttat, Jacques-Albert. *Expérience chrétienne et spiritualité orientale.* Bruges: Desclée de Brouwer, 1967.

D'Costa, Gavin. *Theology and Religious Pluralism: The Challenge of Other Religions.* Oxford: Basil Blackwell, 1986.

D'Costa, Gavin (ed.). *Christian Uniqueness Reconsidered: The Myth of a Pluralistic Theology of Religions.* Maryknoll, N.Y.: Orbis Books, 1990.

dal Covolo, Antonio. *Missioni e religioni non-cristiane.* Roma: Citta Nuova, 1981.

Daniélou, Jean. *The Lord of History: Reflections on the Inner Meaning of History.* London: Longmans, 1958.

Daniélou, Jean. *The Salvation of the Nations.* Notre Dame: University of Notre Dame Press, 1962.

de Lubac, Henri. *The Faith of Teilhard de Chardin.* New York: Desclée, 1965.

de Lubac, Henri. *The Religion of Teilhard de Chardin.* New York: Desclée, 1967.

de Lubac, Henri. *The Church, Paradox and Mystery.* New York: Alba House, 1969.

Dupuis, Jacques. *Jesus Christ at the Encounter of World Religions.* Maryknoll, N.Y.: Orbis Books, 1991.

Forte, Bruno. *Teologia della storia. Saggio sulla rivelazione, l'inzio e il compimento.* Cinisello Balsamo: Paoline, 1991.

Griffiths, Bede. *Return to the Centre.* London: Collins, 1976.

Griffiths, Bede. *The Marriage of East and West,* London: Collins, 1982.

Griffiths, Bede. *A New Creation in Christ.* London: Collins, 1992.

Hick, John. *God and the Universe of Faiths: Essays in the Philosophy of Religion.* London: Macmillan, 1973.

Hick, John. *God Has Many Names: Britain's New Religious Pluralism.* London: Macmillan, 1980.

Hick, John. *Problems of Religious Pluralism.* Philadelphia: Westminster, 1980; London: Macmillan, 1985.

Hick, John. *An Interpretation of Religion: Human Responses to the Transcendent.* New Haven: Yale University Press, 1989.

Hick, John, and Hebblethwaite, Brian (eds.). *Christianity and Other Religions.* Philadelphia: Fortress Press, 1981.

Hick, John, and Knitter, Paul (eds.). *The Myth of Christian Uniqueness. Toward a Pluralistic Theology of Religions.* Maryknoll, N.Y.: Orbis Books, 1987.

Hillman, Eugene. *Many Paths: A Catholic Approach to Religious Pluralism.* Maryknoll, N.Y.: Orbis Books, 1988.

Hospital, Clifford G. *Breakthrough: Insights of the Great Religious Discoverers.* Maryknoll, N.Y.: Orbis Books, 1985.

Jeremias, Joachim. *Jesus' Promise to the Nations.* London: SCM Press, 1958.

184   Bibliography

Joannes, Fernando Vittorino (ed.). *Incontro tra le religioni*. Verona: Mondadori, 1968.

Keenan, John P. *The Meaning of Christ: A Mahayana Theology*. Maryknoll, N.Y.: Orbis Books, 1989.

Kern, Walter. *Ausserhalb der Kirche kein Heil?* Freiburg: Herder, 1979.

King, Ursula. *A New Mysticism: Teilhard de Chardin and Eastern Religions*. New York: Seabury Press, 1980.

Knitter, Paul F. *No Other Name? A Critical Survey of Christian Attitudes Toward the World Religions*. Maryknoll, N.Y.: Orbis Books, 1985; London: SCM Press, 1985.

Kraemer, Hendrik. *The Christian Message in a non-Christian World*. Grand Rapids: Kregel Publications, 1938; London: Edinburgh House Press, 1947.

Kraemer, Hendrik. *Religion and the Christian Faith*. London: Luttherworth, 1956.

Kraemer, Hendrik. *Why Christianity of All Religions?* London: Luttherworth Press, 1962.

Küng, Hans. *Christianity and World Religions: Paths of Dialogue with Islam, Hinduism and Buddhism*. Maryknoll, N.Y. Orbis Books, 1993 (orig. ed., Doubleday, 1986).

Lane, Dermot A. *Christ at the Centre: Selected Essays in Christology*. Dublin: Veritas, 1990.

Le Saux, Henri. *Hindu-Christian Meeting Point*. Delhi: ISPCK, 1976.

Le Saux, Henri. *Saccidananda. A Christian Approach to Advaitic Experience*. Delhi: ISPCK, 1974 (rev. ed., 1984).

Lyons, J. A. *The Cosmic Christ in Origen and Teilhard de Chardin: A Comparative Study*. Oxford: Oxford University Press, 1982.

Maurier, Henri. *Essai d'une théologie du paganisme*. Paris: Orante, 1965.

Mooney, Christopher. *Teilhard de Chardin and the Mystery of Christ*. London: Collins, 1966.

Neuner, Joseph (ed.). *Christian Revelation and World Religions*. London: Burns and Oates, 1967.

Panikkar, Raymond. *The Intra-Religious Dialogue*. New York: Paulist Press, 1978.

Panikkar, Raymond. *The Unknown Christ of Hinduism: Toward an Ecumenical Christophany*, rev. and enlarged ed. Maryknoll, N.Y.: Orbis Books, 1981; London: Darton, Longman and Todd, 1981.

Pannenberg, Wolfhart. *Revelation as History*. London: Macmillan, 1969.

Pannenberg, Wolfhart. *Systematische Theologie*. Vol. 1. Güttingen: Vanderhoeck & Ruprecht, 1988.

Pathill, Kuncheria (ed.). *Religious Pluralism: An Indian Christian Perspective*. Delhi: ISPCK, 1991.

Race, Alan. *Christians and Religious Pluralism: Patterns in the Christian Theology of Religions*. Maryknoll, N.Y.: Orbis Books, 1983; London: SCM Press, 1983.

Rahner, Karl. *Foundations of Christian Faith: An Introduction to the Idea of Christianity*. New York: Crossroad, 1978; London: Darton, Longman and Todd, 1978.

Rahner, Karl. *Theological Investigations*. 23 vol. New York: Crossroad, 1961-92.

Richard, Lucien. *What Are They Saying about the Uniqueness of Christ and World Religions?* New York: Paulist Press, 1981.

Richards, Glyn. *Toward a Theology of Religions*. London: Routledge, 1989.

Ries, Julien. *Les chrétiens parmi les religions. Des Actes des Apôtres à Vatican II*. Paris: Desclée, 1987.

Rossano, Piero. *Il problema delle religioni*. Catania: Paoline, 1975.

Rouner, Leroy S. (ed.). *Religious Pluralism*. Notre Dame: Notre Dame University Press, 1990.

Saldanha, Chrys. *Divine Pedagogy. A Patristic View of non-Christian Religions*. Roma: LAS, 1984.

Samartha, Stanley J. *Courage for Dialogue*. Maryknoll, N.Y.: Orbis Books, 1982.

Samartha, Stanley J. *One Christ — Many Religions: Toward a Revised Christology*. Maryknoll, N.Y.: Orbis Books, 1991.

Schillebeeckx, Edward. *Christ the Sacrament of Encounter with God*. New York and London: Sheed and Ward, 1966.

Schillebeeckx, Edward. *Church: The Human Story of God*. New York: Crossroad, 1990; London: SCM Press, 1990.

Schlette, Heinz R. *Toward a Theology of Religions*. New York: Herder and Herder, 1966.

Sullivan, Francis A. *Salvation Outside the Church?* Mahwah, N.J.: Paulist Press, 1992.

Swidler, Leonard (ed.). *Toward a Universal Theology of Religion*. Maryknoll, N.Y.: Orbis Books, 1987.

Theisen, Jerome P. *The Ultimate Church and the Promise of Salvation*. Collegeville: St. John's University Press, 1976.

Tillich, Paul. *Christianity and the Encounter of World Religions*. New York: Columbia University Press, 1963.

Tillich, Paul. *The Future of Religions*. New York: Harper and Row, 1966.

Tracy, David. *Dialogue with the Other: The Interreligious Dialogue*. Grand Rapids: Eerdmans, 1990; Louvain: Peeters, 1990.

Troeltsch, Ernst. *The Absoluteness of Christianity and the History of Religions*. Richmond: John Knox Press, 1971.

Whaling, Frank. *Christian Theology and World Religions: A Global Approach*. London: Marshall Pickering, 1986.

Wiles, Maurice. *Christian Theology and Interreligious Dialogue*. London: SCM Press, 1992.

Subject and Person Index

Scripture Index